To my father - Who taught me the joys and
wisdom in books - a story of a favorite
"Hoosier" hero & heroin,

Love,
Sara Jane

MARVELLA

MARVELLA
a personal journey

by

Marvella Bayh

with

Mary Lynn Kotz

INTRODUCTION BY
LADY BIRD JOHNSON

EPILOGUE BY
BIRCH BAYH

Harcourt Brace Jovanovich
New York and London

BOOK DESIGN: RONALD F. SHEY

Printed in the United States of America

LIBRARY OF CONGRESS CATALOGING IN PUBLICATION DATA
Bayh, Marvella.
Marvella, a personal journey.
Includes index.
1. Breast—Cancer—Biography. 2. Bayh, Marvella.
I. Kotz, Mary Lynn, joint author. II. Title.
RC280.B8B39   362.1′9′6994490924   [B]   79-1809
ISBN 0-15-157557-6

First edition
B C D E

To the two men in my life,
Birch and Evan,
And to other friends from the past and present
Who have touched my life in such important ways
Especially Jane Sinnenberg

Introduction

Looking back across the years and ties of friendship, I recall my introduction to Marvella Bayh as remarkably appropriate.

It was spring, with the crocuses beginning to show and the golden forsythia in bud, the waves of daffodils along the parkways forthcoming.

I say it was spring, yet the calendar dates it Valentine's eve, February 13, 1963. We reach for spring in Washington. Januaries are so gray, colored only by the ceremony and excitement of the Congressional cycle, the opening, reuniting with old friends, meeting the new faces. When that Congressional excitement subsides into committee work, we mush through rain and snow and yearn, really yearn, for a robin, a bud, a promise that the city will soon burst into the rapturous bloom that is most especially Washington. Sometimes that comes after two or three sunny surprises in February, or early March—only to be interrupted by a late snowstorm, and to retreat until April brings the cherry blossoms.

I don't remember what the weather was in February, 1963. But I do remember that meeting Marvella *was* spring. She enters your life with a lilt, her warmth and friendliness cascading over you like some laughing mountain rivulet. And that was the way our meeting was.

Lyndon had scooped them up—Birch and Marvella, the new young Senate couple from Indiana—on a minute's notice and brought them home to dinner on Valentine's night to The Elms, the handsome French home that we had during his short years as Vice

President. I loved that house, and while it represents only a brief and hurried interlude in our lives, it holds so many moments of deep emotion that it lives in my mind's eye: luncheons for the wives of visiting chiefs of state, dinners for good friends from Congress, the somber return from Dallas after the tragedy of the assassination.

That night of February 13, 1963, The Elms overflowed with joy and happiness: everyone lifting their glasses over the candlelight to Valentine's Day . . . and to the new couple from Indiana . . . Birch responding and then Marvella, looking so small and young and happy, at one end of the long rectangular table next to Lyndon, laughing and confessing, "This is a very special day for me because tomorrow is my birthday," and then with a laugh, "it's terrible to be saying goodbye to your twenties."

Her twenties! We all laughed and groaned because that was a long-ago milestone for most of us and, of course, we burst into "Happy Birthday!"

The rest of our Washington years were filled with such occasions shared with the Bayhs—teas, luncheons, dinners, receptions, musicales—at the White House. Birch and Marvella were not only wonderful friends but wonderful guests, mingling to make someone from out of town seem right at home. Marvella was the kind of person I could call a few minutes before a state dinner and ask to "look after" someone who might need a little special attention to feel relaxed in the White House.

Of course, politically, they were Democrats and strong allies of Lyndon's, the kind of people you "would go to the well with," as Lyndon categorized his friends with the definition of loyalty coined on the frontier. So when the 1964 campaign rolled around, they were the spark plugs in a big rally for the formation of the Young Citizens for Johnson, and went out on the campaign trail to help the Democratic ticket of Johnson and Humphrey. Our daughters, Lynda and Luci, were also campaigning, and when their travels coincided, Marvella's presence was comforting to me because I knew things would just be more fun for them.

Life intertwines along the Potomac as it only can when you are sharing the hard work of it, the heady successes of it, and the deep disappointments of it.

Since they waved us goodbye in January, 1969, we have kept up our friendship by visits and telephone calls, followed the growth of their son, Evan, and kept up with news of mutual Senate friends still there or departed from the Washington scene.

And, of course, we agonized and prayed with Marvella's battle against that most dreadful disease—cancer. Somehow, Marvella took that cruel blow and transformed it into constructive use and knowledge for the rest of us. Her gift of selflessness in that regard may be one of the links that lead to victory.

But I know this. In her story she has brought springtime to all of us. That in itself is victory.

—LADY BIRD JOHNSON

MARVELLA

Chapter 1

Each life is a gift, a precious possession. This personal journey has been a search for meaning in my own.

⤴

She was just a little slip of a woman then, my grandmother Hern, crippled and bedbound in her last illness. But even at eighty-three, her blue eyes crackled with the same fire that lit the face of a girl of the plains. My father, her youngest son, leaned over to tell her goodbye.

"Now you be good, Mama," he said.

"Oh, I will, I will," she replied. Then in a wicked stage whisper: "I sure don't want to catch that disease Marvella's got!"

I was seven months pregnant at the time.

Two weeks later, she was gone, but her strength is still with me, her warmth, her laughter and teasing, and her love of life and the land. She could feel the land and call it hers, and God's, and ours, drawing us into her spell as she told of racing across the plains in a wagon to stake her claim, when she was only twenty-one. I felt as though I were riding with her.

Her name was Laura Vercilla Murphy Hern, and when I was little she would share her big puffy featherbed with me, and teach me how to make quilts in the wintertime, or how to stir up a batch of cornbread every night and bake hot biscuits for breakfast every morning (baking wads of cotton into the batter on April Fool's Day), while telling the girl I was about the girl she'd been.

She rode with her parents and brothers in a covered wagon

from Pike County, Missouri, to Oklahoma in 1889. Her father, Thomas Jefferson Murphy, had made the famous "run" into Old Oklahoma on April 22, to drive a stake in the ground indicating that this quarter-section of rich, grassy land was to be his family's farm. Those acres were called "Unassigned Lands," former Indian Territory opened by Congress to white settlement on that day. My great-grandfather Murphy had made that first run with hundreds of others, hardy pioneers of the new frontier who risked their lives as their pioneering forefathers had, to lay claim on the vast, rich earth of America. It was not until I was grown that I came to realize the true impact of that run, and the ones that followed, upon the lives and culture of the Indian people who lived on the land but did not presume to own it. I grew up believing that the Indian heritage was a rich part of *our* Oklahoma heritage, and not that we, who forced them there on a "trail of tears," had been a tragic part of theirs.

The clear hindsight of history shows the unwitting destruction of the land itself by those first energetic plows on the horse-high grasses of the then moist plains of Oklahoma. My great-grandfather was a strong-willed, God-fearing man, descended from railroad builders who migrated from Kentucky to Iowa to Indiana to Missouri, proud of an ancestor who had fought in the Battle of New Orleans. This Thomas Jefferson Murphy, born in Indiana, whom I remember as a white-bearded old man like a Biblical patriarch, was a Union soldier who eloped with his Mariah (née Glover), daughter of a Confederate colonel, to Hannibal, Missouri. It was their family of eight, including their seventeen-year-old daughter Laura, who set out that fall of 1889 in covered wagons to homestead near Harmony, Oklahoma. Their hearts were open to the new opportunity; they worked hard, man, woman, and child, to prove themselves worthy of that opportunity of free land, which they perceived was given to them by God's grace, and not by the generosity or opportunism of the U.S. Congress.

My grandmother, Laura, told me about staking her own claim during the last, most spectacular "run," into the 58-by-100-mile Cherokee Strip in north central Oklahoma, when it was appropriated for settlement on September 16, 1893. She was engaged, at twenty-one, to Earnest Hern, a neighboring farmboy from the Hennessey community, who also made the Cherokee run. They were delaying their marriage until they had staked *two* 160-acre claims.

It was 100 degrees in the sun that historic day, when 100,000 people stormed into the Strip.

"The gun went off at noon, and you never heard such a clamor," she recalled. "All those people running and screaming, horses rearing, fights breaking out. Earnie's horse went wild and ran into a tree, and he was badly hurt. He couldn't stake a claim. But I jumped out of Papa's wagon and ran as fast as I could across the ground to claim one for us!"

It would be a while before she and Earnie would get that farm, however. As she stood in the long line at the tent that served as a land office, a man who'd claimed the same piece of ground bribed his way into line ahead of her. But she and my grandfather persevered. Another man who wasn't able to make a living on his land forfeited his claim, and they acquired it in exchange for a team of horses.

My grandmother Hern worked alongside my grandfather "like a man," she told me, clearing the land to plow, following behind my grandfather's plow with an axe, splitting the chunks of sod, dropping seeds of corn into the crevices. Together, they built first a sod house and then a one-room log cabin with dirt floor and dirt roof, where finally she could begin to raise a family.

"We were as proud of that house on the prairie as anybody could be of a landscaped mansion," she said. She told me about washing clothes with a scrub-board—which she still did when I knew her—drawing water from an open well, and doing battle with coyotes, not to mention bedbugs, fleas, and mosquitos. "In 1896 I lay sick with typhoid fever for six weeks, without the help of ice, or no protection from flies," she recalled. "Earnie paid a bushel of corn to the country doctor who saved my life."

Together, they planted wheat and corn and cotton; the weather was kind, the earth fertile—and so was my grandmother Hern. She bore three sons at home, Orville, Otis, and Clarence, with no doctor attending. By the time my father, Delbert, arrived in 1910 (three years after the Oklahoma Territory became a state), she'd thought her child-rearing days were over. She was thirty-eight, her older boys eighteen, seventeen, and nine. "You'd think I could at least have had a girl," she said, and dressed my father as such, until his brother Orville took it upon himself to cut off the six-year-old child's long curls. "I spoiled your daddy," she confessed.

But she taught my father to love the land, and he taught me, his only child. It was our link to each other, to our pioneer heritage, and it was something more. It was a raw, gusty, clean-smelling feeling, a spirit of "I can do anything I set my mind to and nobody better try to stop me!" In the Choctaw language, "Oklahoma" meant Red People. But to me, growing up, it always meant red land, and it's in my soul.

Oklahoma! I don't think anybody has said it better than Rodgers and Hammerstein: The wind *does* come sweepin' down the plain, pushing waves and ripples through my father's wheat field that I thought looked like a wide green ocean. Everybody worked hard. Everybody knew life at its most basic. Everybody had a touch of manure on his boots, and laughed about it. Their language was of the earth, and my grandmother Hern could tell farmyard jokes along with the best of them. Everybody had an outhouse, and everybody thought outhouses were funny.

Oklahoma. A sudden thunderstorm can tear up the world. Then, at peace, a sunset fills the entire sky. "Yes you can, you *know* you can!" fills your mind, because people support and encourage each other. At least that's the way I remember it.

I grew up on a farm near my grandparents', near Lahoma, Oklahoma, which is twelve miles from the town of Enid. My father, Delbert Murphy Hern, farmed 160 acres he came by because his brother Orville died in World War I. When they read Orville's Army insurance policy, it was made out "to my baby brother, Delbert." Grandpa took the money, in 1917, and made a down payment on a quarter-section for my father, then only seven.

I was born on February 14, 1933, and by then my family was clinging to their land by their fingernails. Some of our neighbors had been swept away to California, to the poorhouse, to oblivion, along with the dry red earth of their mortgaged farms. Steinbeck wrote about our kind, the Okies whose land was blown out from under them. But the *real* Okies, the Herns and others like us, stayed.

We stayed on our little hard-scrabble farms and fought foreclosure, and when the crops failed and prices dropped at the same time, we grew what we could to feed ourselves. Mother and I fled into Enid to her sister Lillian's house when the dust storms came—because the weather that had brought the abundant crops for Thomas Jefferson Murphy turned out to be only a freak spell; the real climate was drier. But the homesteaders had cleared and farmed the land as if it were like the land they had come from, and would stay forever as rich and moist as it had been for those few years at the turn of the century. Now, following the drought, the topsoil was blowing away. During each gritty, blinding storm, we moved to Enid, where we sat with wet handkerchiefs over our faces. Afterward we would shovel out our little farmhouse until the next storm. The Herns hung on.

"Marvella" was my mother's idea. She wanted to give me something from her Norwegian heritage. She named me for her grandmother and her sister, Lillian Morvilla, and only changed the spelling because Morvilla seemed a bit too harsh. (My middle name, Belle, was for my mother's mother, Belle Koetke Monson.) My unusual name was a gift, and if I heard someone call "Marvella" at a basketball game, there was only me to answer. It pleased my mother when I told her I liked my name.

It pleased my mother to have me, she said, although my birth ruptured her vertebrae, and she would suffer for many years. Mama was an orphan who dreamed all her childhood of someday having a daughter to love as she had not been loved. She once wrote about me: "On her I have poured out all the hopes and ambitions that for some reason have been denied me."

My mother, Bernett Hern, was born in 1908 to Elef and Belle Monson, on the rolling prairies of North Dakota, just south of the Canadian border. At home, they spoke her father's native Norwegian. But before she was two, he was killed by a train during a blinding snowstorm, and her widowed mother died the autumn just before Mama turned six. The four orphaned children—Ernest was ten and the two older girls fifteen and sixteen—stayed alone out there on the prairie all winter, fighting illness and hunger and cold, keeping their chickens alive so they could at least have eggs to eat. The following spring, their mother's mother, a widow who had married a Mr. Wolf and moved to Oklahoma, took a train to North Dakota to fetch the girls, leaving eleven-year-old Ernest behind with an uncle. Ernest had told six-year-old Bernett that "Mrs. Wolf" would have a long tail and big, sharp teeth, scaring the child half to death.

Life was harsh and unpleasant on her grandmother's farm. My mother's toes were always stunted and gnarled because the thrifty Wolfs refused to buy new shoes for the growing child. The two older girls soon left to make their own way, leaving the youngest to endure the strict conditions imposed by these older, tired grandparents, who had already raised one large crop of children. There were no games, and few playmates. When a neighbor, moving away, offered my mother a pony, the Wolfs refused. Feed would be too costly. As children will, she filled her mind with fantasies of how perfect life would be, had her mother only lived. She endured the lonely, austere life until, at the age of twelve, she went to work as hired help, living on other people's farms, working in their houses and cooking for harvest, all the way through many schools until she finished high school.

"Some of the families were nice," she told me, "but others were just terrible. The men treated the women and children badly." Some took advantage of the child-worker, reneging on promises to clothe her; others worked her too hard, treating her unkindly.

In Drummond, Mother found the Andersons, who became a real family to her. She called them Mother Anderson and Papa Joe, and worked in their nice house across the street from the high school in Drummond, where she went for her last two academic years. Her dream was to go to college, but there was no way she could afford it.

She met my father in high school; they fell in love. After graduation, he enrolled at Phillips University in Enid, and she went to work for the telephone company there. In 1929, he dropped out of college to marry, and to work the quarter-section of land on which my grandfather had put the down payment with Uncle Orville's insurance money. He was nineteen and she was twenty-one, and they were very happy together on that farm. My mother milked the cows and helped in the field at harvest those first years. When times were hardest, Mother Anderson and Papa Joe loaned them money, because they knew they'd always get it back. As friends and relatives lost their land and left for California, Delbert and Bernett harvested their crop of wheat and then drove up north, through Kansas, demonstrating and selling aluminum cookware. It brought in pennies, but they managed to keep the farm. Three and a half years later, along with the blowing dirt that killed people and cattle, the bad weather, and a wheat-freeze, I arrived.

For my mother, I was nearly a calamity, for I came early, while her doctor, Dr. Harris, was in Texas attending a funeral. Instead of having me by Caesarean section, she endured hours of pain, and then the doctor in Enid's General Hospital extricated me with forceps, rupturing her spine. When he returned, Dr. Harris was furious. "I would not treat an animal the way you have treated this woman," he told the other doctor. "I am going to run you out of town." And he did.

"Depression Baby," they called me. Just existing was a struggle for my parents, with the drought shriveling to dust year after year of baby wheat shoots, then a driving rainstorm flattening the 1936 crop, the grasshoppers killing off the rest. My mother tried to work in the fields alongside my father, but often as not, she fell ill with excruciating spasms in her back for weeks on end.

But I was adored. I was happy. I was oblivious to their struggle and suffering, because they made survival seem a wonderful challenge.

We lived in a little frame house with no plumbing or electricity, with kerosene lamps, and a wood-burning stove in the dining room the only heat. An Oklahoma winter can be as cold as Chicago —I'd nearly freeze while my mother filled the round tin tub with water heated on the stove for my nighttime bath on the kitchen floor. (Or, when it was even colder, while running through the snow to the outhouse. Brrrr.)

Winter was butchering time, with fresh sausage and then making soap in the big black pot; winter was ice-cream time, with chunks of ice snatched from the cattle-watering tanks fueling the hand-cranked ice-cream freezer; winter was blizzards piling snow higher than the fence posts. I'd take my old dog Jake, who was part something and part something else, and we'd go out rabbit hunting when everything drifted over. We would find a little hole in the snow, which I always opened up enough for Jake to get his head and shoulders into, and he would go in after the rabbit, reappearing way down the road at the other end of the snowdrift, sometimes with a rabbit and sometimes not. And winter was the long, lax period when wheat farmers did not have to work from sunrise to sunset, when my daddy was at home a lot.

I thought my daddy was the most wonderful daddy a girl ever had. I was his little buddy. His pal. Anywhere he was, I was, hopping into the pickup with a "let's go," if it were ten miles or a thousand. When Daddy went scouting for some custom wheat cutting in Colorado or Kansas, Mother would braid my hair and throw some clothes in a sack, and off I'd go with him. Or if he was out in the field, I was in the field. He built for me a little seat beside his on the combine, another on the tractor. He always pulled my wagon behind the hay baler.

He rode a big, high-stepping horse, Babe, and he bought me a Shetland pony, Punky, to trot along beside him. He picked me up and brushed me off when ornery Punky deposited me in the sand-burrs, which was often. I was his towheaded tomboy, making a daredevil climb to the top of the barn roof or the hay mound, play-ing with the chickens or Donny and Leoral Scheffee, the neighbor boys, up and down trees, on the hay baler and threshing machine. Sometimes I'd have to yell for Daddy to get me down.

He was handsome, a farmer who dressed in khaki pants and shirt, not overalls like most of his neighbors. He always wore a straw hat, smoked a big cigar, and carried a pocket knife. When we were out driving around in the summertime, we'd buy watermelons. He would take that pocket knife, wipe it off on the side of his pants, split open the melon, slice out the heart for him and for me, and we'd sit down by the side of the truck and eat it, juice dripping down our chins. We'd find an outside water pump and Daddy would work the handle, to set the water rushing. He taught me to cup my hands, scoop the water up and drink it, cold fresh water in the Oklahoma dust. Sometimes we would splash that water all over our faces, our heads, and laugh with the fun of it.

He drove a red pickup truck with "Delbert Hern, Auctioneer" painted on the side. I remember riding on the running board, or on the front fender, hanging on for dear life as he drove slowly across the fields. I loved to watch him at auctions, listening to the strange language that rolled off his tongue, mystified as to how he or they, the farmers who stood around the auction ring in their over-alls, knew exactly who had bid what for which calf. He supplemented his income that way, as well as by "custom cutting"—following the harvest up north after our wheat was cut in June, driving his big combine on the highway from Kansas to Colorado, clear up to the Dakotas, hiring out to other farmers until summer's end.

He was meticulous, precise; he expected good performance from other people, he gave good performance in return. He took pride in his work, kept his equipment in perfect condition. He had a great respect for land and machinery, and for life itself. When meat was scarce, he'd shoot a rabbit for food, but he abhorred killing for sport. "Never kill a living thing, Marvella," he'd say. "God loves every life as much as He loves yours."

He told me I was his pride and joy, and he encouraged me to do anything I wanted to in life, and to do it well. Many times, when I was in a play at school or a recital, he was the only daddy there.

My parents laughed a lot, and were affectionate with each other and with me. My pretty mother, who had snappy brown eyes and blond hair, mended my father's trousers over and over again, turned his cuffs and collars, sewed for me, rolled and combed my hair, taught me to make my bed, hang up my clothes, and clean house. In the evening my father would make up stories, or my mother would read to me, and we all listened. We all kissed each other goodnight, and goodbye. They didn't spare the rod. I was spanked soundly for disobeying, or for being sassy. There was no liquor in the house—they were strict teetotalers then. We said prayers at mealtime, and we went to the little country church every Sunday, where my mother taught my Sunday School class.

One Sunday, the church was filled with lilacs from Grandma Hern's yard. I'd been told to discard my ever-present chewing gum before church, and when I set about to do so that Sunday, my father caught me just in time. "Don't throw that gum in the yard," he said. "Somebody might step on it."

"Where can I put it?" I asked.

"Behind your ear," he joked, but I took him literally. The wad caught my mother's eye all the way across the church, and I caught the devil.

The elocution lessons were my mother's idea, from her determination to give me all the opportunities "to develop your talent" that had been denied her. From the time I was three, when I began mimicking voices I heard on the old battery radio, she saved a dollar a week—a dollar she sorely needed for clothes, furniture, groceries—to pay Judge Byrd's wife to teach me "expression" every Saturday. Mama wrote out my lessons in her beautiful script, and then taught them to me, word for word.

My first performance was that same year, when, in a yellow crocheted dress, I took to the stage of the Enid Convention Hall and recited "The Little Flirt." Daddy applauded louder than anybody, though I didn't win the contest. It was the first of many years of competitive public speaking.

My days on the farm were spent in coveralls and overalls, romping with Donny and Leoral, or tramping down the road with our shoeshine stand (polish courtesy of Mama; we charged extra for cowboy boots). It was another matter for public speaking. Mother would spend hours washing, starching, and ironing to get those ruffles just so. And then, "Now be careful and don't wrinkle your dress"—and I'd sit on the car seat, ruffles spread out around me, elbows bent and arms up, for the ride to whatever church or auditorium would be presenting the speaking contest. Those contests, where I would recite "readings," poems, short essays—bringing home the prizes—were a great source of pride for my parents. "You talk too much, Marvella Belle," they teased me, but they never tried to shut me up.

On my first day at Lahoma school, the teacher looked around and said, "Well, class, I see we have two children, Billy Carlson and Marvella Hern, who are left-handed. What shall we do about that?"

I blurted right out, "If it's all right with Billy, it's all right with me if you just leave us that way."

At Lahoma school that year, I was forever getting into trouble because I could never remember to raise my hand whenever I had something to say. I would just say it. The teacher talked and talked to me about disrupting the class. Finally she took action. It was so humiliating. The bell would ring, and as those big important high-school kids trooped by on their way to gym, there I would be, sitting out in the hall in my little red chair with a big piece of tape across my mouth. (The tape didn't cure me, however. I still forget to think before I speak!)

As I look back, I realize what an extraordinary effort my parents made to give me the best head start in education that they possibly could. When I was five, alone out there on the farm except for my playmates Donny and Leoral, Mother felt I needed the companionship of other children. As there was no kindergarten at Lahoma school and, with a February birthday, I'd soon be school age, Mother had gone to the Lahoma teacher with her request: "Marvella needs to be with other children. Will you let her start here in first grade, a year early, but not pass her on? Let this be like a kindergarten year."

At the end of first grade, however, the teacher said I was doing as well as the other children, so she passed me on to second grade.

Mother was not so sure. She knew that I had not learned to read. At the beginning of second grade, she and Daddy visited Lahoma school, to see what was being taught so that they could help me at home. The new method of teaching then was the "look-say" technique of reading. They saw the teacher hold up a card, with "there" printed on it. One child would holler out, "There!" and so would everybody else.

Only I didn't say anything.

At home, Daddy tried to help. He took little cards, printed words such as "there," "the," "they," "those," and pinned them on the curtains. It was like a game. I was to go around the room, and tell him what the words said. But he very quickly realized that I couldn't do it.

Because of my success with the "expression" lessons, memorizing and delivering readings that she read to me, Mother reasoned that old-fashioned phonics might crack the literacy code for her child. Phonics were taught at Spencer school, the little one-room schoolhouse which was two miles down the road from our farm but not in our school district. My mother enrolled me in Spencer school to complete the second grade.

I wouldn't take anything for the experience. All eight grades were in that one room, which had a potbellied stove in the middle, and the cloakroom was curtained off to conceal our lunch pails. It was at Spencer that I began to learn to read.

Armed with the knowledge that this method would indeed work for me, Mother set about to find a larger school that would offer phonics as well as educational opportunities missing from the one-room school. Miss Croft, the second-grade teacher at Drummond, roomed at Grandma Anderson's, where my mother had once lived and worked. My parents paid her a visit. Yes, she taught phonics, but Drummond was a two-hour school bus ride, way outside our school district; there would be extra tuition, which my parents could ill afford. But they scrimped, sending me off to catch the bus at Grandma Hern's corner, for the opportunity of learning at a bigger school, an experience as enriching as the one-room school, though in a different way.

I loved the long bus ride, watching the older children flirt and pair off, learning to sing "You Are My Sunshine," looking out the window at the new winter wheat waving at the sky. I had one great moment of triumph on that bus, when a bigger boy tugged at my long curls one time too many. The next day I purposely sat behind him and without warning slammed my lunch bucket down on his head. "Don't mess with Marvella," they teased him.

At Drummond, I learned to study, and, partly because of the speech competition experience, to excel. I was lucky. For children who have difficulty learning to read today, sophisticated tests have been devised to determine just how they can learn best. My parents had no such tests at their disposal; they had only the determination that somehow I would be educated, and kept looking until they found the right way.

The Drummond school bus stop at Grandma Hern's corner gave me a chance to enjoy even more good times with that remarkable lady. Sometimes I'd ride Punky over to her house and leave him in the barn until the school bus came back in the afternoon, and sometimes mother would fetch me. "There was such squealing and carrying on coming out of the house I was sure there was a birthday party going in there," Mother would say. It was just Grandma Hern and me, slinging rolled-up newspapers at each other across the dining-room table.

Grandma had waited a long time for a little girl. She was full of fun and ideas for my cousin Patricia and me. There was a swing in her yard, hanging from a big tree, and a little gizmo with a wheel and handle to run up and down her narrow sidewalk. When I was tiny, she'd rig up reins out of rags, and hitch up the stair-bannister for a fine horse. She taught me how to string buttons or spools to make a toy, how to hammer nails into the ground to make a design. She let me go fishing in the kitchen sink—pumping a sink full of water and filling it with rubber jar rings. She bent a pin and tied it to a string for fishing gear, and we fished for the jar rings as if they were fine lake bass. She had a milk house and a cave, or cellar, where she stored her home-canned fruit and vegetables. I would sit spellbound, watching her make butter, chanting as she churned, "Come butter come. Marvella Belle wants some."

I remember once when Patricia, Uncle Otis's daughter, and I were spending the night at Grandma Hern's. She popped into our room to tell us goodnight. "Now each of you name the four corners of the room for four boys you know," she said, "and when you wake. up in the morning, the first corner you look at—that will be the boy you marry."

Grandma's sprightly spirit, her fun and attention, meant all the more to me because my mother was so often confined to her bed. Mama could get along for months and be just fine, and then she might step up to get into the car when we were in town shopping, and freeze, locked in pain. In the first years, it would go away after a few days, but then it got worse, and she would have to lie flat for weeks at a time. At her worst, she had difficulty feeding herself, because she could not use her arms. By the time I was in Drummond school, her pain was more frequent, more intense, and I knew that it had been caused by my birth.

About that time I began to put on layers and layers of fat. I was as wide as I was tall. The kids called me "Lardy" or "Fatty." Though I still made public recitations, I felt everybody was snickering at my fat. For a year, I had desperately wanted a pair of cowgirl boots. But when my parents took me to the store for my birthday, and I tried to pull on the boots, my legs were so fat they wouldn't go up over my ankles. It broke my heart. "*We* love you, Marvella Belle," my mother would say. "Don't call me Marvella *Belle*," I shouted back. "That sounds like a cow!"

The fat was especially uncomfortable during our scorching Oklahoma summers—but now, at least, we had an electric fan. The New Deal, and the rural electricity that came with it, profoundly changed our lives. It meant that we had an electric pump, which brought cold water into the kitchen (although we never had an indoor bathroom at the farm). It meant that we had a refrigerator. An electric vacuum cleaner. A heating pad for my mother's back. The luxury of an electric radio. And the blessed, blessed relief of the electric fan. My grandparents never did have electricity— Grandma continued to do her wash on the scrub-board, drawing her water into the kitchen by hand-pump, as long as she lived on the farm.

The new wonder of electricity had taken some getting used to. The first winter after it was installed, somebody told my parents to put an electric lightbulb under the covers to keep my feet warm, as the only heat in the house was that wood-burning stove in the dining room. At daylight, they would go out to milk the cows, leaving me asleep upstairs. One morning, when they returned, they smelled something burning. The lightbulb had burned a hole almost all the way through to the top of my pile of blankets, scorching the feet of my pajamas. It was, I suppose, my first narrow escape.

Dangers notwithstanding, electricity was an incredible boon, a gift, we felt, from the President. We gathered around the radio, hanging on to every word from Franklin D. Roosevelt. "He's going to be our savior," predicted my father, and he set about to involve himself in Democratic politics.

But it was December 7, 1941, that altered our lives drastically.

I was performing in a piano recital in Enid that Sunday when one of the fathers rushed in to announce the news he'd heard on the radio. My father, who owed so much to his brother Orville, the soldier who died in France, was impatient to join up. He was thirty-one when he enlisted, heading for Officers Candidate School. There were farewell parties for him, and Mother and I cried, but he explained that it was his patriotic duty. The day we took him to Fairview to catch the bus for Oklahoma City, we stopped by the mailbox. There was the paper with the headline: FARMERS DEFERRED. MUST RAISE FOOD FOR THE TROOPS. I cried and begged. "Daddy, you don't have to go now. Please stay here. Mother's health is bad. Grandma is sick." But he went ahead to Oklahoma City. The next day, he came back. They told him he was needed to raise food for the troops.

He felt embarrassed and guilty about not serving his country, as all three of his brothers had served in World War I, and so he began to raise food with a vengeance. He wanted to be of service, and the first thing we knew, he was running for the state legislature, from Major County. I remember my father going out in the truck at night, trying to meet people out in Major County, campaigning and working his farm at the same time. He lost.

He worked twice as hard as before. Prices were up, the weather was better; he added more acreage and another mortgage, and bought more machinery, including electric milking machines. But there was a shortage of help.

The summer I was ten, he had only an old man to drive the truck to haul wheat at harvest, one woman to drive the pickup, himself to drive the combine, and nobody to drive the tractor that pulled the combine.

"I can't pull a crew together," Daddy moaned.

"Let me drive the tractor," I offered. After all, hadn't I practically driven it from my little seat all those years?

"It's too heavy, Marvella." It was one of the big old tractors of the days before self-propelled combines, big enough to pull the huge harvesting machines.

"Please, please let me try," I begged.

Finally, he told Mama, "Let me take her out there and let her try it, just to show her she can't do it."

I couldn't even drive a car, of course, but I was determined. I've never strained so hard in my life: Drive a straight row. Don't let the machine go dead. Shift gears. When we came to a corner I'd have to stand up and throw my whole body on the steering wheel to get it to turn the corner. But I did it. And Daddy hired me, at five dollars a day, to help harvest. I took pride in rounding those corners close, so there wouldn't be any wheat left standing. The strong Oklahoma wind blew the chaff all around me, into my eyes, even behind my goggles, and down the back of my neck, and sometimes my daddy would stop the combine, whip out his big old red bandanna handkerchief, and wipe my eyes. At evening, I'd be covered with red dirt, and totally exhausted, but I'd worked all day in the fields, like a grown man.

"Do your best," my mother always told me. "Do your part." Every year thereafter, until my senior year, I helped at harvest.

The air was always charged with excitement at harvest time. It was a race against the weather: one hard rain could destroy the crop, driving a year's income into the ground.

Big family dinners at Grandma's house after church on Sunday were always an occasion. There were cousins, uncles, aunts, Grandma's plain home cooking, story telling, practical jokes. During harvest time, Sunday dinner was a feast, with hired hands, sometimes the neighbors, sometimes the preacher, all digging into a mountain of fried chicken, cornbread, homemade cakes, big purple plums.

Aunty would be there, my mother's sister Lillian Morvilla, who treated me as a daughter (she had two boys), and her husband Oren Tharp. Aunty is a wisp of a woman, but she has glowed with a love and gentleness that has touched family, friends, and neighbors ever since I first knew her. Like my Hern grandparents, Aunt Lillian is deeply religious. The peace of soul that faith brings her is something to be envied. She prays for God's will to be done. (And through her many acts of kindness through the years, I'm sure she has been doing it herself.) Aunt Lavern, mother's other sister, had moved to California during the Depression. It is Aunt Lillian, who lived in Oklahoma during most of my childhood and lives there still, who is Aunty to me.

Aunty cared for my mother and me in the house in Enid for the first few weeks after I was born; it was to Aunty's house that we fled during the dust storms. When I was sick with measles they took me in to Aunty's. On Saturdays, when Mama drove into Enid to do the week's shopping, after my lessons she would park me at

Aunty's while she made her rounds. Aunty would stand in the kitchen, baking scrumptious cinnamon rolls, cakes, pies—and miniatures for me—and stand me in a chair beside her to stir raisins in a bowl of water for "raisin soup."

Aunty's husband, Uncle Oren, had a way of making you laugh when nobody else could, without trying to. One Sunday when they arrived at Grandma Hern's for dinner, Grandma was standing on the front porch with her washtub turned upside down, holding a small rope that led underneath the tub.

"Oren, we caught a big white owl," she said, "the biggest one I ever saw. We got him under there and I'm afraid he'll get away if I let go this rope. Will you hold on to him while I finish with dinner?"

So she handed him the rope, and he stood there holding the rope for about thirty minutes, talking to everybody as they gathered around. At last Grandma came out.

"Dinner's ready," she announced. "And by the way, Oren, you want to show everybody the owl?"

Uncle Oren lifted the washtub, and there, with the rope tied around it, was a big white chamber pot.

Grandma Hern never let him live it down.

When Grandma took sick, not long after, I wanted to be of help, for Grandpa Hern was old and stiff, and couldn't manage the house. Every Saturday, I'd go over to mop and wax the floors. I'm afraid I waxed right over some dirt, but at the end of my job, Grandpa would creep over to his desk, take out his old leather coin purse, and hand me a quarter. I was very proud of earning that quarter.

One Saturday, as I was finishing, I mopped backwards down the hall until my leg bumped into the bucket, and I sat, with a thump, in the filthy mop water. I couldn't get out and I began to holler. Grandma, from her bed, called out, "Earnie, Earnie, she's stuck!" I'll never forget Grandpa, moving like a snail down that hall, or Grandma's jolly laughter at the indignity of it all.

I was so fat.

Mama went down in her back that fall when I was ten, and the doctor said she'd never walk again. Daddy cared for her as best he could, then made the decision to move us from the farm into Enid, into a little two-bedroom bungalow where my mother could be near doctors, where we had an indoor bathroom, and where a hired girl could come and help cook, as Mama had done for others when she was a girl.

My father was not satisfied with the diagnosis, however. "Somewhere in this country of ours there must be somebody who can help you, Bernett," he said. "I don't care if it costs a million dollars." And taking all his precious war-rationed gasoline stamps, he drove us to Rochester, Minnesota, to the renowned Mayo Clinic, removing one front seat of the car so Mother could lie on a stretcher.

She was told, to our great joy, that there was a chance, with spinal surgery, requiring a ninety-day hospitalization period.

"And by the way, young lady," my father said to me. "What shall we do about you?"

I weighed 125 pounds and should have weighed 90, a flour sack of a girl with a string tied around my 32-inch waist. In my autograph book, my classmate idol Benny Garner had written, "Dear Marvella, if you get any fatter, I shall render you for lard." It hurt.

The doctors agreed with my father that something should be done, and, sure enough, they discovered a thyroid imbalance and began medication. And then they started me on my diet. "You'll have a lifelong battle to keep your weight down," the doctor told me, "but you can do it." For two weeks, I ate in the Mayo diet kitchen, with each gram of specially prepared food weighed on a scale, and the dieticians drilled me on the foods that I could and could not eat.

We took Mama to Oklahoma City, to McBride's Bone and Joint Hospital, for her surgery. She was there two months. Since I was beginning fifth grade at a new school, I lived at home in Enid, taking evening meals and sometimes spending the night with the Rex Esques, the kind family next door. My father was either in Oklahoma City with Mama or out on the farm, and could not supervise my diet. He sat me down for a serious talk.

"This battle is yours alone, Marvella. I can't do it for you," he said. "I won't spend the money again to send you to Mayo or any other clinic. You have to choose now, if you want to spend the rest of your life fat or thin."

I was lonely for my mother. The temptations were great. Everybody munched on candy bars at recess; after school there sat our refrigerator, the mecca for any growing youngster. It became a challenge. Each week we weighed, and sent my progress chart to Mayo Clinic. Each week was a skirmish won. Between September and Christmas, I lost 25 pounds. And I kept it off.

That first victory, at ten years of age, was a grand experience. Not only did I enter puberty with a new pride in my appearance, but I gained something else of great value: I was in control. Nobody else did it for me. Forever after, I knew I could be in control of myself.

It helped me take responsibility when Mama came back home, to lie in bed for her slow recovery. "Marvella, you must do this because I can't," she'd say in her quiet voice, and off I'd go on the strange bus, a little country girl in the big wide city of Enid, to pay the gas bill and the electric bill, do the banking, buy the groceries. Although a hired girl came to help out when mother was down, I learned to look after my own clothes and my hair, and in that bustling, can-do young city of Enid, Oklahoma, I grew up fast.

Chapter 2

The war that came to an end with a celebration in the streets of Enid brought sadness to our family. My cousin Orville, Uncle Clarence's oldest, had been killed when his plane crashed on a training flight in Florida. Grandma Hern grieved the most, for he was her only grandson, namesake of the son killed in World War I.

For my father, World War II did not bring the prosperity that lifted so many American farmers out of the Depression. He was able to add to his land, over the years, but the medical expenses for my mother, at a time when there was little medical insurance, were so incredibly heavy that he never did get very far ahead. He studied the latest farming methods, he planted crops suited for the climate; his yield was high if the weather was favorable and the "green bug" could be controlled.

These near-microscopic pests came in swarms, turning a beautiful field of wheat brown overnight. We thought the costly new pesticides a great boon. My father would hire a light crop-dusting plane to swoop low over the wheat field and drop a white cloud of DDT that would settle on the wheat and kill the green bugs. Airplanes weren't all that common in those days, and I remember hanging on the fence to watch the plane spray the fields, inhaling the pungent odor as the poison blew right over us. Nobody knew then about the dangers of DDT.

If they had warned us, I know my father would have been more careful, because he never spared any expense when it came to the health of his family. He was concerned about proper diet and fresh air, and thought of the body as the most finely tuned machine in Creation.

When I was eleven, I caught pneumonia, and to alleviate the after-effects of asthmatic bronchitis I was taken to Oklahoma City every Saturday for x-ray treatments on my bronchial tubes. The x-ray treatments left me ill each time, but no one worried then about the danger of excessive radiation.

Mama continued to be in ill health much of the time, which frightened me. After several major operations, with migraine, and with a painful nerve disorder, she was "down" (sick in bed) for weeks at a time, suffering silently. Doctors became an important factor in our lives. We revered them, these holders of the secret of healing. Dr. Harris in Drummond had been like a member of our family. In Enid, we came to depend on Dr. Leroy Gau. Dr. Leroy, an osteopathic surgeon, and his brother Dr. Vernon bought an old rooming house, revamped it, and turned it into Gau Hospital. It was there I lay in bed with pneumonia, there my mother was operated on, there each medical crisis in our lives seemed to be solved.

It was to the Gau Hospital that they took Grandma Hern when she fell ill in 1946. She had refused to go unless Grandpa came along too. "Nobody can take care of me like Earnie can," she said. I remember sitting on the hospital porch with Grandpa, watching the Cherokee Strip parade. He and Grandma, who had opened the "Strip" that day in 1893, had ridden in many of the colorful commemorative parades. It was Grandma who wasn't expected to live, but instead, my Grandfather Hern died of a stroke in that hospital. Grandma was so sick they delayed his funeral, expecting her to join him in death, but Dr. Leroy saved her, that October of 1946; she survived for nine years.

She came to live with us in Enid, in a little house my daddy built for her in our back yard, along with a practical nurse he hired to take care of her. Now there was nobody in the old farmhouse, but Daddy still farmed the land and I hired on again at harvest, taller, slender now, sure I was stronger, sure of myself on the tractor.

I didn't particularly want breasts. When they arrived, small though they were, sprouting on my chest during the next harvest season, I resented the intrusion. Driving the tractor, bouncing across the field, was suddenly uncomfortable. I complained to Mama, and she brought home a brassiere for me, which was embarrassing. I liked being a tomboy. But except for harvest, my tomboy days on the farm were over. With Grandpa gone and Grandma in town, home was now Enid, once the magical city on the plains we had only visited on Saturdays, as country people do.

In no time flat, I was attached and bonded as though by glue to a gaggle of girls, whose main preoccupation, outside of bubble gum, was giggling. It was epidemic. We giggled at school if we saw somebody's secret "crush" in the hallway; we giggled at church if somebody's grandpa went to sleep. We giggled until the tears streamed down our faces, and sometimes until we wet our pants, at which we laughed even more.

We shared secrets, collected movie-star posters, kept diaries, learned to blow bubble-gum balloons while trying to execute intricate maneuvers on our roller skates, raced around on our bikes, and swapped comic books and movie magazines. We had the Krazy Kat Club, with a black cat as our insignia, and the Hern Hornets girls' basketball team, of which I was an undersized forward—and, finally, we began dating boys, rather than just giggling at them.

Football and basketball games were our supreme social events, along with the "hops" afterward, when we slid around the gymnasium floor in our socks to "Cruisin' Down the River" or "Lavender Blue." To "Ballerina," Max Meyers or Dwayne Hedges and I would dance until we nearly dropped, or we would cling together during the Mills Brothers' "Till Then," which survived three worn-out records at my home. We "put up" our hair every night (mine was twisted around rag curlers) and collected, more as trophies than as pledges of affection, boys' class rings, which we fit to our fingers with rounds and rounds of adhesive tape, or strung on a velvet ribbon around our necks.

Were those the last of the innocent years? Or was I just sheltered and protected? I remember happiness, excitement, energy, laughter, fun. "Patriotism" was at a premium, the American ideal; "citizenship" was the participatory role toward achieving that ideal. Crime seemed a foreign word—something that occurred in Chicago, maybe. Drugs were the realm of pharmacists; sex was wait-until-you-are-married; the word "homosexual" was not in our vocabulary, or in my consciousness; ours was a "dry" state and I had never laid eyes on a drunk person, until the school band took a trip to Dallas, where I saw a man staggering around in the hotel lobby.

I also was unaware of discrimination. I had no idea which of my friends was Jewish, or Catholic, or Baptist—it never occurred to me to wonder. (I knew of course who was Methodist. We saw each other in church every Sunday.) We knew, by their names, who was Indian—Joe Fishinghawk was hard to miss—but in Enid the Indians were well-integrated, popular members of our high-school life, some, like Betty McGugin, class leaders. On the other hand, segregation of blacks was taken for granted. I never even wondered about it, even when I saw it with my own eyes. Once Frances Long and I boarded a bus and took the only available seats, which were at the back. When a black woman got on the bus, and demanded a seat there, I couldn't understand what the fuss was all about, for I wasn't aware that she couldn't sit anywhere else. And when I went across town to swim at Government Springs Park, I noticed little black children staring in from outside the chain-link fence. I thought they enjoyed watching us swim, not realizing that they were not allowed to join us. Our society conditioned what we were able to perceive. I remember how people who visited us on the farm would complain about our terrible drinking water. I thought they were crazy. After all, didn't we drink it every day? It was the only drinking water I knew. Later, after I'd moved away, I came back one day and pumped a drink of water. It tasted awful. It would be many years before I would come to realize that life was not perfect, not in Enid nor in my own home.

But Enid was a safe place, a clean place, and I think it provided a very special atmosphere in which a country-born girl, flushed with the success of losing all that ugly weight, could flourish. I had an ongoing love affair with Enid, Oklahoma. I liked the way it looked: built around two squares, with neat lawns and sidewalks, trees and flowers; clean, angular buildings on the flat land, dominated by enormous grain elevators towering like Spanish castles on the skyline north of town. A small city on the plains, a *new* city that had sprung up from the tents of the first families who settled the Strip, Enid was a thriving, bustling town of the frontier, where about 40,000 people seemed to be working together to create a good life for us, their children. After all, Oklahoma had been a state only since 1907, and most of the town fathers were just that, not even grandfathers yet. It was as though they'd planned and built a city in which they said, "nothing is too good for our children," and provided us with excellent schools, parks, swimming pools, auditoriums, and plenty of opportunities for talent to develop. At least, that's the way I remember it.

There was a citywide attitude of "Anything is possible"—and if faced with doubt, they'd thrust their chins out and say, "Don't tell me it can't be done because we're going to do it!" And then they would, and they taught us that we could, too. They participated themselves, they helped us to participate, and they showed us how to acquire the tools for leadership.

One of those tools was the competition in citizenship activities and in public speaking. I thrived on that competition. Practically all my after-school time was taken up with speech training and in competing in talent shows or speech tournaments, or simply in performing at farmers' gatherings, 4-H Clubs, home economics clubs, and church meetings. We memorized "readings," poetry, and famous speeches, then learned to write our own speeches and to compete in a category called "extemporaneous speaking." That, perhaps because I was used to talking out of turn, was my specialty.

As I developed, and the giggling subsided, I began to build confidence with a series of small successes that made me eager for each new challenge. I shot through my youth like a small missile, propelled by a drive and determination that I didn't quite under-stand, guided and supported all the way by my parents. It was as though their main goal, their singular focus, was to make me happy and to develop whatever talents they saw emerging in me. They encouraged me to go as far in life as I could go—and even further. My father's brother Clarence was the only college graduate of their families; I would be the first female to have a college education. "The sky is the limit for you, Marvella," my father would say. There was never a suggestion that because I was a girl, I would be restricted in any way. Around our table, everybody had a right to his or her opinion, and spoke it. They listened to me and my endless recitations of school trivia as earnestly as if I were Edward R. Murrow on the evening radio. They gave me lessons in self-sufficiency—and yet they were always there, my great mainstay.

Part of the self-sufficiency came from necessity: my mother's ill health. Whenever she went "down," I had to run a household—a mixed blessing. I can remember setting the alarm forty-five minutes early every morning, when I was in the eighth grade, to clean the house and hang out the wash before going to school. After school I had to iron my clothes. A country girl, Claunda Kain, moved in to help cook while Mama was down, and, because there was no-place else, shared my bedroom for the duration of Mama's illness.

When my mother was well, however, there was no end to her imagination, or devotion, or energy for me. I thought she was beautiful. She played out my girlhood as if she were making up for her own. When Frances Long and I decided to have a "stand" in the front yard, to buy and sell Cokes and candy, comic books and movie magazines, Mama set it up, made gallons of lemonade and iced tea, and kept us in business. She would stage circuses in the back yard, dressing one girl as a fortune teller, setting up one booth where you could throw rings over jars, and another with a dartboard, and then she stayed in the kitchen popping corn by the barrelful, for our popcorn sales. She taught the auburn-haired Frances and me songs from a record, dressed us up in baggy pants, and entered us in the Talent Contest at Convention Hall against people with real talent, singing "Bigfoot Joe was a so-and-so, as mean as he could be, why just last night he started a fight, he was picking on poor little me. . . ." She would traipse around the countryside, ferrying the Caldwell sisters and me about with our "act," as we dressed up in stovepipe hats or pinafores to sing and dance or recite at country churches, Home Demonstration meetings, and the like. She was always ready with a costume or an alteration, or a fresh change of clothes. She was always dressing me up, enrolling me in all kinds of speech tournaments, helping me learn to recite "The Poor Old Maid" or "Suds, the Prize Baby," listening to my rehearsals of "The Mountain Whippoorwill" or "The Touch of the Master's Hand." She kept a meticulous scrapbook titled "Accomplishments of Our Little Girl." I later wrote: "The main enjoyment I get out of winning anything or receiving any title is that it gives my parents so much satisfaction and thrills them so."

During these years I grew even closer to my father. "Daddy's little tomboy" had grown into a perfectionist of a girl, who would spend an hour ironing a skirt to get every pleat just so, but who still helped at harvest. He survived my giggling stage, perhaps because of his own sense of humor, which, like Grandma Hern's, ran to prankish practical jokes, and now, as father to teenager, he guided me, gave me advice ("Roll with the punches, Marvella; always roll with the punches"), and was always available for a heart-to-heart talk. He was gentle with me, and with everybody else.

"I didn't want to have Delbert," Grandma Hern said, "and now look. I couldn't live without him." After Grandpa died, my father cared for her, supported her. He helped others, too, giving people work when there was none, loaning people money (some of which he'd never see again) even when he himself was in debt, and guiding young men who had no parents. "Work as hard as you can, for yourself," he taught me. "But you aren't anything at all if you can't lend a helping hand to others."

He worked hard at farming in those days, but had time, after the wheat was harvested, to do things with the family. He'd take my Sunday School class on excursions, and once he drove Mother and me to California to visit Aunt Lavern, and once to visit the nation's capital. It was Daddy who drove me all over the state to enter speech competitions, coaching me, giving me honest critiques, but always telling me over and over, "You can do it, Marvella, you can win."

It never occurred to me to notice that others had more than we did, that I had fewer and less expensive clothes, that our five-room bungalow at 2024 West Oklahoma was very modest. It was my haven. Home was home, and I loved it. My mother did without many things. The furniture was old and, as I look back, nondescript, but I never thought about it with an eye to appearance. A sofa was good if it was comfortable; a chair was a chair; a lamp was for light.

One week the Krazy Kats would crowd into our little living room-dining room one afternoon after school, and hold a grand old meeting, and the next week we'd spread out in a mansion across town, and nobody thought about comparisons. We all went to school together, ran around together, spent nights in each other's homes, and mine, because of the love that lived there, was a mecca for all my friends.

My parents' bedroom was tiny; mine was as small. Daddy had made a desk table out of plywood; Mother had sewn a ruffled skirt for a dressing table that we painted, and added bows to the ruffles; I had a second-hand bed, cut down from a four-poster. On the floor beneath pictures of Raymond Massey and Dana Andrews and Peter Lawford and Van Johnson stood two huge Truman-Barkley posters that I'd sequestered from a Democratic county convention. I was as ardent a Democrat as my parents. (When Frances Long came to spend the night, she'd insist that Truman and Barkley be turned to the wall: "I can't undress with *them* looking at me!" Her family was Republican.) My father had put up a basketball hoop for me on the garage. I worked out there until I left home, shooting baskets to relax after intensive bouts of studying.

I studied until late every night, determined to stay on the honor roll, striving for grades, memorizing the parts of a leaf quickly for a botany test, forgetting just as quickly the next week. I worked to please my parents and my teachers, and because one job well done led to another, I soon was accepting more than my share of "leadership" roles—because my family expected it of me, and praised me for it. Scholarship didn't come easy for me; I always felt that I had to study twice as hard as my friends, especially after other school responsibilities started snowballing: student council, yearbook, class plays, Oklahoma Honor Society, class presidency—and band.

The Enid High School Marching Band was our great pride, with its splendid uniforms, its half-time spectaculars, its trips to perform in other cities. Our white-haired band director, G. Ray Bonham, had studied under John Philip Sousa—and everybody in three states could tell it, from the sound of our band. Though I wasn't musical, I volunteered to join—keeping track of the sheet music and carrying the American flag. "School spirit" at Enid High, not only for band and athletics but also for student government, forensics, music, drama, and scholarship, was infectious, stemming from principal D. Bruce Selby, the former football coach who ran the school like a head cheerleader. At Christmas, he'd dress up in a Santa suit and hand out outrageous presents. One year mine was a chain of bubble gum (not so outrageous, considering that I was an addict). Most of the students liked Mr. Selby, and responded to his encouragement to "get involved."

At the end of my junior year, I began to reap some rewards from all those involvements. I was elected president of the 900-person student body, the first girl ever to have won that responsibility. But even before the honor of that election could sink in, I was whisked off to the beginning of the key experience of my young life.

The summer before our senior year, five girls were selected to represent Enid at Girls' State that June of 1950. There would be a statewide "convention," an enclave at Oklahoma College for Women at Chickasha, where we would learn, and actually live the steps for local and county and state electoral politics. The Enid American Legion Auxiliary enlisted many of the town's service and social clubs to help sponsor our representatives. My parents were impressed with the fairness of the competition. "Just think," my father said, "we aren't members of any of those organizations, and yet our daughter was selected to represent Enid." Daddy was running for the state legislature from Garfield County that year, trying to campaign and get the planting done at the same time. This would be the first year that I wouldn't be around to help at harvest (at fourteen I had graduated from the tractor to driving the pickup truck).

Off we went to Chickasha, to live in dorms and begin our week-long careers as representatives of twelve model "cities" of Oklahoma, members of two mock political parties: the "Boomers," named for the early professional promoters of the Oklahoma Territory, and "Sooners," that minority who sneaked in to stake claims before the 1889 run officially opened (a name lifted to respectability by the University of Oklahoma football team). I was a Boomer. We held party caucuses, then "city," "county," and "state" elections, and wound up with a governor, a lieutenant governor, a cabinet, and a legislature.

In the city elections, I was named mayor of "Johnson City," and that evening, friends from Enid and I sat down to plot my campaign for governor. Each of us organized her own dorm and laid out elaborate campaign strategy, scheduling rallies and meetings at which candidates would come round and speak. They enlisted new friends to make posters, write songs, buttonhole friends, invade the cafeteria with campaign speeches, and build up a groundswell of young, soprano Boomers.

By midweek, at the nominating convention, I was hoarse, sleepless from hours of preparing speeches and studying the next day's strategy. In addition, I was astounded by my backers, most of whom I'd never met before, who put in as many hours as I did, working together in an ever-enlarging team for my candidacy. It was my first lesson in the reality of politics, and one that continues to fill me with awe: friends working together with a common purpose.

That Wednesday night, I was nominated Boomer candidate for governor. My Sooner opponent was Betsy Klein, from Ardmore, an articulate, poised, and charming girl.

One morning during the campaign, as I was walking toward the flag-raising ceremonies, a dark-haired girl hurried up beside me. "I heard you speak last night, and I want you to know I'm going to vote for you, even though I'm Jewish."

"Thank you, but why would that make a difference?" I asked.

"Well, so is Betsy," she said.

I was so ignorant of other people's religions that I had never thought to wonder what Betsy's was, nor did I have any knowledge of the special bond of Judaism that would make this girl's choice a hard decision.

c✎

On election day, all 370 of us sat in the auditorium, half-listening to a lecture, while they counted the ballots, Betsy on a front-row seat on one side of the room and me on the opposite side. Our names were called out last.

"For Governor of Oklahoma, the winner is . . . Marvella Hern of Enid." At that second, before the cheering broke out and I tried to breathe, Betsy Klein shot out of her chair like a rocket, and raced across the auditorium to congratulate me. She was one of the most instinctively gracious people I'd ever met.

Governor of Oklahoma. If only pretend, for a year, for Girls' State. It would be days before I could breathe normally. My parents drove down for the inauguration, beaming with the pride I didn't dare show, almost beside themselves as the real governor, Roy J. Turner, delivered the oath of office to me the last day. I fairly floated, as the Governor of Boys' State, Fallis Bell of Tulsa, led me down the promenade for the Boys' State-Girls' State ball. ("Boys at last!" was the cry in our dorms. Some of our delegates became physically sick after a week without their "steadies.")

There were interviews, pictures in the paper, and a welcome-home parade for me in Enid. My father interrupted his farming and his campaign, just to run around being proud of me. We were good people, country people, proud-and-barely-getting-by-people, and, well, we'd never produced a celebrity before. I knew full well that I couldn't have won anything by myself, that those four other Enid girls and scores of others had worked their socks off for me. My parents, my Aunt Lillian Morvilla, and Grandma Hern felt enough glory for all of us.

There was something else to look forward to: going off to Washington, D.C., in August, to represent Oklahoma at Girls' Nation.

My parents were a little hurt; they couldn't understand why I was so adamant about going without them, on a train all the way to Washington with Betsy Klein, whose graciousness had so impressed the Auxiliary that she was chosen as the other Oklahoma representative. But I had felt a surge of independence at Girls' State: at seventeen I was branching out from Enid and my parents.

All Enid, it seemed, gave me a send-off. The Coulters, good

friends of my parents, even lent me a set of brand-new luggage, which I could unpack with pride at Mount Vernon College, in Washington. There were a hundred girls, two from each state, Washington, D.C., and the Canal Zone, ready to divide into "Federalists" and "Nationalists" and conduct a mock national administration. Taking part gave us an understanding of national government that no amount of textbook teaching could match. At the Capitol, we met young Senator Hubert Humphrey from Minnesota, who urged us to participate in politics and stressed the importance of the individual, and Senator Margaret Chase Smith of Maine, our own heroine, who took us through her day in the Senate.

It was Margaret Chase Smith who said to us that most of us would be housewives and that we should build strong homes because "the home makes the community, the community makes the state, and the state makes the nation." Such was the prevailing thought about women's priorities in 1950—even from the highest elected woman in the nation. India Edwards, the vice-chairman of the Democratic party, gave us more concrete encouragement, however, about our possibilities of taking part in government.

As impressive to me as the high officials was meeting other seventeen-year-olds with vastly different backgrounds: a Mormon from Utah; a Yankee from Maine; a Georgia belle; a Greek-American from Massachusetts; a black from New Jersey. In that pre-television, pre-jet-travel summer of 1950, those encounters were real eye-openers for me. They gave me the idea for my campaign—I spoke about the need for a Girls' World, a miniature United Nations, where we could get to know one another as people. I was running for President.

The election here was more intense, more serious. Each girl was ambitious, for most had won statewide contests and were under pressure to return home with a higher position—President or Vice President, the only elective offices. The issues were real: Statehood for Hawaii, a strong national defense, a permanent U.N. army. I studied these problems until late at night, made speeches in my earnest Oklahoma twang to my Federalist cohorts, lined up support from Arizona and Michigan and New Jersey, and laughed as we placed little cards on everybody's dining hall trays, "She's Ours, We're Hern!" But voting broke down mostly into party lines. The Federalists, it seemed, had worked harder. I was elected President of Girls' Nation.

There were squeals; I was suddenly on the platform. "—With the greatest humility, I accept this offer—I mean, this honor," I stumbled.

My acceptance speech was filled with polite, patriotic platitudes. I moved through the Candlelight Inauguration and the selecting of my cabinet as though in a dream. Our Congressman, George Howard Wilson, came to the Inauguration, and had it filmed. The other girls teased me because Oklahoma sent not one, but two big purple orchids for my corsage: "If we had oil wells on our state-house lawns, we'd have two orchids, too," they said. There were radio interviews on NBC and MBS, a broadcast for the Voice of America, and, of course, a visit to the White House.

We were all dressed up in our best dresses and white gloves, standing outside the door of the President's office. Sally McTague of Pennsylvania, the "Vice President," and I had a special citation for President Truman. A military aide appeared. "I'm sorry, but due to a sudden development in Korea, the President won't be able to spend the time with you as planned."

But before we could wilt, the President sent word: "I always will have time for the young people of our nation," he said, and invited all 100 of us into the Oval Office. Somehow, he made it seem more casual than ceremonial, like a personal visit. He was bouncy, healthy, and suntanned, and as we stepped out into the garden for the formal presentation, there was the sound of hammering, the renovation of the White House, in the background. "It wasn't always called the White House," he told us. "It was simply the President's House. But after the British burned it during the War of 1812, it was painted white—and the name has hung on." Of course, he predicted that some of us might live in the White House ourselves someday.

Congressman Wilson offered to send Betsy and me to New York, but I declined. I was getting homesick. They had stopped a baseball game in Enid to announce my election over the public-address system, Daddy reported. And homecoming would be a real Oklahoma celebration. My parents met me at the train in Oklahoma City, and we went straight to the State House, where Governor Turner welcomed me with reporters scribbling and cameras clicking, and then to a luncheon in my honor. At the hotel, when we finally had a moment alone, my father said, "Come on, let's have a Coke."

We traipsed down to the coffee shop, my daddy and I, and sat down at a table. He took a deep breath. I shall never forget the look on his face. There was pure adoration in his eyes. I was almost uncomfortable, feeling that some corner had been turned. "How did you do it?" he asked. "Marvella, how ever did you do it?" He had just been defeated in his own campaign for the legislature.

There was another big parade in Enid; the key to the city, our front porch decked with flowers, the Aztec movie theater with my name on the marquee the day the "News of the Week" newsreel was shown with President Truman welcoming me at the White House, speeches about my experience. And everywhere I went, people saying to me, "Marvella, you're going to be the first woman governor of Oklahoma. Just you wait and see!"

It was a great, frothy, all-American whirl, in which I was too caught up to notice the underlying pain at my house. I was stung, however, by the unwitting cruelty of the man who introduced me to the Kiwanis meeting: "Here our Marvella is, President of the whole United States, and her daddy can't even get himself elected to state legislature." Daddy laughed, loudly. I would not know until later how wrong the timing was, or how very hurt he had been.

In fact, I saw very little of the undercurrents at home that senior year, and what I did feel was very confusing. There was so much activity centered around me that it was all my parents could do to keep up their support system: I made ninety-eight speeches to civic clubs and organizations throughout Oklahoma, and made trips to Los Angeles to address the national convention of the American Legion Auxiliary and to Indiana, birthplace of Thomas Jefferson Murphy, to address Girls' State there.

In addition, there was the constant struggle to make A's, the time spent presiding over student council, learning a role for a play, falling in and out of "love" with Dwayne Hedges, W. D. Jones and Kenneth Franklin, and, glory of glories, being elected Band Queen. In a time and place where beauty was at a premium, I never thought of myself as a beauty—not like Patty Cordonnier, the doctor's brunet daughter, or Doris Ackerson, last year's blond Band Queen. My friends and I constantly tried to "improve ourselves," with our pincurls, side-bangs, and neck scarves, analyzing and hoping to conceal our "flaws" and trying to emphasize our "good points." I was concerned about the "Hern hump" on my nose, the shape of my legs. I wished for a milk-white complexion like Joan Gentry's, and developed a fetish for neatness, perhaps to compensate for my "flaws." With Lana Turner and Betty Grable setting certain standards to turn young men's heads, some of my friends stuffed Kleenex into their bras to fill out their strapless "formals." I scoffed. "If anybody ever gets me he'll get me just as I am, small bosom and all," I said. "I want to look natural—no dyed hair, very little makeup." But I worried constantly about my weight, watching every bite. For the former little fat girl from Lahoma, with all those "flaws," being elected Band Queen was a special thrill, though it was not the only decorative post available by a long shot. The high-stepping Bravettes pep squad, cheerleaders, the May Queen and her court who paraded across the concrete bridge over Government Springs Lake, Basketball Queen, Football Queen, Aquaettes Water Queen, and Band Queen—"If there is anything Enid High students love, it is Glamour," reported our yearbook.

As Band Queen, I marched in costume on the arm of the assistant drum major, behind the drum major, in front of the twirlers; at Christmastime they dressed me as Mrs. Santa Claus. I loved it. But aside from the glamor, I loved it for another reason. "This means more to me than Girls' Nation, even," I told my mother. "Anybody can put on a good front for a week, and win an election, but these kids have known me all my life."

I couldn't imagine life without that group of Enid buddies. Norma Jean Hoover, another farmer's daughter, Mary Alice Caldwell, who performed on stage with her sisters and me, Joan Gentry, whose house had two staircases to run up and down, Billie Mitchell, who could sing like an angel, Sally Malone, who could outswim all of us, Jane Wilson, our congressman's daughter, and Connie Hill and JoAnn Biggs and Virginia Nichols—some or all of us were never apart. We were driving our parents' cars now. We were all in love, some more deeply than others, and we shared our secrets, gathering in little groups after Methodist Youth Fellowship on Sunday nights, or huddling for hamburgers at the Three Towers drive-in restaurant. Some of us, Barbara Oliver and Marian Adams and myself, were "only children." We clung to each other like sisters. I felt sustained, nourished by those friends.

At home, however, tension grew up between Mother and me, and it bothered me. We clashed often. I was always aware that she was not well, and I worried that something I did would make her worse. Was I too demanding, too impatient? With me, everything was out in the open: I wanted quick decisions. I was rather high-strung, with sweeping enthusiasms and sudden flashes of temper that washed over as quickly as they appeared. Her displeasure, however, lasted for days, with silence as thick as fog. Neither of us knew that mother-daughter conflicts were a common part of growing up. She idealized her own mother's memory; having lost her at six, she never had the opportunity to grow away from her. Having had no older sisters, I was paving new ground as a daughter. My father was in the middle, my confidante and advisor, explaining her to me, explaining me to her, gentling the friction between us as best he could. My pleasure was her great pride in my accomplishments. It thrilled me to please her so. I was crushed when she was unhappy with me. That my mother might be bottling up troubles of her own, or feeling distress that I was growing up, was as unthinkable to me then as would have been the possibility that her marriage to my father was less than perfect. They were not separate people, for goodness' sake, they were my parents. My support.

My sense of home that year was a closeness to my father. Mama kept things inside. And at those times of strain, I fled for female sustenance to Aunty, her older sister, whose patient, listening voice kept saying to me, "Keep on trying."

Our senior play, like so many in America in 1951, was Thornton Wilder's *Our Town*. On stage every night I listened to Nancy Tindle as Emily, a young mother who came back from death to relive her twelfth birthday on earth. I thought her words about the wonder of life were beautiful. I wanted to cherish them, for they meant to me my friends, my Enid, my home.

Our band played "Pomp and Circumstance," as we always had for graduations. There were caps and gowns, Mr. Selby handing out diplomas. I was standing, as always, between Norma Hawke and Billy Joe Holcomb, marching down the auditorium aisle with our Enid High School class of 1951, 240 strong. There were tears because I knew an important chapter of my life was closing. Just how important I would not realize until much later, when I would look back and wonder if I had bloomed, had "peaked," in high school. But suddenly, and with no time for such introspection as hindsight brings, I was away from home and into college.

My father wanted me to be in government or politics someday. All the adults who helped sponsor my public speaking encouraged me in that direction, and I was enchanted by the notion.

"First Woman Governor of Oklahoma" was a flattering thought. I wanted to bite out every chunk of life, to widen my horizons, to get that college education, go to Europe as an exchange student, have that career, whatever it might be—and then, only then, get married and raise a family. If I were ever to enter politics, I'd still be a wife and mother, but—later.

Although I had been offered a scholarship at a woman's college in Ohio, I enrolled in our own coed land-grant college, Oklahoma A & M at Stillwater. Not only did I have a case of incurable Oklahoma boosterism, but also, most of my high-school friends, from whom I'd become practically inseparable, were going to A & M—and that seemed to me a most valid reason for selecting a college. Stillwater was a ninety-minute drive from Enid, a surprising Williamsburg replica of a pretty college town on the Oklahoma plains.

It would seem that for a young woman who had shown potential and interest in those areas, someone would have advised me to study political science, or government, or history, or public administration. However, Enid High School did not offer career counseling for girls (perhaps not for boys, either). It was assumed that we would quickly settle down in our own homes to raise the future Bravettes, Aquaettes, and Band Queens. "What shall I study?" I asked my father. "It's up to you," he said. College courses, semester hours, majors, minors—all that was a foreign language to my parents. They just couldn't help. And so, because we had to declare a major when we enrolled as freshmen, I wrote down "Home Economics," because my favorite high-school teacher, Lois Vance, taught home ec.

To this day, I am astounded by that decision. In sewing class, I was a disaster. In desperation, I took the assigned skirt to a professional seamstress in Stillwater. The woman laughed, "You're the fifth one of those home ec girls to bring in a skirt this week!"

Home economics was the most popular course for women. But it was not for me. Although I rather enjoyed the foods and nutrition courses, in which good grades came more easily, four years of domestic science loomed drearily ahead. In one of my other courses, we were given an aptitude test, the results of which ended in "job suggestions." Mine, in order, were "diplomat, director of public relations, politician, radio announcer, actress, journalist, editorial writer." Home ec never surfaced. I determined to change my major next year. But that first semester, just coping with A & M itself was all I could handle.

College turned out to be much more difficult than I'd expected, being away from home a lot lonelier than I'd imagined. My father wrote me funny letters addressed to "Running Mud, Oklahoma." Mama sent big boxes of crispy fried chicken surrounded by the crumbs she knew I liked, and angel-food cakes, and on my birthday a huge, three-layer, heart-shaped cake, big enough for all the girls on the dorm floor. I survived, I think, because of the warmth of my roommate and high-school friend, Marian Adams, and our sorority, Pi Beta Phi, which elected me president of the pledge class and began entering me in contests. Soon I was off to Kansas City, as Oklahoma A & M's Queen, for the American Royal Livestock Show, and on to various speaking tournaments. Social life was a happy flurry, both on campus and at various other colleges in the state. I marched out onto the playing field during halftime at Oklahoma Military Academy in Claremore on the arm of Kenneth Franklin, as Football Queen.

But I didn't feel very queenly. I was harassed and overworked at school, a plodding student driven more by desire to excel than by scholastic aptitude. How was it that grades seemed to come so easily for others when I had to set my alarm for four A.M. to study for exams?

It happened that the Farm Bureau's countywide extemporaneous speaking contest was in Enid, so on one weekend when I was home from school, my father coaxed me to enter. When I won, he wanted me to enter the district and then the statewide contests. "There's absolutely no way I can do that," I protested. "Midterms are coming up. You don't realize how hard I have to study." If that state contest had been anywhere in Oklahoma but Stillwater, he couldn't have dragged me, even after I'd won in the district. But as it turned out, I only had to walk over from my dorm to the Student Union building, draw my topic from a hat, study for thirty minutes, and begin speaking. Our main topic was "Foreign Policy and the Farmer," something I knew quite a bit about, having listened to Daddy and his friends for years. I went to the library for facts and figures to support my position, which advocated aid for war-ravaged and developing countries.

There were no age or education limits in this speaking contest; the man who preceded me was a young minister, a college graduate with plenty of oratory under his belt. Daddy, who had driven over from Enid for the contest, watched me slink down in my seat as I looked over the other contestants. "There's no need in my even trying," I told him. "These people are professionals. Look at that preacher. I can't compete with them." And Daddy snapped back, "Okay, just forget it. With that set of mind, it is a waste of my time and yours even to draw your topic. Just forget it. With that attitude, there is no hope for you." But then he put his arm around my chair and grinned. "I think you can beat him, but first, *you* have to think you can." I smiled back at him, my wonderful, strong arm of a daddy, drew my topic, and won the state contest.

The national finals, in Chicago, would be in December. "My own final exams are right after Christmas, and I need that time to study!" I protested. But of course I wound up going, on a train with Daddy as chaperone, with Mama's strict instructions "not to let her out of your sight for one minute!" She was not well enough to travel herself, and Chicago was a wicked, sinful city for an innocent eighteen-year-old from Oklahoma.

We stayed at the Congress Hotel, Daddy and I, with our friends from the Oklahoma Farm Bureau and contestants from the other states. The morning of the contest, December 10, 1951, all the entrants met to discuss the general topic, "The Farm Bureau's Role in International Affairs," as well as the specific subtopics which we'd be assigned, and to go over the general rules of the contest. The four regional contests would be held that afternoon, Oklahoma being included in the South. "Meet me in the hotel room and we will go to lunch," Daddy said. "We'll go over your material."

Outside the meeting room was a reception room, full of contestants. There were no empty chairs, so I sat down on the end of a big, heavy coffee table and began talking to a girl from Michigan. But there was somebody else listening to my southwestern drawl.

"You're not from Michigan, are you?" he said, and I looked up into the bluest eyes I'd ever seen.

"No, I'm from Oklahoma," I said.

"Well, come on over and join Indiana, Oklahoma," he said. "My name is Birch Bayh." I forgot all about Daddy.

He took me to lunch at the Glass Hat, this tall, striking young man with the brown curly hair and stubborn cowlick, the clean square jaw and the sky-blue eyes, and he told me about Indiana and about himself. He was twenty-three, a college graduate, a farmer like my dad. He'd worked his way through college raising tomatoes. He'd grown up in suburban Washington, D.C., where his father was director of physical education for the public schools, but he and his sister had lived with his grandparents in Indiana for some time after his mother's death, when his father went overseas in World War II. He had graduated from high school and gone to college in Indiana. Now he and his grandfather were alone on the farm, with a housekeeper to take care of them.

This was no ordinary young farmer, I thought, as he told me more: president of his senior class at Purdue, president of Alpha Tau Omega, and winner of that fraternity's national achievement award. He was a boxing champion, a baseball star, and had won two State Farm Bureau speaking contests; I was sure he'd win this, the national. He was an Army veteran, who had taught German children how to raise vegetables in his spare time overseas. He brought his own seeds from Indiana—a one-soldier predecessor of the Peace Corps. There'd been an article about him, "G.I. Ambassador," in *Reader's Digest*. We were both churchgoing Protestants, both Democrats, and though I couldn't vote yet, both more than interested in politics. Birch Bayh had something special—the kind of drive that I had, that I'd seen in no other boy. "What a team we'd make," I thought.

He asked me for a date that night, after the finals. We wished each other luck, and I floated back up to the hotel room. Daddy was in the hall, locking the door. He glared at me. "Young lady, don't you remember you had a luncheon date with me? Everybody in this hotel is looking for you—even the hotel detective!" Missing an appointment, or even being late, was so unlike me, I was bewildered at myself.

"Oh, Daddy, I'm so sorry," I wailed. "But I've met the most wonderful boy."

We didn't have time to go over my notes. I rushed to the Southern Regional contest room, and drew a topic: "Can American Technical Assistance Raise the Standard of Living in Underdeveloped Countries?" I spoke, extemporaneously, for ten minutes. We were timed carefully, and I felt as if I'd run out of time before I could use the ending—including a Franklin Delano Roosevelt quote— that I'd prepared. I was by far the youngest, and the only girl. And I wanted the judging to be over soon so that I could hear Birch Bayh speak in his contest. "It didn't go well, did it?" I said to Daddy.

"I've heard you do better," he replied.

When they announced the winner, I was shocked to hear my

name. But then we rushed over to the Midwest competition just in time to hear Birch Bayh speak.

"That's the one," I told Daddy, "right there," and Birch made an impressive, forceful speech. I was crushed when the boy from Ohio was selected as the Midwest winner. Daddy and I both thought that Birch was the better speaker.

That evening, before the huge convention of the American Farm Bureau at the Grand Ballroom of the Stevens Hotel, three young men and I drew our topic from a hat, to enter the final competition before thousands of farmers in the audience. If I had one goal, it was to out-speak the boy from Ohio who had beaten my new friend from Indiana, who was now sitting beside my father in the audience.

When my turn came I flashed them a smile, waited, as I'd been taught, to gain the audience's attention, and began: "Should the United States Follow the Method of Controls Which Has Destroyed the Free Enterprise System in Other Countries?" Later, when Allan B. Kline, the president of the American Farm Bureau, presented me with the large gold cup, he announced that "Marvella Hern, a farmer's daughter from Enid, Oklahoma, is the first girl ever to win this annual national speaking contest. By this token, we regard you the most outstanding young orator in the nation." It was, appropriately, a loving cup. I wished Birch Bayh had won it. I was mightily in love.

Daddy was as charmed by Birch as I was. They talked farm prices, parity, overproduction, and always wound up with politics. Daddy was our county Democratic chairman then, and Birch asked his advice: "Sir, how does a young man go about getting started in politics?"

"This is a good beginning," Daddy answered.

We three went to the Museum of Science and Industry, and Birch, who was from coal country, took us on a trip through a mock coal mine. We toured Chicago in a taxi, shaking our heads at the slums we'd read about and were seeing for the first time, staring wide-eyed at Chinatown; we stood in the middle of that madhouse called the Board of Trade, and went to the Chicago Art Institute and to the theater.

The last night of the convention there was a grand ball, after which Birch had asked Daddy's permission to take me out, alone. I bought a gardenia for my hair, wrapped my new white imitation-fur cape around my shoulders, and stepped into his 1950 blue Studebaker. He handed me a gift-wrapped package. "Oh, you shouldn't have—" I said, glad that he had.

"It's not for you, it's for your father," he said, passing the box of cigars through the window to Daddy.

He took me to the Ivanhoe Club, a nightclub like those I'd seen in the movies, with candlelit tables and strolling guitarists. I'd never tasted alcohol before, but somewhere I'd heard of an Old Fashioned. I felt so grown-up, so sophisticated. (I took one sip, just to show him, then let it sit on the table the rest of the evening, afraid of it.) We danced. We talked. We went down to the underground "Catacombs," through the Tunnel of Love. We threw darts, and Birch won a false moustache. We put a quarter in one of those little booths, and had our picture made together. We drove around and around Chicago, talking and talking, until the gray light began to appear over Lake Michigan. He kissed me. "I've always looked for a girl just like you," he said, "but I'd begun to believe I'd never find one." It was five in the morning when we said goodbye. (I stammered through Don McNeil's "Breakfast Club" radio interview two hours later, and when he asked, inanely, "Do you prefer farm boys or city boys?" I answered, inanely, "Both," mindful that Birch, from the farm, had his car radio on as he drove back to Indiana, and Kenny Franklin, a city boy from Enid, was listening at Oklahoma Military Academy.)

Her arms full of telegrams and clippings about the contest from the Enid newspapers, Mother met Daddy and me at the Santa Fe railroad station in Perry, Oklahoma, so that we could drive straight to Stillwater. I bounced off the train, and threw my arms around her. "Mother," I announced, "I have met the boy I'm going to marry!"

She just glared at Daddy. All those orders about not letting me out of his sight!

❧

Poor Birch. The telephone bills were enormous. He sent roses at Christmas, and drove down to see me during my semester break in January, bringing a record of "Getting to Know You." We shot basketballs at my hoop, in our shirtsleeves, and sat on my front steps studying the moon. He was surprised, coming from frozen Indiana, by the warm weather. "If you don't like the weather in Oklahoma, just stick around," I told him, repeating an old saw. "It's bound to change." (Sure enough, we had a blizzard the next week.) He drove that same little Studebaker, which he said was made in Indiana, and I noticed that he wore deep-blue lizard shoes and a leather jacket, not exactly in the latest Oklahoma fashion, causing me to wonder if people dressed differently up there in Indiana. He was too tall for our living-room sofa, and so he shared my room with my father during his visit, while I moved in with Mama. I took him out immediately to meet Grandma Hern, who fell for him, as I knew she would.

Mama was a problem. She had never been so adamantly opposed to any of my romances as she was to this one. Birch was five years older than I, and I'd never been permitted to date anyone more than two years older. He'd been in the Army, he'd been around, he'd fed her little daughter a long tale, and I had swallowed it. She was disgusted with Daddy, disgusted with me, and I was afraid she would be rude to Birch. Daddy chuckled about it. "He doesn't know what he's walking into," he said.

When Birch walked in, he just put his arm around Mother and gave her a squeeze. It took him about thirty minutes to win her over. By the time he drove away, three days later, it was "Birch this" and "Birch that."

He left his fraternity pin with me, and she didn't object.

In those days, "pinned" was serious, a college pre-engagement ritual announcing to all that the wearer does not date other men. When he was in college, Birch had never parted with his ATO pin. We wrote every day, and talked every Sunday night, but after a couple of months, sitting in the dorm night after night while my intended was on a farm in Indiana began to wear on me. After all, I'd just turned nineteen, and absence was making my heart grow . . . fainter. I didn't want to miss out on everything at school, and so I began dating again.

"I'm going to send back his pin," I told Daddy.

"Oh, no, you won't!" he said. "I don't care if you give it back or keep it, but if you do return it, you're going to do it in person, like a lady."

Birch had retained close ties with Purdue University, as president of his alumni class. He invited me there to the Junior Prom, in April. I didn't want to go. I got on the train for Indiana, determined to return his pin. Should I tell him at the station, immediately, and get it over with, or should I wait until after the prom? What would I say when I saw him?

The train arrived in Terre Haute, and I didn't see him. I got my luggage, sat down in the waiting room, and wondered what to do. After about ten minutes, I had decided to try to call this Mrs. Henley, the lady he called Auntie Katherine, who had written me a letter, when, all blue-eyed and breathless, Birch Bayh charged in. "I stopped to get the car washed," he apologized, throwing his arms around me, and rattling off our weekend plans so fast I didn't have time to think.

I checked into the Pi Phi house at Purdue, my resolve only slightly weakened by having seen him at the station. There was a knock on the door, and five or six girls came into my room. "We want to see the girl who finally got Birch Bayh," they said. These northern sorority sisters waxed eloquent about Birch's campus days —most popular, most outstanding, "best catch."

"He's going to be President of the United States someday," one of them said.

I couldn't tell them I had come to return his pin to this paragon. And I didn't. On the way home, I didn't get off the train at Claremore, where Kenneth Franklin was expecting me, but went straight back to Stillwater, where I remained in long-distance love with Birch all semester.

❧

My parents were worried about this sudden, deep involvement; their ambitions for me had not yet been fulfilled. Mother often told me how each of my accomplishments repaid her for her sacrifices. And my father, driving me back to college one weekend, suddenly said to me, "Marvella, I am a failure." I protested. "You are the only thing I have ever accomplished of which I am proud," he continued, "the only thing that keeps my life from being a complete loss and waste. All my hopes and dreams rest upon you." At that moment, I felt a sudden, great burden, one that I did not understand. Never before had I questioned or even thought about (except to want to please them) the fact that my parents were living *through* me. I did not know what to say, only to try to reassure him.

They knew I had to see Birch again, that six days in six months was not enough on which to base a realistic appraisal. His courtship was too imaginative, too romantic: funny telegrams and poems, flowers, a big live white rabbit in a crate at Eastertime. My parents thought, perhaps, that daily exposure might slow the momentum a bit, and so they agreed to send me to summer school at Indiana State Teachers' College in Terre Haute, about twelve miles from Birch's grandfather's farm.

After five weeks of fifteen-minute-a-day courtship (after he'd finished in the fields and before I had to be back in the dorm), and after his baseball games, which followed church on Sundays, Birch and I decided to get married right away. We were just plain in love. We called Birch's father, who wished us the best, and then we called my parents. They were horrified.

"You're only nineteen," Daddy said. "So were you," I argued. "But you two kids haven't even known each other long enough to have a real fight yet," he persisted. There was silence on the line.

"Sir, is that necessary?" Birch broke in.

"You have such a wonderful future ahead of you," Mother said.

"So does Birch," I said.

The more they argued, the more stubborn I became.

"What about your education? You just can't throw that away!"

"She'll finish college here in Terre Haute," Birch said.

After a while they seemed to be argued down.

"I want a big church wedding," I said, hoping to perk Mother up. She loved weddings, showers, ceremony. "In August." (I thought I was being practical: as an Indiana bride, I wouldn't have to pay the extra out-of-state tuition.)

"I can't pull together a big wedding in a month," my mother said. "I am not well." She had spent two months in the hospital that spring, in such pain I feared for her life, and was still weak.

"Well, *I* can," I retorted, and did, ordering invitations, studying brides' books, designing a dress, buying yards and yards of pink and blue satin on sale in Terre Haute for my bridesmaids' dresses, planning everything and sending directions in letters surreptitiously written in radio class.

There was no time to stop, to reflect, to wonder. It was my first big social event, and I was the social director. The wedding would be beautiful, a success. Birch was in his busiest season on the farm, and I was up to my neck in summer school finals as well. The Bayh name was revered at Indiana State, for Birch's father had been on the faculty; I couldn't let them down by not making good grades. Birch and I saw even less of each other.

Birch's father came out to Terre Haute to meet me. He was a muscular, athletic man, a physical-education teacher whose passion for athletics had been passed on to his son. He was phys-ed director of the Washington, D.C., school system, a former Army colonel. I felt slightly overwhelmed. My one sport had been girls' basketball; Birch was a baseball player at Purdue, and light-heavyweight boxing champion. My father, like most farmers, got his exercise in the fields, not on the courts. I wondered what Mr. Bayh and I would have in common.

Everything. He was courtly and old-fashioned in his treatment of women, and immediately I was up on a pedestal. He asked me to call him father; I called him "Daddy Bayh" for the rest of his life. He looked at my finger, and noticed that I wasn't wearing an engagement ring. (I was getting pretty nervous about that, myself. Every time I'd come into the dorm from a date with Birch, my Indiana State roommate would say, "Did you get your ring yet?" My parents would be driving me to Oklahoma any day now, and what would I do if I didn't have a ring to show off to my friends?)

On the way back from the train station after picking up Daddy Bayh, I noticed a big, heavy box in the trunk of Birch's Studebaker. When we arrived at the farm, Birch said casually, "Oh, by the way, this box came for you, to my address." I began opening it, and it was filled with *U.S. News and World Reports.* And there was another box inside. And inside that, yet another. And another, and another, on down to the sixth, tiny box, in which was . . . my ring. I ran squealing upstairs to show everybody. A little while later, Birch came up to me, a crestfallen look on his face. "I want you to give me the ring back."

"WHY?" I nearly had a heart attack.

"Dad called me on the carpet," he said. "He said that's a terrible way to give a girl an engagement ring. Not romantic at all. If you'll give it back to me, I'll give it to you again tonight." But I wouldn't give it back to him. After all, wasn't I the daughter of the biggest prankster in all of Oklahoma? "That's just the kind of thing my daddy might do," I said.

When I arrived in Enid two weeks before the wedding, Mother was in one of her moods. "Of all times!" I complained to Daddy.

"Whatever is the matter? What have I done?" It came out that Daddy was the culprit. It seems that he'd gone off and bought a wedding present impulsively, while he was in Kansas harvesting, without asking her. The gift was a splendid little brown-and-tan Chevy Bel Air, so that I wouldn't have to drive Birch's pickup truck (he'd sold the Studebaker to get the truck) from the farm to school in Terre Haute. The wheat crop wasn't good this year; Mother wondered just how they were going to pay for it. "I'm going to divorce him," she told me. "Oh, Mama," I pleaded, "I don't want the car if you feel that way. Please, please don't ruin my wedding." Birch offered, however, to pay my tuition at college, and so we ended up accepting the car. Sometimes, even now, I wish that we hadn't.

There were showers, there was a to-do. My parents' friends, the two Coulter families and the Carltons, pitched in as if it were their daughter who was getting married. Mother canceled me out of the Miss Enid contest; Daddy said, "I'm going to miss watching you win a big contest on the average of twice a year." He stood and held my wedding dress off the floor as I ironed it.

Grandma Hern cried at my wedding. It was a beautiful wedding, that steamy Sunday afternoon, August 24, 1952, in the Methodist church in Enid, as inexpensive as it could possibly be, with bridesmaids in their long pastel gowns, flowers decking the altar, with the nonalcoholic punch ready to be served afterward in the church basement. Birch's father was there, and his pretty sister Mary Alice from New York, who was my maid of honor; there were his dear Aunt Katherine and Uncle Henry from Terre Haute, his cousin Bill Bayh and Uncle Bernard, the best man, P. A. Mack, and a good representation from Enid. But sitting in the side of the church in her wheelchair, Grandma Hern wasn't crying because it was beautiful. She had left her own home at seventeen and never went back to Missouri. "We'll never see her again," she said.

I carried the white Bible she gave me. Walking down the aisle on the arm of her son, I suddenly thought, "I am leaving my father." It was a dreadful, wrenching emotion.

Birch wrote me a letter on our wedding day, which P. A. Mack delivered to me just before the ceremony, a letter full of love and promise and hope for our life together, for our children, and for their children. Now we were husband and wife, he at twenty-four, I at nineteen—and we still hadn't even had a "real good fight yet," as my father put it.

Actually we had had one fight, one that was still unresolved. "I want to have a career," I had told Birch one day after class in Terre Haute. We had discussed this once before. On the way home from that first trip to Terre Haute in April, Birch had driven me down to St. Louis to catch the train to Oklahoma. That's when I first told him that I had always dreamed of a career. We didn't talk much about it—except that Birch was just disgusted. Later he told me he was ready to "junk the whole thing, if you were going to be like that." But shortly after I got on the train for Oklahoma, a porter delivered a telegram with an adoring message from Birch. We were too madly in love to give back a fraternity pin, or break up over my wanting a career. In July, the night we called my parents about getting married, I wrote in my diary, "Birch told me he believes a woman's place is in the home, and that's been worrying me. Got to talk to him about that."

In Terre Haute, that day after class, he repeated those sentiments. "I agree that my first commitment is to family. But I need something else. A purpose," I tried to explain. "Besides, I don't want all this training to go to waste."

"You'll have me," he said.

We argued. After all, I felt it very important to be in control of my life, and it looked as though he were trying to control me. But we compromised. After I finished college, we would raise a family. And after the children were old enough, I could teach.

People who know us today are surprised that Birch held such traditional ideas about the role of a wife, and that I, with all my stubbornness, accepted them so readily. Many are puzzled as to why I, who had become accustomed to being "the first girl" or "the only girl" to win competitions, a person who was beginning to show potential for helping break down barriers for women, should marry so young, too young.

Birch was shaped by his upbringing. His mother had died of cancer when he was twelve, he had been raised by strict, old-fashioned grandparents. A woman's role was in the home. Period. I pictured marriage as more of a partnership, where each role was clearly defined, yet each partner held his own, doing his or her share.

My parents, opposed at first, liked Birch immensely, seeing in him the son they had almost raised me to be. After their initial reluctance, they were in full support of the match. They, and I, only wished he'd move to Oklahoma.

But it was society's conditioning to which I succumbed. No matter how many times my parents told me "Go as far as you can," the subliminal message in books, magazines, movies, among my friends and sorority sisters, was "Marry!" In 1952, society said to young women: "You can achieve anything you want, up to a point. Get your education, win your contests. But your *real* purpose in life, dear heart, is to find a good man and make him happy." (And to add a touch of hindsight to that love-blinded young woman, I was weary, bone-tired from driving, driving, driving, being an overachiever. I remember telling one of my teachers, Miss Correll, "I'm ready to try at some point to find a good man and help him get ahead, because I'm so exhausted doing it all myself." For women in those days, marriage was not only expected, it was also an easy "out," a way to postpone the hard track of one's own life.)

At nineteen, I married Birch Bayh and headed for Niagara Falls. He was a very good man—intelligent and ambitious, warm and witty, poetic and charming, corny and wonderful. Magnetic. Imaginative. Strong. Honest. Energetic. Kind. Handsome. Loving. He adored me.

And I would never become the first woman governor of Oklahoma.

Chapter 3

In 1732, the French governor of the Louisiana Territory ordered that a fort be built on the high ground, or *terre haute*, of the Wabash River. Birch used to tell people that he was from Terre Haute.

"Where in Terre Haute?" they'd ask.

"Well, actually my mailing address is West Terre Haute, on the other side of the Wabash."

"Where in West Terre Haute?" they'd press, if they knew the town.

"Well, I don't actually live in West Terre Haute. I graduated from high school in New Goshen, which is about ten or twelve miles outside of West Terre Haute."

"Oh, you're from New Goshen, then?"

"Well, I don't actually live in New Goshen, but two miles on down the highway from New Goshen is a crossroads with two little stores, two taverns and a little restaurant. It's called Shirkieville. I don't think more than a hundred people live there."

"Your home is Shirkieville, then?"

"Well, actually, I live a mile and a half south of Shirkieville. . . ."

It was a plain, no-nonsense farm as Midwest farms go, 450 acres of soybeans, corn, wheat, and tomatoes, with a few cattle and hogs, but to those who feel at home in such settings, it had its charm. There was a big, white, two-story farmhouse with a front porch, surrounded by tall locust trees, a couple of cedars that had greened the place through many a winter, and one lonely old catalpa. I thought the land was beautiful, especially in the spring, with the dark earth upturned, different from the red land of Oklahoma, yet holding that same fresh-and-waiting smell. There were lilacs, too, around the yard, bringing each May a memory of Grandmother Hern.

Birch's grandfather, John Harrison Hollingsworth, had acquired the land piece by piece, by selling the mining rights beneath it. Though the coal mines had been depleted years before, there remained two huge piles of black gob on either side of the Shirkieville road, an eyesore reminder of a once prosperous era in southwest Indiana. Those were our only hills. I would learn to long for winter, when for a few short months they would be mercifully covered with snow. Birch's grandparents built the house, and they raised their only child, Leah, there. She grew up to be a schoolteacher like her mother.

When Leah married another schoolteacher, with the German name pronounced "buy," the young couple moved into Terre Haute, where Birch, Sr., served on the faculty of Indiana State. As the college was only twelve miles away, however, Leah spent many hours in her parents' home. Their two children, Birch, Jr., and Mary Alice, two years younger, were born in Terre Haute, where their father had become athletic director for the public schools, but they spent practically all their childhood summers with their grandparents on that farm. When the family moved to Washington, with the appointment of Birch, Sr., to the D.C. public school system, Leah felt such a pull to the Indiana farm that the minute school was out, she'd pack up the two kids and make the long drive across the Allegheny Mountains to spend the entire summer there.

In the spring of 1940, Leah developed cancer of the uterus. After her surgery, she rested at home until school was out, and then packed up for the 675-mile drive to Indiana, as usual. She felt fine, she said, helping her mother with summer canning and fall housecleaning. After she drove back to Washington, however, she began hemorrhaging, and was taken to the hospital. Birch has never forgotten the day his father was visiting his mother and he called to ask his father a question. "May I please speak to Mr. Bayh? He's in Mrs. Bayh's room."

"He wouldn't be there," answered the hospital operator. "Mrs. Bayh died this afternoon."

Birch was twelve years old, all alone at home. He screamed and screamed.

Birch's father found it difficult to function as both mother and father to the two children. When war broke out, he enlisted, serving as an Air Force colonel in charge of physical education and recreation in the China-Burma-India theater, while Birch and Mary Alice, then thirteen and eleven, moved to the Indiana farm to live with their elderly grandparents.

Mary Alice was lonely and miserable under the strict no-lipstick, no-bathing-suits, no-dating surveillance of her fundamentalist grandparents, and vowed to return to Washington as soon as her father came home from the war. Birch loved the farm. He became a 4-H Club champion at the Wabash Valley Fair, raising first a calf and then a stellar fifteen-acre crop of tomatoes. He worked at all the farm chores, scooping wheat with a heavy shovel into a truck to take to market, developing the biceps that slammed home runs for the Sunday afternoon baseball team. Birch majored in agriculture at Purdue, hoping to use the latest mechanized techniques to increase the yield on the Hollingsworth farm. When he moved me there in late August, 1952, we were sure it was for the rest of our lives.

Our marriage began, in proper Indiana fashion, with a shivaree. (Actually, it was proper Oklahoma fashion as well.) Our second week on the farm, we drove to Terre Haute in the evening for a Purdue alumni meeting in a private home. Suddenly, Donald Foltz and a couple more old friends of Birch's burst right into the meeting room and grabbed him. The ex-Golden Gloves contender started to fight, but he was afraid he'd damage the furniture. They surrounded him and dragged him out. Three strange girls swooped in and blindfolded me, pushed me into a car, and drove me around and around. Then they took off the blindfold, stopped the car, and let me out on an old deserted river road. Being as independent as Grandma Hern, I just started walking, terrified, into the pitch-black September night, down that old dirt road. Pretty soon, the car appeared again, but I refused to get in until one of them wailed, "But we're having a party for you over at Hutchinson's farm. The boys are bringing Birch."

I got into the car.

When the men appeared, laughing, without Birch, I asked

them, "What have you done with my husband?" "He'll be here any minute," Don said. But after an hour or two and no Birch, the men left again. When they came back, I could see they were worried. And I was frightened.

Had I known Birch better, then, I wouldn't have worried. That man can get out of anything. They had stripped him of all his clothes, fastened his hands behind his back with state police handcuffs (filched from Don's uncle), and locked him in a shed way out back on Hutchinson's farm. When they went out to get him, they tossed firecrackers at the shed, then threw open the doors, intending to take him, naked, to the party.

But he was not there. And they couldn't find him anywhere. "There was no way," they kept saying. "That shed was locked. Houdini himself couldn't have gotten out of there."

About midnight, Birch sauntered into the party in an ill-fitting new suit, dangling a pair of sawed-open state police handcuffs.

He was, of course, very strong. He had maneuvered his arms and feet until his manacled hands were in front of him, scooped up some feed into a big pile in the corner, climbed up on it, and literally pushed the roof off the top of the old shed with his head so that he could climb out and drop to the ground. Unlike me, he quickly knew where he was, and ran to a neighbor's farm. Everything was dark, thankfully, as he banged on the bedroom window. "Uncle Olin," he called to the farmer. "It's me, Birch. Can you help me?"

"Oh, yes, Birch, just a minute," answered Uncle Olin, "I'll turn on the yard lights so you can see."

"Don't turn on the lights!" Birch yelled. "I don't have any clothes on."

Uncle Olin laughed for the rest of his life about sawing open Birch's handcuffs and dressing him for his Indiana shivaree party.

Indiana. I didn't dare tell them how I really felt about the shivaree, because I wanted them to like me, those boyhood friends of my new husband. But as I walked along that dark, muggy river road, with the unaccustomed humidity hovering around my hair, my skin, filling my nostrils with strange, wet smells, I felt, suddenly, a long, long way from home. I ached for a whiff of the dry, dusty air of Oklahoma.

I was homesick for quite a while, though I didn't admit it. I just began telling Birch that Oklahoma was the best, the most forward-thinking, progressive, cleanest, healthiest, liveliest place in the whole wide world, in contrast to you-know-where. It would take a while for this Sooner bride to convert to Hoosier. How he tolerated me, I will never know. Waiting at a traffic light, I'd point out that "Oklahoma had right-turn-on-red a long time ago." Noting that Terre Haute kids whose parents weren't wealthy enough to join the country club had to swim in the dangerous "strip pits," I'd fume that the city fathers of Enid would rob a bank in the next city before their kids would go without a swimming pool. The top floors of the main Terre Haute high school, the same building Birch's mother had attended, had been condemned by fire inspectors for years. "They come all the way from Kansas to look at Enid High School as a model for their own," I boasted. I complained, loudly, about the soot. Going into church after having parked a block away, I'd look down and there would be black soot streaks on my pink wool coat. "I had it cleaned once a winter in Oklahoma," I pointed out. In Indiana the familiar sound of cooing in the spring didn't come from turtle doves, as in Oklahoma. They called the birds "rain crows."

Terre Haute was twice as large as Enid, an industrial city of 90,000 that in 1952 was still struggling to survive the depression that had followed the coal boom. Indiana seemed old to me, having become a state in 1816, ninety-one years before Oklahoma, so old that no one could agree on the origin of the Hoosier nickname. (Some said it was from Samuel Hoosier, who built a canal on the Ohio River; others said early settlers answered a knock on the door with "Who's yere?" Some trace it back to an old Anglo-Saxon word meaning hill or highlander, or backwoods man.) In Oklahoma, everybody knew what "Sooner" meant. In Oklahoma, I was used to hearing "we're going to change things." I found that the Indiana attitude was "now, we have gotten along like this for years, so don't get excited."

For example, I bought some ballerina slippers at Sears for $4.95 and dyed them yellow to match my skirt. Terre Haute girls wore black or white shoes, and stared at mine. Word got around Terre Haute that the Bayh boy had married a "rich Oklahoma oil-man's daughter" who wore pastel shoes and a pink-blanket coat. I learned rather quickly to dress more conservatively, as Terre Haute did, and wore my new, sensible-heeled black shoes to teach my Sunday School class of fifth-graders.

Back then, however, I'd plead with Birch, "Won't you please

go back to Oklahoma with me? We can buy a farm there. . . ."
Later, after I had become a Hoosier to my toenails, I came to appreciate the wisdom of growing at one's own pace. Progress in Terre
Haute since 1952 is highly visible—and lasting. And, of course, I
came to love the people as my own.

From the beginning, I learned the bedrock quality of their
friendship. The night I woke up to discover flames shooting out of
our corncrib (and Birch, who sleeps through alarm clocks, jumped
out of bed and flew down the stairs in one mighty leap that burst
the stair step), Max and Marge Lenderman, on the next farm,
awakened a brigade of neighbors, who quickly arrived with buckets,
hoses, pipes, pumps, everything they could think of at four A.M. on
an icy morning, to help us. Katherine Henley, Birch's mother's best
friend, who had been like a mother to him, opened up her home
and heart to me as completely as if I were a blood relative. Gaynell
Poff, who rented a house on our land, helped me when I needed
her, and became a close friend.

Our farmhouse was far nicer than any house I'd ever had, but
over the years it had run down, as old houses do, and was in need
of work, inside and out. Birch took every penny of his tomato crop
savings to remodel the house to the specifications of his inexperi-
enced nineteen-year-old bride.

Some of the things I did to that fine old house were criminal.
I was determined to make it "modern," cutting down fine tall doors,
carpeting those good oak floors. We moved the steep, ladderlike
stairs from the kitchen to the living room, added a landing, and
then proceeded to remodel the kitchen, adding the cabinets that
were lacking in most old farmhouses. I don't know why I chose
red—perhaps because my mother's kitchen was red; I only know I
chose too much red—long counter tops and table. My kitchen was
twice as big as hers. In the morning when I ran down to make
breakfast before dashing off to Indiana State, I learned to long for
a calmer kitchen.

I attacked Grandmother Hollingsworth's attic with a vengeance, tossing out old tables, chairs, and beds, mostly just plain,
honest farm furniture, but also a few pieces that I wish could be
retrieved for my grandchildren.

I had the living room walls painted a medium-bright pink, one
of my favorite colors, and then bought two big overstuffed chairs
covered in velvet, half gray, half purple, another favorite color.

They were awful. Birch and I designed our own sofa, combining features from two pictures we'd clipped from magazines. When it was delivered, covered in a bilious green, even my unpracticed eye could tell something was wrong. It dominated our pink-purple-and-gray living room like some huge, growing thing. Our new bedroom suite, with its "modernistic" huge-mirror dresser and uncompromising headboard, was gray, as was the carpet that crawled all over the house.

After extending the porch and creating a circular driveway, and a great deal of remodeling and landscaping, we didn't have any money left over to backtrack and cover my mistakes. I had to live with them.

But at nineteen, taste was something on the end of my tongue.

Birch loved that land, that farm. I'd watch him cock an eye to the sky, when I couldn't see a cloud in it, and rush out to pitch hay before the rain. Sometimes he'd work into the night, until dew began to form, to get in the hay if it looked like rain. When that corncrib burned, Birch was devastated to see the corn he had planted and harvested go up in flames. He was a conscientious farmer, who weighed new agricultural discoveries as a scientist would, but who still felt the mystical wonder at new green sprouts or the birth of animals every spring. He'd head for the fields on a tractor or combine, our dog Dixie running behind; he'd plow, or scoop wheat at harvest, or clean out the barn, come back in for midday dinner, and then go out to the field again. It was diversified farming, crop after crop ("in Oklahoma, you can take the winter off," I would say), and he was out working on the farm all year long.

I didn't get involved with the farm. An old lady had told me at my wedding reception, "Marvella, never learn to milk a cow." So I took her advice to heart. I was a full-time student, and my realm was the house. Except for the laundry, I took care of everything inside; I cooked hearty farm breakfasts and then baked a meat loaf after school, or stewed chicken or a pot roast in the pressure cooker, for dinner for the three of us.

Grandfather Hollingsworth, at eighty-eight, was a dear old man who regaled me with tales of the coal boom, of his family, of his big Hudson automobile which he said "passed everything on the road except a filling station." He still puttered around the farm, tending an ancient flock of hens that could barely lay eggs, planting a little vegetable garden, listening with awe while Birch told him about the latest mechanical wonder for farming. But Granddad was getting feeble. We couldn't leave him alone, which kept us on the farm on weekends. He adjusted to me and my attack on his house far better, I confess, than I adjusted to him.

Granddad liked peculiar things to eat, like pigs' knuckles and pigs' feet, and I learned to cook for him because he appreciated me, told me how I reminded him of Birch's grandmother when she was young. Which made me feel even worse about my irritation at the clicking of his false teeth, or the acrid-smelling Green Mountain Asthma Cure that he burned beside his bed.

When Joe and Dorothy Welch came over as our first dinner guests, we laid out the wedding presents, then dined by candlelight. Granddad wandered through the dining room on his way to the bathroom, flipping a switch to bathe us in glaring light. "Why, you can't see a thing in here," he announced, as one who was old enough to really appreciate the marvel of electricity.

Birch had decided he was going to make his fortune by trucking Indiana corn down to Tennessee, and bringing fence posts and pigs back to Indiana. Auntie Katherine said when she saw the figures on the yellow pad, "I don't understand why everybody in the country isn't in this business if there is that much money to be made." So Birch bought a secondhand semi-trailer and the night that Eisenhower was elected President, we headed south. We couldn't find a place to spend the night, so we ended up having to pull over and sleep in the cab of that truck. Finally, we got to our destination in Tennessee, unloaded the corn, and went out to the backwoods to pick up the pigs.

There was no chute, no fence, nothing for loading those hogs. The farmer sent his son out to help Birch. They would try to corner those squealing, filthy razorback hogs and Birch would grab one up and sling it into the back of the truck, and then go and get some more. Then the pigs started jumping out of the truck, so Birch got me a big limb and I had to keep poking those dirty pigs back in. I was scared out of my wits. They were all mixed up, going GRUNT, GRUNT, GRUNT. Finally, he got them all loaded.

Birch had on a flannel shirt over an undershirt, and now *he* stank. As we headed home to Indiana, I rolled down the window, hanging my head out of the cab of that truck. Birch couldn't smell himself because he had been out there among the pigs, and he said,

"Oh, you are always exaggerating." But he took off the flannel shirt and put it in the back. We stopped at a truck stop to get something to eat and, wearing his tee shirt, he still smelled so bad that the people sitting at the next table got up and left.

Then he went into the pig business. Birch decided he would plan the birth of baby pigs in the heart of the winter, so when they were ready there wouldn't be many pigs on the market and the price would rise. The only problem was that the baby pigs might freeze to death, or the mother pig might roll on them or eat them. So when baby pigs were expected, Birch spent the night down there with those old sows, and then he'd come in for breakfast stinking like a pig. I would make him go to the basement, take off his clothes and clean up. He thought I was just "carrying on."

Then he decided he would build a hog-farrowing house according to Purdue's instructions, with concrete floors, drainage, and little crates to put around each sow so she couldn't move around and mash the little pigs. I think we had only one sow use it, because the first year the pigs came down with rhinitis, a new hog disease. We didn't know then that rhinitis remains in the ground for several years until there are quite a few hard freezes. The first year the pigs got the disease, and we lost our shirt. The next year they got it, and we lost the top layer of skin as well. To say I hated those pigs was an understatement.

The sports I tolerated, even though I had lost interest in them myself. Birch was so good at baseball that he was one of the best semi-pro baseball players in the Wabash Valley—and had once tried out at a major league scouting camp. During baseball season, every Sunday after church I'd go down and sit in the bleachers while he pitched, trying very hard to appreciate all the nuances of his performance so I could praise him on the way home.

When Daddy Bayh came for a visit our first summer on the farm, Birch was thrilled to have his dad watch him play ball. But as he sat beside me on the bleachers that sweltering summer day, he must have noticed my eyes glaze over.

After the game, he went up to Birch. "Bud, you'd better hang up your cleats. Your ball-playin' days are over."

Daddy Bayh was my ally, a great support to us both. Perhaps the finest wedding present for both of us was his talk with Birch the night before we married. "Over the years, I have taught you to believe that your mother was perfect," he said. "She was not. Leah was a wonderful woman, but we had our strong disagreements, as you and Marvella will inevitably have. You must be tolerant." Another piece of advice that Birch and I took to heart: "Never go to bed angry," he told us. "No matter how bitter your argument, if you make it up at the end of each day, your marriage will be a happy one."

It was a happy one. I now had the house under control, our daily routine was worked out; college, if not a breeze, was certainly much more satisfying now that home ec was out of the way. Granddad Hollingsworth was dear to me. When my parents came up for a visit, he told my mother, "I've never seen anybody move as fast in my life. Why, Marvella comes running down the stairs every morning and has a big breakfast ready by the time it takes me to get to the table."

On our first wedding anniversary, August 24, 1953, Granddad took sick. We didn't realize it would be his last illness. We drove him to the hospital in Clinton that night, and ran out of gas on the way. He sat in the car, patiently, and talked to me while Birch walked over the country roads to find some gasoline. At the hospital, he lingered for four weeks. He had been Birch's salvation as a boy; he had lived to see that boy follow in his footsteps in the farm, heir to his promise as a homesteader. After he was gone, the house seemed empty. It was a week before I could face his hens. Then it began: chicken and noodles, chicken and rice, chicken soup, chicken croquettes. Even now, whenever I eat chicken, I think of him.

❦

If you remember, 1954 was the year of "Togetherness." For Birch and me, it began with such hope, and happiness, the first period of time alone together since we'd met. It was a perfect time for a young couple in love. He called me Shotsie, his version of the German word for sweetheart. Birch farmed, driving truck, tractor, combine; I kept him supplied with string beans, homemade ice cream, and chocolate angel food cake, his favorites. I was enjoying college, our group of young friends, our trips across the state to football games and to meetings, our evenings together alone at the farm. At last, I was beginning to feel a part of the community, involved in church and in our Home Demonstration club (where everybody except me reported faithfully how many jars of beans she'd canned or cucumbers she'd pickled—I had school for an excuse). Auntie Katherine Henley had become a dear, older friend to me, like my Oklahoma Aunty. She treated me like a daughter. I felt love all around me. I wanted nothing more out of life. My gregarious Birch was active in the Junior Chamber of Commerce in Terre Haute, on the Fair Board, with the Volunteers of America, in the Indiana Rural Youth Organization, with the JayCees' basketball tourney; he was one of their Three Most Outstanding Young Men, and president of the Vigo County Farm Bureau. Just after he turned twenty-five in January, he decided to run for the state legislature, which met in Indianapolis for 61 days every two years.

My parents, along with Daddy Bayh and Mary Alice, had been up to spend Christmas in our home, my first holiday away from Oklahoma. Our previous visits home had been traumatic for Birch: When we'd drive away from 2024 West Oklahoma, I would cry all the way to Missouri. Somehow Christmas in our own home in Indiana, around the tree Birch chopped down, so big we had to take the door off the hinges, seemed to turn the tide of my homesickness. We were "the children" to my parents, but Mother and I were establishing a new, closer relationship as two married women. Instead of bringing home awards to please her, I mailed her my latest Indiana white fruitcake. We wrote to each other every week and traded easy, companionable conversation about our lives as homemakers, and became real friends.

For my twenty-first birthday, Valentine's Day 1954, Birch planned a surprise visit to my parents. I'd packed a lunch and filled a thermos with orange juice. He picked me up at Indiana State, in the little brown Bel Air my folks had given us. We took turns driving. Birch had taken over the wheel on the two-lane hilly country road about eight miles south of Fort Leonard Wood, Missouri, just before dusk, and I had leaned over to open the thermos and get him a glass of juice. They told me that reaching for the orange juice probably saved my life. I came to in an Oklahoma City hospital three weeks later, unable to move, an intense pain throbbing inside my head, my mother standing beside me, smoothing my matted hair.

A car coming the other way passed a truck on that uphill grade and smashed into us head-on. No one else, thank God, was hurt seriously. My clavicle was broken, as was my foot; my knee was badly cut, and where my head had hit the steering column, I had a concussion that left me unconscious for two and a half weeks. Part of this time was spent in a Lebanon, Missouri, hospital until I was transported by air ambulance to Oklahoma City. My parents came to Lebanon to help Birch care for me, day and night, taking shifts, and when he had to go back for spring planting, Mother stayed with me in Oklahoma City, and then they took me home to Enid. Home, 2024 West Oklahoma, with a hospital bed in my old room, where I lay in pain so intense I cannot begin to describe it. The muscles controlling my eye were damaged; the right eyelid drooped, the left eye rolled back into my head. I could not focus. There were two images of everything. I lay there, in a shoulder cast, in my mother's care and Dr. Leroy's, until Easter, when Birch came to drive me back to Indiana.

My old life seemed to have ended. I remember months of piercing headaches, icepick pains in the back of my neck, trips to osteopaths, and worst of all, being unable to do anything. I felt horribly, achingly alone.

Never had I realized how much I valued the company of other people. More than the physical trauma from the wreck, I suffered from the silence. I could not use my eyes, so school was out of the question. I could not read, or write, or drive. The rural telephone lines were down and I couldn't phone. I dreaded waking up in the morning to that awful double vision. When we would go into town, Birch would have to hold onto me, to help me up and down the curbs. I couldn't exercise or do anything to make me tired, and therefore I wasn't sleeping. The doctor said I'd have to have rest in order to mend—and put me on sleeping pills. Then I became addicted to the sleeping pills.

Birch was into his first campaign for the state legislature; his evenings were spent all over Vigo County, meeting precinct committeemen, going farm-to-farm, introducing himself to prospective voters. I had so enjoyed my few weeks of running around with Birch, knocking on doors, meeting people. Now I was an outsider. One night I cried, pounding on Birch's chest with my fists. "I want to be with you, making speeches, meeting people, living our lives. Not here in this house, seeing double!" He held me quietly until I stopped crying.

Every day, I spent two hours trying to gain control of my eyes. I'd sit on that horrid green couch, focusing on a dark doorknob, determined that there would be one, not two, until I'd finally burst into tears. All my cheer was gone, all my delight in playing house. All I had left was my will. And that, too, was shaky.

Birch won the election. My goal was to see him sworn in on January 7, 1955—to see *one* of him. It was not to be. Instead I was in Oklahoma City with my mother during the complicated major surgery on the back of her neck to repair the diseased nerves in her wrist. The painful, long hours in the hospital with my mother had not helped my condition. Eleven months after the wreck, the pain in my neck, head, and eyes had not let up. I called an old friend, Shirlee Stoll's mother, who recommended Dr. Ruth Payton.

Dr. Payton restored hope to me. "Your life is nowhere near over," she said. "You are only twenty-one. Mother Nature is marvelous. She wants you to be alive and well. And there is no reason why you are not going to regain your health. We are going to get on top of this." And her treatments began to help me.

After my mother's crisis had passed, her recovery predicted, I flew to Indianapolis to be with Birch. My interest in government was too intense to miss all of his first legislative session. I met Governor George Craig, who said to Birch, "Birch Bayh, your dad's the only man who ever threw me out of a football game." We stayed at the Lincoln Hotel, near Mrs. Walter Maehling, our good friend from Terre Haute whose husband, the brother of Birch's mentor, Jake, also served in the legislature. Birch threw a surprise twenty-second birthday party for me at a cafeteria, but my headaches were so painful I could barely focus on the fun. Despite treatment, the headaches persisted and my neck got progressively worse.

There was only one thing to do, it seemed: return to the person who had given me relief and hope. About two weeks before the legislative session was over, I flew back to Oklahoma City, and rented a room about two blocks from Dr. Payton's office.

Every day for three weeks, Dr. Payton made "adjustments" on my taut neck, which relieved the headaches somewhat, and put me on a regimen of diet and exercise that began to put shape into my body and mind. Every day I walked the two blocks to her office, forcing my eyes downward as I walked, training them to see only one curb. Double vision was more than annoying, it was dangerous. Meanwhile, Mama was recuperating from her surgery at Grandma Anderson's house in Drummond. On weekends, sometimes I'd ride with an old school friend, or take a bus, or else

Daddy would drive the eighty-five miles to Oklahoma City to bring me home to her. With Mama, Grandma Hern, and me, Daddy had a handful of ailing women.

When I returned to Indiana that spring, my spirits were on the rise. Pain was still with me, but I had strengthened the muscles of my eye so that it wouldn't roll back in my head when I spoke to my new friends in the Indianapolis Democratic Women's Club. Extended reading was still out, however, and I couldn't go back to school. So after Birch's first session in the legislature, we decided to have a child. That had been our plan for after my graduation, anyway. As my hormones had always behaved in an unpredictable manner, I checked in with Dr. J. Lewis Stolting for advice on temperature charts, etc. As it happened, I was already pregnant.

෪ↄ

"I hope it's a boy," Grandma Hern told me that October, the same day she told Daddy she didn't want to catch my "disease." "Why, Grandma, you always told me you wanted a girl," I said.

"But you need a boy," she answered. Grandma did not live to see her first great-grandchild. She died on October 16, 1955, sixty-two years and one month after she had made the historic run into the Cherokee Strip. Her great-grandson was born in Indiana, the day after Christmas.

When we brought him home, Gaynell Poff took one look at the fat, healthy baby and said, "I can't believe celery and cottage cheese produced this!"

Birch Evans Bayh, III, whom we called Evan, delighted his father, who wrote poems to his new son, diapered him, held him in his arms, and during the long crying spells walked the floor at night with him, singing "Lullabye, please shut up. . . ." As he grew, Evan was so active I didn't need double vision to see two of him. Running after Evan was more exercise than I'd had since the Hern Hornets girls' basketball team in Enid.

Motherhood put me into a state of perpetual wonder, and brought back the sense of purpose that had vanished in the car wreck. Bearing a child sank my roots ever more deeply into the Indiana soil. It "takes awhile," yes, but when a Hoosier becomes a friend, you have a friend in truth. Gaynell Poff was such a one, this neighbor farm wife who came to me when Evan was born, because my mother was ill, and taught me the fine art of diapering and formula-making, and guided me over the postnatal terrors ("Now, Marvella, he won't break.").

All was well in my world, except for the pigs. The fences had gone down and before Birch could rebuild them those pigs began roaming over the countryside. People would call from five miles away saying, "Mrs. Bayh, there are pigs down here in my garden ruining my flowers and vegetables, and I know they must be yours." One day, I put Evan outside in his playpen while I was washing dishes. Suddenly everything was very quiet out there so I went out to check on him, and there was one great big old white boar scratching himself on the side of the playpen. Evan was reaching his chubby little fingers out at the creature, which could have taken a bite out of them. I stomped and screamed and yelled, and that old boar backed off, then turned around and looked at me, as if he were daring me to do something. And I just dared him right back. If looks could kill, that pork wouldn't have made it to market.

The flies, who seemed to enjoy the company of pigs, were equally low in my esteem. Every summer I'd wage war with my swatter, and inspect the screens for the tiniest holes through which they could wend their way from the barnyard to my kitchen. By fall, they were usually gone. But in December, 1956, we had a warm spell, and one day I began noticing the flies were back. When I carried Evan upstairs to bed, I found the bathroom full of flies. I told Birch when he came home and I heard the bathroom door open, and then slam shut. "Oh, my God," Birch yelled. The bathtub was half full. Only the flies weren't confined to the bathroom. They started coming out of the walls, out of the cracks around the sliding doors. By this time, dead flies were six inches deep in the light fixture, and still coming. Birch went down to Lendermans' and borrowed their barnyard spray pump. I stood at the walls and vacuumed as fast as I could, and still they kept coming, crawling over everything, over Evan's face, over the kitchen, like a plague in the Bible. The next morning Birch discovered the source. They had laid their eggs in the insulation in the attic, and the unseasonable warmth had caused them to hatch there in December, in great proliferation. When he sprayed up there, they dropped like black snow from the eaves.

᠊ᢒ

Although he will deny it to this day, Birch was not cut out for farming. I could see it the minute he left for Indianapolis and the legislature. He loved politics too much, sparring with his elders about the state withholding tax, ferreting out errors in the governor's proposals, defending a constitutional amendment allowing Indiana towns and cities to choose their own form of government, sponsoring an amendment to give nineteen-year-olds the vote. In his freshman session, the *Indianapolis Times* wrote that "Young Bayh, with a reasonable share of breaks and some good guidance, may be in the running for higher offices than the General Assembly in future years." Running for reelection was more fun for him than running a tractor; my husband was just too gregarious for life in the fields, no matter how much he loved that farm.

Moreover, he won those elections partly because he just worked harder at it than anybody else, tromping up and down the county until all hours. He was always rushing off to the Vigo County Fair Board or the church board, or a Farm Bureau meeting, or across the state to a farm management conference.

Farming 450 acres profitably would have taken more time than Birch could spend at it and still fulfill his legislative duties in Indianapolis, not to mention all his civic duties in Terre Haute. All our earnings were tied up in machinery, and we were struggling to keep up payments to Birch's sister for her half of the farm. I watched, and worried, as Birch tried to live two full lives, working harder at both than anybody should have to. The answer seemed very clear to me, as clear as the windows I was washing the day he rushed in from the field to change clothes for the Hog Growers' Association meeting at Purdue.

He ran down the stairs, all dressed up, and announced, "I'm running late." Purdue was a two-hour drive.

I left the windows, a job I despised, and sat myself in one of those gray-and-purple chairs. "Sit down a minute. I have to talk to you," I said.

"But I have to go. I'm late already," he protested.

"Just sit here with me," I insisted. "I've really got to talk with you right now."

He sat.

I looked across at him.

"You know, don't you, that you've really got to stop farming," I said.

Had I told him he would be the first man on the moon, he'd have been less surprised. "Farming is not fulfilling you," I went on. "We are not making money. If your great joy is in making laws, then you should consider law as your real profession." He protested, and argued, and drove off to Purdue. But when he got back, late that night, he said, "You know, you are right."

As he was advised by the dean that he'd have a rough time as a first-year law student while trying to serve in the state legislature, Birch postponed law school and went to work as an executive trainee with Anton Hulman, Jr., a civic-minded Terre Haute millionaire who believed in his abilities from the very beginning. Tony Hulman had developed shopping centers and airports, owned the Terre Haute newspapers and television station and other businesses, but perhaps he was best known as owner of the Indianapolis Speedway, where the famed "500" race is held every spring.

Jim Poff, Gaynell's husband, came to manage the farm, while Birch drove to his office in Terre Haute each day. The next year, Birch took a leave of absence from the Hulman Company to serve his term in the 1957 legislature. This time I joined him in Indianapolis and got involved in Democratic women's activities. Mother and Daddy came up to stay with Evan on the farm during the entire session, with Daddy doing most of the work because Mother was not well. Daddy diapered our wriggly one-year-old and helped him learn to walk by putting adhesive tape on the bottom of his shoes to give him traction.

At twenty-seven, Birch was elected minority leader of the House of Representatives—and he plunged into politics with both feet. At the end of the session, Birch decided to give up his job and enter law school. Then he decided to take the gamble of selling our house so that we would have money enough to live on.

Mother was aghast when we told her: "I've never lived in a house as nice as this, not in all of my life."

"Mother, this is a *dump* compared to the house I'm going to live in someday," I answered.

The price we got for the house, nine rooms of furniture, and 120 acres would support us for the next two years and pay off our debt to Mary Alice, as well. It was an emotional struggle for Birch to decide to sell the house and part of the land that his granddad had cultivated. But he truly wanted to study law and continue his political career.

"Look," I finally told him. "Your granddad used this farm the way he wanted to use it. He would have wanted you to use it in your way. Besides, he loved politics."

In October, 1957, we moved off to Bloomington, to the University of Indiana. I never looked back.

In our old truck, with the green sofa and our bed in the back, we laughed all the way to Bloomington, feeling like Okies in *The Grapes of Wrath*. Our new home was not far removed from my Oklahoma life, either: two rooms of married-student university housing. Evan's crib was next to our bed; the sofa and a small dining table were in the other room. We weren't allowed more space because we had only one child. Evan's recreation was the green sofa. He used it as a trampoline, as a banquet table. (As far as I was concerned, he couldn't destroy it fast enough.) We had no desk, no place to store anything. Our research papers and everything extra were filed underneath our bed.

But we had never been happier. Nobody had any money, everybody drove an old car, everybody exchanged ideas on a thousand ways to fix hamburger—the cheapest meat in those days. Unable to afford a perm, I yanked my stick-straight hair back into a ponytail and looked even younger than twenty-four. The children ran in a pack; Evan was an "only child" only until breakfast was over. Those were magic years, warmed with smart, stimulating friends. How I had missed the joy of learning, the exchange of ideas!

I was a student again. Even though I had only a year and a half to go, I arranged to stretch my secondary education/social studies courses over three years, to be assured of enough time to take care of Evan. Three mornings a week, I left him with a friend and neighbor, who supplied playmates as well, and went off to classes. And though I had really dreaded my semester of student teaching in the local high school, to my surprise I loved it.

At last, my health was better. The double vision was under control, except when I was tired, or driving at night, blinded by oncoming cars. The neck hurt only occasionally, when the injured spot on the left side, where the head sits upon the neck, would slip out of alignment, bringing back the icepick-sharp pain. One trip to an osteopath, however, would usually be enough to pop it back in place. Dr. Leroy told me that as I got older it would go away altogether. Another problem, however, was worrisome. For two years

I had had no monthly periods. I'd feel high-strung and weepy, for no reason at all. In Enid for spring vacation, I entered Gau Hospital for a D and C. After the surgery, Dr. Leroy reported that Evan, indeed, had been a miracle. My reproductive organs were those of a menopausal woman. Soon I might need estrogen shots, he said.

But back in Indiana, my energy returned. As a student-wife-mother, life could not have been better.

"Three mornings a week, I walk out the door with Birch, each of us working happily at our own choice," I wrote my mother. "I want it to be like this for the rest of my life."

Meanwhile, in 1959, when he was only thirty, Birch was named Speaker of the House for the Indiana legislature, the youngest Speaker ever. Winning an election was one thing; winning leadership, so young, was something beyond that. It took more than being gregarious or well-liked, more than a strong sense of values and convictions. Because of Granddad, and the Maehling brothers who'd helped guide him, Birch had learned to work well with older men, listening to and respecting their ideas. We became friends with them and their wives. He had a tenacious quality they admired—he'd stick to a project after everybody else had given up. But the deciding factor that impressed those older Indiana Democrats was his courage, especially in standing up for constitutional reform against the strength of the party "pros." Even though the amendment lost, they saw his integrity and ability to reason, and gave him the state's most powerful position as a lawmaker.

He was a senior in law school, pulling down top grades, too. I felt sorry for him, having to study night after night in the bathroom seated on a cushion on the hard toilet lid.

One evening the president of the university, Herman Wells, invited us, with four other couples, to dinner. To me, Dr. Wells seemed a remarkable man, knowledgeable about the arts, politics, and science. At the dinner that night, I was seated next to him, and said with a twinkle in my eye: "I know we only have one child, but we desperately need another bedroom. Do you as a citizen feel safe with your important state documents filed underneath the bed of the Speaker of the House?" Dr. Wells laughed. And we got another room.

By this time, Evan was attending I.U. Nursery School co-op, and when I took my turn assisting the teachers, I must confess that I couldn't wait to get back to my teenage students.

Birch, on the other hand, was, and is, wonderful with little people. He likes to play with them, and make up little games for them. We used a big red tarpaulin to cover those of Evan's toys which were kept out on the deck. Birch would take that tarp, wrap himself in it, and roll around on the ground with the children, playing big bad wolf, or a giant, or a big red punching bag in the tarp.

Just after Birch was elected Speaker, we invited my parents up to celebrate with us. While we were sitting in our living room describing the election, there came a little knock at the door. My mother, who was closest, got up to answer it. At first she thought nobody was there. Then she looked down to see a little girl, not more than three years old. The little caller asked: "Can Birch come out and play?"

Mother looked back at us. "So *that's* what the Speaker of the House of Indiana is supposed to do!"

Mother and Daddy were frequent, welcome visitors. They came up for Christmas, along with Birch's father and Mary Alice, and stayed with Evan a few days so that I could take a bus to Indianapolis for the legislature. During the 1959 session, I was active in the State Democratic Committee women's division, in Indianapolis, and vice president of the Indiana Democratic Women's Club. That was the year I was also elected President of the United States—in a clever farce, "Jenny for President," written by the National Democratic vice-chairman, Katie Louchheim. The playwright herself came to the program, and I found Katie to be a dynamic speaker.

Each accomplishment of Birch's, each speech of mine, each new antic of Evan's (whirlwind Evan with his inseparable once-white bunny that trailed its stuffing all over the house), I shared with my parents as eagerly as if I were still winning contests back in Oklahoma. I still counted the days until our next visit home, each summer for ten days. We alternated holidays with my parents in Indiana and Oklahoma. Daddy would write us long, loving letters expressing pride in his son, his grandson, his extended family.

It was a shock, therefore, when I received a letter from Daddy soon after their visit in 1959, in which he confessed that he was in love with another woman, that he wanted a divorce. "I have not been able to tell your mother," he wrote, "hoping that you will help me. I have, however, talked to your Aunt Lillian. . . ." I called Aunty immediately. We decided (wrongly, we now believe) that under no circumstances should Mother be told, that Daddy was going through what is now called a "mid-life crisis," that he would soon get over it. We conspired to keep it secret, and Daddy wrote me later that the affair was over and that he appreciated my understanding. Aunty and I breathed a relieved sigh. My greatest concern, now, was finishing college.

On March, 29, 1960, I sent a postcard home: "I finished! Wow! Hurrah! Yippee! Cheers! Hallelujah! All my love, Marvella."

My parents and Birch's father came to Bloomington to celebrate the family milestone: Birch and I donned our caps and gowns, and marched into the football stadium with our graduating class at I.U. During the ceremony, President Wells called out only two students' names—ours—announcing that we both were graduating with honors, Birch as a doctor of jurisprudence, I as a bachelor of science.

Afterward, Daddy gave me a hug. "I'm so proud," he said. And so, I must admit, was I. It had taken nine years and three colleges, but finally, I had earned the first college degree in the Delbert Hern family. I planned to wait another year, until Evan was in first grade, to begin teaching.

Birch joined a law firm in Terre Haute, where we bought a little six-room rambler—a modern, light-blue house I could feel was my own. Evan and I took off for Oklahoma, to give Birch peace and quiet to study for his state bar exam.

If Daddy had been a splendid father to me, he outdid himself grandfathering. He took Evan fishing, where they would lie on their backs and talk about nature. They would take an old skillet, build a fire to fry potatoes, weiners, and bacon, and then take a walk along the railroad tracks. Daddy built Evan a little "zoo" in the back yard, with cages for Oklahoma specimens such as coyotes and rabbits. When Evan had learned about each, they'd return the animals to the fields. "Always love God's creatures," Daddy would tell Evan, as he had told me. "Never hunt or kill."

We called Birch to see how he was getting along with his studying. Instead of studying all the time, I discovered, he'd been watching the Democratic Convention in Los Angeles on television. He was beside himself—our political hero, John F. Kennedy, had just been nominated Democratic candidate for President of the United States. I was as emotionally involved as Birch was, swept off my feet by Kennedy's acceptance speech: "The New Frontier is here whether we seek it or not. . . . A whole world looks to see what we will do—give me your help and your hand and your vote."

He seemed to everybody to have what we were trying to put together in our own lives: the vigor of youth, coupled with a commitment to politics. "I think he has a chance," Birch exulted. "I'm going to start campaigning for him as soon as I get this exam finished."

"But when are you finding time to study?" I asked.

"I'm doing fine, fine," he assured me.

Every day after Evan and I returned from Oklahoma, we expected the bar exam results to arrive. Finally, that third week in August, while Daddy Bayh was visiting us, the letter came in the morning's mail. I ripped it open, eager to share his score with his father before calling Birch.

I did not call Birch. Instead, I quickly got dressed and drove down to the law office. They told me that he was over at the Terre Haute House Hotel, having lunch with a client. I walked to the hotel, went into the dining room, and found Birch. "I need to talk to you," I said. "I'll be waiting in the lobby until you're finished."

They came out, the client went on his way, and Birch and I walked back to the office, me talking a blue streak about everything I could think of, until we got there. And when we were alone, in the office, I told him.

He had failed the bar exam, by one point.

Neither of us could believe it. Birch was at the top of his law class, a straight-A student, Law Review, had piled up achievements in law school as he had everywhere else.

It was so hard, such a blow for him, embarrassing, causing headlines to match his fame as "Youngest Speaker."

(I have always thought it was political, a blow below the belt, although Birch doesn't agree with me. But that is a wife's prerogative. The examining board was composed of Republicans, all appointed by the Republican governor whom Birch, as an up-and-coming Democrat, had opposed on many bills. Jim Capehart, who was in law school with Birch, called long distance to say if there was anybody in our class who knew the law, it was Birch. He was a top student. Not long ago, a Law Board member, checking on his own, dug back through the old files to look at Birch's first law test—and said it was outstanding.)

I felt anguish for Birch, and yet he grew by learning. It was a loss that made him know defeat, but know it early enough in life so that he would be hardened to it later on.

He served in the next state legislature as minority leader, making gains for education, tax reform, highway department reform, flood control, unemployment compensation—building a reputation for leadership there. The following March, he passed the bar exam with flying colors.

And now, I thought, we were ready to settle into a normal life, that of young professionals, in Terre Haute, Indiana, a city I had come to appreciate. But with decorating a new house, all the details of moving, coping with a lively preschooler—all of a sudden my energy dropped to zero, the weepiness and irritability returned, my hormones started acting up again. The doctor in Terre Haute began weekly shots of estrogen and my energy and equilibrium returned. Soon I was rarin', as we say in Oklahoma, to get involved in my community.

Chapter 4

My husband. Was there ever a man as dear as Birch Bayh? I didn't think so. That breath-catching, love-at-first-sight feeling I'd had at nineteen lingered, and blossomed, until sometimes I felt my chest would burst. He left funny little notes around the house for me—and still does—brought flowers for no reason at all, sent telegrams to commemorate odd anniversaries, wrote loving, sentimental poems that I cherish. Looking at the back of his head as he walked out the door in his new business suit, at the cowlick cutting a cleft in his dark curly hair, watching him stomp around the back yard with Evan on his shoulders, seeing the farm-hardened muscles in his arm tense as he clenched a baseball bat—I'd feel I might simply explode with love for that man.

There were other explosions as well. My father once said that he couldn't understand how three such strong personalities as Birch, Evan, and I could exist in one little house without the roof flying off. The roof quivered at the eaves more than once as we clashed wills, standing toe-to-toe, the Hern chin and the Bayh chin set at stubborn angles—until somebody budged. But somebody always budged, sooner or later, and the storm would fly out the window.

In some ways, we were very, very different. My inner clock was punctual; Birch's always ran a little late. Birch was masterful at comprehensive, long-term planning and analyzing complex ideas; I was better at keeping track of details. (I learned early on that I'd have to. On our honeymoon, he lost all our money and travelers' checks. Even now, his eyeglasses tend to disappear, and he seems destined to leave his raincoat on airplanes.) He had endless physical energy; after the wreck, mine was in short supply—Daddy Bayh used to tell me that I had a "hundred-horsepower engine in a thirty-horsepower chassis." But we learned to live with our differences, and to complement each other.

Our explosions were always over little things. Birch likes to put things off, and I like to do things yesterday. Sometimes I'd do things too quickly, when it would have been better to pause; sometimes he'd wait until too late—and miss the train. He would get mad at me for speaking "out of turn" and saying just exactly the wrong thing to somebody. I'd go straight up the wall about his being late, for airplanes, for meetings, for social engagements—all those occasions for which I would be early.

When it came to big decisions, our values were the same, our goals clear. We both taught Sunday School classes at the Centenary Methodist Church, Birch the young marrieds class and I the fifth grade, and both took very seriously the lessons from the Bible concerning our responsibilities toward our fellow man. To translate those responsibilities into programs of social action seemed to Birch and me almost a "higher calling." We were acutely aware of the opportunities that we ourselves had been able to seize, through the help of Providence and circumstance; we felt that America could not fulfill its promise unless people who were denied those opportunities by their own circumstances were allowed to share in the society. We saw government as being the only vehicle by which we could do our part to help bring about those opportunities. After having been allowed to participate in it, we felt that government was more important than ever before—it affected the world we lived in, the education we and our children received, the jobs available, the extent of freedom and security we enjoyed. Democratic government works by means of politics. Birch and I believed that if we were to make a contribution to our society, it would be through politics. We were afflicted with the idealism of the young, and the optimistic belief that anything is possible, through hard work.

The election of John F. Kennedy fueled our enthusiasm with hope—that what had seemed a future possibility might turn into reality sooner than we had planned. Our political dream had been for Birch to run for the U.S. Senate someday. Now, youth no longer seemed a liability. During the 1960 campaign, Birch had stumped the state in behalf of our Democratic friend, Matthew Welsh, in his winning campaign to become governor. But the Republicans once more gained a majority in the Indiana House of Representatives and Birch stepped down from Speaker to minority leader.

However, in his trips across the state, he sensed a stirring in Indiana. Everywhere Birch went to speak somebody would say, "You ought to try for the Senate. Look at Kennedy." But we had no funds with which to launch a campaign. My father advised Birch to wait—"make your money first." In August, 1960, after Kennedy's nomination, Birch had told the Indiana Democratic Editorial Association that he would "weigh" the Senate race in 1962, setting up immediate speculation that he might run. A few biting editorials pointed out that Indiana was not yet considered part of the New Frontier.

Positive signs were Birch's selection as "Most Able Representative" by newsmen covering the Assembly, and the enthusiasm of fellow Democrats at the state Jefferson-Jackson Day meeting in Indianapolis in May, 1961, who repeated that the state was "ripe" for change. Birch realized the best hope for change in Indiana would be to defeat the eighteen-year veteran conservative Republican, Senator Homer Capehart. The election of Matt Welsh as governor had made serious inroads into Capehart's Republican strength. In the spring of 1961, Birch began his forays around the state, seeking support from county chairmen and precinct leaders. Many times it would be turning daylight before he got home, and he'd be off to his law office with two hours' sleep. By autumn, he had visited all ninety-two counties at least once, discovering that though there was hope, unless people had followed the state legislature closely, they'd never heard of Birch Bayh. It would be a tough campaign just to become known. Together, we made the crossroads decision: We couldn't afford to climb the slow, safe ladder of politics. We would "go for broke" now, investing all our energy and resources in this one big race. If Birch should lose, he would leave politics and concentrate on a career practicing law.

On October 19, in the Claypool Hotel in Indianapolis, Birch formally announced his candidacy for the U.S. Senate, pledging "close cooperation with President Kennedy's excellent programs." He was primarily concerned with the solution of problems facing our senior citizens, proper care for the unfortunate and the mentally afflicted—and the defense of our country against Communist aggression in whatever form it appeared. But it would take more than Kennedy's programs to elect Birch Bayh in Indiana, we knew.

Our "it takes a while" state was not quite sure about JFK, who had lost Indiana by more than 200,000 votes in 1960. The Berlin Wall, in August, had seemed an affront. Some thought, as they tend to focus blame on a President, that it was somehow Kennedy's fault; others saw the Wall as a battle call. Bayh would have to campaign for Bayh, and for Kennedy as well.

In the fall of 1961 we took a trip to Washington to visit Daddy Bayh, and attempted to seek the counsel of our Democratic Senator, Vance Hartke, and Representative John Brademas, who, speculation had it, might be a candidate. Both of them were friendly; John assured us that he didn't plan to run, but neither offered his support.

We paid a call on Larry O'Brien, who was President Kennedy's chief of congressional relations, at the White House, and then were fortunate enough to get an appointment with Attorney General Robert F. Kennedy in his office in the Justice Department. Before the nomination, however, it is difficult for a national figure to offer a state candidate more than advice, because there are other Democrats running. Both Larry O'Brien and Bobby Kennedy wished us friendly, noncommittal good luck. We felt little enouragement, though no *dis*couragement.

In the beginning, with barely enough room in our new house for a typewriter, much less a campaign office, it was just the two of us. We operated out of a borrowed garage. The O'Connors, our Young Democrats friends a few blocks away, donated the space, with college volunteers putting press releases through a borrowed typewriter. I went to the stationery store and bought a file box. On the living-room floor, I spread out all the resource materials and clippings I had been gathering while Birch was out meeting the county leaders, to organize and put together his "issues" files— "Health Care," "Education," "Charges Against Birch." At first, I was his only full-time researcher, and in the process I began to learn the issues as well.

Our team first met in the living room. But after those first sessions, we decided not to allow the campaign to invade the house—except by telephone, which soon became an extension of Birch's ear. We wanted Evan's life to be as normal as possible, under the circumstances. We wouldn't drag him to meetings or parade him around with a sign saying "Vote for my Daddy." Besides, Evan wasn't very good at that sort of thing. I took him to one political picnic, armed with a lapful of coloring books and crayons, which held his interest for about five minutes. He just wanted to get out of there. No. Evan's place was at home, with normal hours for meals and bedtime, and vitamins and shots and shoes checked for fit, and his daily task, clearing our street of bad guys and Indians. I would leave him only with a family in our neighborhood who had children he knew and liked, the Charles Crispins, who even had a permanent bed set up for our Evan. In Indiana, neighbors are like that.

From the beginning, the team decided to use me as more than a researcher, although I continued that role as well. Our objective was to become known, to introduce Birch to as many of Indiana's 5½ million people as we possibly could before the state Democratic nominating convention in June, 1962. He'd need as many speaking engagements as could possibly be scheduled—and so would I. We tried to place ourselves in different parts of the state, to garner as much local publicity as possible. Birch would speak at a Democratic meeting in Rochester, while I spoke to one in Greensburg; he'd speak to the JayCees in Evansville, while I'd speak to a group in Tipton. After all, if we were together on the same platform, there would be one news story; if I were speaking in another part of the state, there would be two.

We didn't have resources for paid advertising, so the campaign was built around little more than our energy. The Democratic opponents seemed to be formidable: the mayor of Indianapolis, Charles Boswell, with the wealth of Marion County and City Hall behind him; the mayor of Marion, Jack Edwards; and Judge John Gonas from South Bend. We would have to contact each one of the 2,578 delegates to the June Democratic nominating convention. No meeting was too small, no road too long, no hour too late—or too early. If Birch was at factory gates at dawn, he'd be out on some farm road at a delegate's house at midnight.

At first contributions were tiny—somebody would come up after a speech and stuff a twenty-dollar bill into Birch's hand—but they soon increased. The biggest initial donation was not cash, however; Birch's former boss, Tony Hulman, lent Birch his 1957 Mercury to drive those thousands of exhausting miles, so that I could keep our car in Terre Haute. At first Birch drove it alone. But after nearly falling asleep at the wheel several times, he was joined by Bob Hinshaw, who volunteered his services as a driver.

My trips kept to the same pace as Birch's, if not quite the same quality. Chewing bubble gum was my secret relaxation in the car, while Larry Cummings, the volunteer who drove me from town to town, played the radio or stopped to fix the motor with my fingernail file. After Larry went back to college, another young volunteer, Allen Flory, took over, dodging my clouds of hairspray as well as the ever-bigger bubbles I blew.

At Christmastime, we took a break, driving to Oklahoma to visit my parents. Daddy, ardent Democrat that he was, was all wrapped up in our campaign. He'd even picked up a pen and written to former President Truman: Could his daughter and her husband the candidate stop by to see him on our way home? Truman's invitation, in response, was one of our Christmas presents. Mother and Daddy drove with us as far as Independence, Missouri, where we all spent an afternoon.

Mr. Truman was grayer, of course, than when I'd met him at Girls' Nation—but still feisty. He told us a story about the Republican opponent, Senator Capehart, and then said, "Of course, I can't be quoted on that."

Evan (who had just turned six), dressed in his best clothes and filled with instructions on how to behave, sat quietly on the sofa beside "Gran" while the former President told his Capehart story. There was not a word out of Evan, which was unusual, but rewarding to a parent. After about forty-five minutes, however, Evan spoke out in a loud voice: "I have to go to the bathroom." I was undone. It was not a whisper, but an announcement. But Harry Truman got out of his chair, walked over to Evan, and took his hand. "You know, son, I do, too. Let's go." And Truman took Evan to the bathroom.

Birch was thrilled to meet Harry Truman, to elicit his encouragement. "Tell you what, Birch," he said. "You win that nomination and I'll come up to campaign for you."

All the fall and winter, we had hoped for some sign of encouragement from our friend, Governor Welsh. However, Welsh's people were pushing for Charles Boswell, who, as mayor of Indianapolis, had a heavy organization and a large staff, and was in a stronger position to influence the governor's advisors than we. Matt Welsh's advisors had told him that there would be no hope of winning a Democratic majority in the State House without the mayor of Indianapolis at the top of the ticket.

Birch was pacing the floor. "If Mike Sperling will stick with me, we've got a chance," he said. Mike, a close friend and strong financial backer of John Kennedy, had heard Birch speak and liked him enough to put some cash on the barrel. A Hungarian-born industrialist, millionaire founder of the Merz Engineering Company in Indianapolis, Miklos Sperling was a Renaissance man, I thought, an art collector and philanthropist who was especially astute about politics. Mike stuck with us.

Fannie Mae Hummer, too, was on our side. Indiana runs on patronage, and she was a beneficiary. A longtime Democratic operative, she was a hard-working, hefty, working-class woman from Kokomo. In 1962, she had earned the state License Branch, the best job of her life. She simply marched into the governor's office and announced, "Now look, Matt. I supported you and you are an outstanding governor. I am eating better than I have ever eaten in my life, but I am going to be for Birch Bayh and I don't care what you say."

I remember a February meeting in Fort Wayne, where nobody thought I'd show. I was driving, alone, from Terre Haute (a far piece away under the best of conditions) to represent Birch; Dr. Bob Risk, a dentist who strongly supported the Kennedys, was driving from Indianapolis. The most awful blizzard hit. The road was icy, the kind of conditions in which you have no control of the car. Even at 20 miles per hour, scared to death, I made it to that meeting, exhausted. So did Bob. Another night, driving home from a meeting in Shelbyville with Jack Mankin, we ran into a blizzard so bad that Jack had to stop every two miles and beat the frozen windshield wipers. In Fort Wayne and Shelbyville and all over the state those delegates wanted us—but we kept hearing that Matt Welsh's people wanted Charlie Boswell.

On May 10, Birch was in Indianapolis preparing to hold a news conference on juvenile delinquency. I was at home in Terre Haute, running a week's laundry, wondering how Evan could manage to get four pairs of jeans filthy in one day. Birch phoned me from the State House. "Matt is in there speaking to the reporters," Birch said. "He's giving us his endorsement." Boswell, of course, was furious, and, seeking Administration support, he took off for Washington.

So did I. As one of Indiana's fifteen delegates to a Democratic Women's Conference, I became reacquainted there with an old personal hero, Senator Hubert Humphrey, at a reception given for us by Indiana's Democratic Senator Vance Hartke. I was elated at the opportunity, but too exhausted to enjoy it. On the plane to Washington, Mary Jo Rock noticed my hand shaking. My left hand, the dominant one, could not get a bite of airplane food from the tray to my mouth without it spilling all over me. But I couldn't rest just then. We had a month to go.

In Washington, besides Senator Humphrey, one person impressed me: Katie Louchheim, vice-chairman of the Democratic party, who had written the play I'd been in. Katie's message was like that of her predecessor, India Edwards: the underrated role of women in electoral politics. I thought long and hard about Katie Louchheim, and the important job she was performing. "I'd love such a job someday," I told Mary Jo Rock, "a real job in politics."

The state convention opened with a swirl of color and noise. Half a dozen bands from all over the state trooped in and out of Indianapolis hotel lobbies, where campaign workers fanned out for last-minute buttonholing of delegates. A man from Fort Wayne brought a donkey up to our fifth-floor headquarters at the Claypool Hotel, then parked it ceremoniously underneath the 40-foot birch tree—our pièce de résistance in the lobby. Mayor Boswell of Indianapolis took an axe to the birch tree, Mayor Edwards of Marion held a "twist" party to attract the young to his cause. We held rallies, singing an old song adapted from my Girls' State campaign: "Put on your Birch Bayh bonnet, his wagon get upon it, and we'll push our party to the top. Every rooster boosting, not a booster roosting, we will never, never stop!" And we didn't. It was pure, corny enthusiastic Americana, a lot of hard work crowned by about seven barrelfuls of fun.

The Claypool reeked with political history—Lincoln even spoke there on his way to Washington after being elected President—but we were afraid it was going to reek with a lot more. Our donkey, all dressed up in its hat, with "Vote for Bayh" on each side, had now been paraded around to the district caucus rooms. He was on the eighth floor, and everybody agreed it was time for him to come down. The donkey, however, balked at the freight elevator door, all four feet planted firmly, refusing to budge. They were pulling, yelling, and whacking him on the rear, and causing a general commotion, when along came elegant, immaculate Mike Sperling. "Stop it," commanded Mike in his Hungarian accent. He walked up to the animal, put his hand behind its ear, leaned over and whispered a few words, and then he took the reins and led the donkey right onto the elevator. He looked back at the people. "You see? You don't know how to talk to the donkey."

The balloting took place in the State Fairgrounds Coliseum on June 22, preceded by a tumultuous demonstration organized by our enthusiastic young volunteers on Birch's behalf. There was a band, of course, led by "Uncle Sam," and sixty pretty girls carrying what seemed like a forest of Bayh posters, followed by not one but two donkeys, "Jack and Jackie." Birch and I communicated by walkie-talkie, crisscrossing the huge auditorium, followed by huge posters with our photographs on a 20-foot pole—so we could locate each other—shaking hands with everybody in sight. Birch was energized, stimulated, buoyed by all that contact. He'd stretch out his hand, give a wink, jab one shoulder while putting his arm around another. "How are you?" or "What are you up to this morning?" or "Good to see you," he'd grin, handshaking his way through the crowd. For the women, he shouted, "Hi there! You look mighty nice in that hat! You look awful cute today!" The women giggled and swarmed in appreciation. It was that kind of a crowd, giving off the sort of electricity that feeds a candidate with a source of energy when he has little left of his own to generate. I felt as if I were about 900 watts that day.

Birch won the nomination on the first ballot.

The victory celebration lifted us even higher. The Claypool Hotel nearly took flight, Birch's father said, and later the parade down Wabash Avenue in Terre Haute, with Evan, Birch, and me perched in a convertible, leading a fifty-car cavalcade, brought the kind of exhilaration that can push a politician beyond endurance. But I was tired, really tired. Birch and I had logged 70,000 miles on that campaign. Sleep we did without.

Mother and Daddy had joined us for the convention, driving Evan back to Oklahoma for a visit until I could join them. "Only 17 more days," I wrote my mother. "Then I'm going to crawl in my old bed and pull the covers over my head—I don't care if it is July." But before I could go to Oklahoma I had a commitment to fulfill, one I wouldn't have missed for anything—as Federalist party counselor and Senate advisor to 750 girls at Hoosier Girls' State in Bloomington. Meanwhile, Birch was regrouping with the state Democratic party, planning the fall campaign. Then he had to go to Washington for a Democratic candidates' conference. I struck out for Oklahoma alone, driving in the daytime because my double vision returned at night. My goal was to make Lebanon, Missouri, the halfway point, by dark. On the St. Louis bypass I took my eyes off the road to look for a cafeteria—and plowed into a car that had stopped in front of me. The only injury was to my radiator, but it was a Saturday afternoon and there was a four-hour delay, what with tow trucks and finding garages. Then after I got going again, wouldn't you know I'd hit a speed trap? I paid my twenty-dollar fine, and went on my way—slowly, nerves jangling.

The next day, I drove into the driveway at 2024 West Oklahoma, in dire need of tender loving care. Heaven couldn't have looked better to me. There was my basketball goal, the Krazy Kats sign on the sidewalk—and my support system, my mother and father. I was ready to be a child again, for ten days.

The next morning we found Daddy lying on the floor. He had taken an entire giant-economy-size bottle of aspirin, trying to commit suicide. Mother was distraught, Evan was confused. We took Daddy to the Gau Hospital, and I got on the phone with the Menninger Clinic in Topeka, Kansas, to seek advice. "Doesn't this give you some clue that he is reaching out to you," the Menninger doctor asked me, "that your first day home he would choose to do this?"

I assumed the burden of Daddy's desperation, remembering that as a child I was the only one who could bring a smile to his face during his midwinter "gloomy spells." Now, what could I do? I talked to Dr. Leroy, our family doctor, and to the hospital in Oklahoma City that Dr. Leroy had suggested. They agreed that Daddy needed to be hospitalized, but that he would have to commit himself.

Every day I spent hours at the breakfast table talking to him, trying to persuade him to go to the hospital, knowing that no one could force him to go, but also that I could not help his depression. My heart nearly broke as he poured out his feelings of failure—his failure to serve his country during the war, his failure to get a college education, his failure to make a good living at farming (now Mother had to take a job at the county assessor's office), his failure to win a political election. He kept saying he had been an "unwanted" child. In my eyes he had been strong, fearless, unconquerable, my daddy, my hero. How could he see himself so differently? I could not leave, knowing he felt so low that he wanted to die. What if he should attempt again—and succeed?

Finally, I was able to talk him into entering that hospital. He put up a good front, my daddy, signing himself into the psychiatric ward, wisecracking with the nurses. They asked him his religion, and he answered "Unitarian"—much to my surprise. We'd always been Methodist. I told him goodbye and he clung to me for a moment, as if he wouldn't see me again.

We returned to Enid; I got our car repaired and our clothes packed, wrote a long letter to Daddy, and then drove by the assessor's office to say goodbye to Mother. She stood on the courthouse steps, my lovely mother, wearing a bright blue knit dress, with a watch I had given her on a chain around her neck, waving to Evan and me as we drove away to Indiana. Evan stood behind my seat and patted my shoulder. The tears came then, for the agony of my father, and from my fatigue. My mother needed me, but so did Birch. My mind was a tug-of-war, torn between loves and responsibilities a thousand miles apart. Evan, at six, standing behind me in that car, proved to be of enormous comfort. When we discovered I had left our suitcase at Mother's house, when we couldn't find a place to spend the night, when my double vision came back as it got dark and I began to panic. "Now, it's going to be all right, Mother, we'll find something. Don't worry," Evan said. And he kept patting me on the shoulder, like my father would have done.

As soon as we got home, we went full steam into the fall campaign, which we were not supposed to win, against Republican Senator Capehart. Evan was furious when he found out that his father had still another opponent. "That's not fair," he said, stomping his six-year-old foot. "Two against one."

❧

I was torn between concern for my parents and the necessity to focus all my energy on this uphill fight of my husband's. If he were to have any chance at all of defeating Homer Capehart, he would need every ounce of my strength during the next four months. "How can you stand up under the strain of a campaign?" a reporter asked me. "You can stand anything for four months," I replied.

In Oklahoma, Mother's health, never strong, was gravely taxed.

She would leave her job at the courthouse, make the two-hour drive to Oklahoma City to be with Daddy when he could have visitors, then drive back and go to work the next day. In addition, she was trying to manage things on the farm. Then Daddy began to write that he knew he had been helped, that he was in control once again and was ready to go home. Only they wouldn't let him out.

Mother would call me, saying he seemed all right to her. She had heard stories about "how these psychiatrists get their hooks in you and they get you dependent on them so that you lose your ability to stand on your own two feet—and they have a good thing going for their income."

Daddy was an actor, he could convince anybody. I finally called his doctor. "No, he is not ready to leave," he said emphatically. "This man is not ready to be released. But we cannot keep him here without his consent. And if he leaves now, we cannot be held responsible. . . ."

Mother signed him out, at Daddy's insistence. "He's as fine as you are," she said. And I was vastly relieved to hear his voice, when he called, profoundly apologizing for having caused so much worry.

His letters were so full of his old optimism that I hoped and prayed this most severe of his "gloomy spells" was over. With this hope, I was able to concentrate all my attention on my husband. By now, I knew that I would see very little of Birch until after the November election. He had scheduled over three hundred speeches between Labor Day and November 6. There were already sixty on my calendar by the time I returned from Oklahoma. During this, the hard part of the election, my neighbor, Lois Crispin, took Evan into her home while we were traveling about the state, although I made it a rule to come home every three days. I fretted that our being in the public eye might affect him. Sure enough, one day he came home from first grade crying. Some children had started to chant: "Birch Bayh is a rat, 'Cause he is a Demo-crat."

With the state Democratic party behind us, we were able to move from the O'Connors' garage into a bona fide headquarters. Suddenly there was a staff—and money was not as much of a problem. Another asset was Harry S. Truman. True to his word, the former President came to Indiana to campaign for Birch—and told a large audience the same story about Capehart that he'd made us promise not to tell. He brought them to their feet.

But this was the quintessential uphill race—the Indiana news-papers already were calling it David vs. Goliath—and we simply had to make more speeches, travel more miles, drink more tea, shake more hands, get more press, create more enthusiasm. Homer Cape-hart was a household word in Indiana. And Birch Bayh, nominated in a closed convention rather than in a statewide primary, was still an unknown upstart. They couldn't have been more different: Capehart, at sixty-five, was a millionaire manufacturer; Birch, at thirty-four, and I were gambling our shoestrings on this race. Cape-hart was conservative, to the right of Barry Goldwater; Birch sup-ported President Kennedy's liberal programs in Medicare, the Peace Corps, civil rights, and Cuba. Capehart had sat in the U.S. Senate for eighteen years; Birch was itching to get that seat.

Our strategy was to attack his conservative record, to convince the voters of the efficacy of President Kennedy's programs, to show up at every gathering of people for any reason in the state of Indiana —and, as in the earlier race, send Marvella to one part of the state while Birch spoke in another. From English to Muncie to Lake County to Evansville, in and out of Indianapolis, from French Lick to Michigan City, to Valparaiso to Versailles to Anderson and Wil-liamsport, Lafayette and Elkhart, Wabash and Booneville and Ko-komo, and all over the back roads and industrial centers of Indiana, we hammered away at Capehart's voting record and introduced Birch as the Candidate for Change, for progress.

Birch and I talked to each other by car telephone as we tra-versed the state, exchanging notes and facts and figures for our speeches. I reported on education and on national health insurance; I invoked Susan B. Anthony, sounding a clarion call for women's involvement in politics. Indiana's women were the backbone of our campaign, arranging parties, breakfasts, brunches, teas, luncheons, dinners, receptions; answering telephones, addressing envelopes, or-ganizing precinct meetings, ferreting out lists of undecided voters. In those days, it may have been somewhat unusual for me, as a candidate's wife, to take to the stumps talking about issues; it was not unusual for other wives to volunteer large chunks of their time and energy organizing the myriad details of a campaign. I shall never forget that terrific trio, Fannie Mae from Kokomo, Josephine Bicket from Indianapolis, and Agnes Woolery from Bloomington, strong, forceful veterans of many a political war, who set the state in order for Birch—as did Paulette Whiteman in northern Indiana, and hundreds of other volunteers. Our future depended on all those women, hundreds of volunteer friends, and they worked as if their future depended upon us.

How can I describe the pace of a campaign? It is superhuman, thrilling, exhausting, demanding. What a price one pays! You are totally caught up in it. Everything, but everything, takes a back seat—family time, sleep, health, friends. Birch was home exactly two and a half days between Labor Day and Election Day; during one five-week period, we didn't see each other at all. I learned to change clothes in gas station restrooms, and live from Dairy Queen to Dairy Queen (those ambrosial puffs of white nothing got the best of my diet), held together by hairspray and bubble gum. We were relying on the old Oklahoma formula for competitive success, "Just work twice as hard as the next guy." I felt like Grandma Hern, following her husband's plow, dropping seeds into the cracks in the sod. A full partner in the family endeavor, I was following Birch's plow as he broke new ground in politics. I felt that, by dint of hard work, I could help Birch win.

That is, until Cuba ("Cuber," as we called it, imitating President Kennedy's Boston accent) became the central issue. On August 27, Senator Capehart, who had long been campaigning for intervention in Cuba, urged a Marine invasion days before President Kennedy announced that there was a large military buildup of Soviet equipment. Birch accused the Senator of warmongering. And so it went, up and down the state: "Invade!" "No!" "Blockade!" "No!"

On October 13, President Kennedy came to Indianapolis to speak in Birch's behalf. Surprisingly, he did not mention Cuba—although he came down hard on "armchair generals who wanted to send others' sons to war." Nine days later, the President announced that because of the building of missile sites there, he was ordering a naval blockade of Cuba—the very thing our opponent had urged! We were crushed, but Birch went on the offensive, praising the President for his actions. The newspapers told us we had "had it." On the front page of the *Indianapolis Star* was a big cartoon: A ship, steaming along, Capehart at the helm. Climbing aboard was President Kennedy. And behind, in a sinking rowboat, rowing as hard as he could, was Birch Bayh. As we approached election day, the *Indianapolis Times* poll predicted that Capehart would win by 61.4 percent to Birch's 38.6 percent of the vote. President Kennedy himself, we heard later, had told an aide ruefully after the Cuba blockade announcement, "We just defeated Birch Bayh."

Now I tried to prepare my husband psychologically for the loss. I didn't want him to be totally devastated. Birch, on the other hand, just hung on to his optimism and said, "We've got to double our efforts." And Mike Sperling never gave up. At the lowest point, Mike just laughed and said, "Remember, you're going on TV." The Bayh television assault had been set up long before "Cuber." It was now our last hope.

The Republicans had poured lots of their money into traditional kinds of advertising: billboards, pamphlets, rotogravure sections—and gimmicks. I remember little sponges that said "Soak me in water." When expanded, they read "Vote for Capehart." We had to concentrate on the most effective use of our resources. Mary Lou Conrad had written a little verse, to a tune from Lucille Ball's Broadway show *Wildcat*: "Hey, look him over, He's your kind of guy. His first name is Birch, his last name is Bayh. . . ." We bombarded radio and television stations with that recording for the last two weeks of the campaign. During the closing days, Birch appeared in "telethons" on local stations around the state, inviting viewers to call in with questions, or to express their views. It was a new and rather personal use of the medium, and judging from the number of call-ins, one that was more appealing than the usual television speech.

We added another television twist those early days of November, the down-to-the-wire days of the campaign, which we called, among ourselves, "Marvella's last-minute appeal." The mayor of Anderson, Indiana, Ralph Ferguson (Mary Jo Rock's father), had the idea. He had heard me speak in Anderson, and immediately called our campaign office in Indianapolis. "Put *her* on television in the last days of the campaign," he said. "It will be different—will catch attention." I wrote and videotaped a fifteen-minute talk about my husband—his record in the legislature, his concerns for the elderly and for teachers, and his character as I knew it as husband and father to our son. Mike Sperling, Merle Miller, and Bob Risk put up the money to buy last-minute TV time. All week long my talk bombarded TV sets across the state. Yet the week before election day, not one correspondent, not one major newspaper, not one poll, not one electronic computer said we would win.

My parents drove up from Oklahoma, three or four days before the election, to see our television appeals. One day Daddy acted strangely when he picked me up at the beauty shop. He gunned the motor and was racing with another driver. "Just let him go," I said. "No, I'm goin' to show him," he said, whirling the car around crazily. "Daddy, don't!" I yelled. And he then lashed out cruelly, criticizing me. I began to cry. When we got home, I ran to Mother, fearful about his mental health. "What's the matter with Daddy?" Tears came to her eyes. "I'd rather not talk about it," she said. Just then Daddy came in, and he apologized. "I had a little to drink," he said, "but I will never, ever, drink again. Because I have hurt you."

"Oh, if you really mean that . . ." Mother said. And he promised her, too. I was astonished. My father had never touched liquor.

❧

On election day, November 6, after we voted, we all got ready to drive down to Indianapolis. Evan was playing with his friend Duffy, a collie that belonged to Ruth and Tom Walton, our Republican next-door neighbors. He ran into the house excitedly: "The Waltons say that if Daddy wins, Duffy can go with me to Washington!"

Daddy Bayh, who had spent two weeks in Indiana campaigning for Birch, flew in from Washington, and we gathered in our campaign headquarters in Indianapolis to hear the returns. By four A.M. the outcome was still up in the air. At five, Dr. Ferguson from Terre Haute, the county coroner, handed me a sleeping pill, and I walked down the hall to my bedroom. Daddy had curled up on the floor in front of Evan's room (so he couldn't get out without Daddy knowing it).

About eleven, I was awakened by somebody beating on the door. "Marvella, let me in. It's Daddy." I staggered out of bed, to the door. "Get dressed," he said. "Birch wants you to go down and attend a press conference he has called."

"Have we won?" I asked, groggy.

"Yes, darlin', you've won," he said, and took me in his arms.

I looked up at him—he knew how much I wanted this—and said, "Daddy, do you know what this means? It means someday I may get to go to Europe." Nobody in our family had ever been to Europe except for Uncle Orville, who had died over there during World War I.

That afternoon, it was announced that Birch's winning margin was 10,944 votes, out of 1,800,000 cast.

Was there ever such jubilation? I look at pictures of Birch and me on that day and see two young faces, thirty-four and twenty-nine, with sparkling eyes and ear-to-ear smiles, caught by the camera before we could really believe that we had done it. The next few days can only be described as pandemonium—with basketfuls of telegrams, a constantly ringing phone, friends who couldn't reach us by phone simply dropping in. My parents stayed to help (we had no staff to help meet this onslaught), my father to provide love and diversion for Evan, Mama to answer the phone and help sort the mail. There were "hate" letters and crank phone calls, too, of course, which she soon learned to handle with aplomb. One of the first calls nearly threw her, however. Birch was in the next room trying to talk to the press, and our phone had been busy all day. The doorbell rang, and my mother answered the door. It was the police chief.

"I have a very important phone call for the new senator—they couldn't get through on your line," he said. My mother answered that we had a whole list of important phone calls here, and he'd return them as fast as he could. "Just give me the name and number and I'll put this one on the list."

The officer grinned. "I think he'll want to put this one at the top of the list—the President of the United States is trying to reach him." I flew into the other room, and begged Birch to let me listen on an extension—promising not even to breathe. I heard the familiar Boston voice of John F. Kennedy say, "Birch, you old miracle-maker. How the hell did you do it—nobody thought you'd do it, especially after 'Cuber'!"

Birch answered that the President's visit on October 13 had made a big difference. But, in truth, nobody ever knows what makes the difference. By the following day it dawned on us that if just one voter in each precinct in Indiana had chosen Capehart instead of Birch, we would have lost. Just one voter. It was something that (sometimes to my distress) Birch kept in the front of his mind for the next six years. You can look at those figures and say, "Boy, I went into those areas and I persuaded at least twenty people in that town that night." But you don't know whether it was going into that town that mattered, or whether it was the ad you put in the newspaper that last week, or the telethon, or the "last-minute appeal," or the President's speech—you don't really know what did it. The *Indianapolis News* reported that "Bayh's campaign was the most furiously active, energetic, and comprehensive ever waged by a candidate in the history of Indiana. He averaged 18 hours a day, seven days a week campaigning from the day the Democratic State Convention nominated him June 22."

I never questioned then whether it was worth it.

I remember our thinking, the day after the election, "Wow! All these thousands and thousands of people believe in Birch and what he can do, all the issues we've been talking about, how he can make a difference, make a real contribution in Washington." The Indianapolis television station had a roving reporter that day, asking people about the election. One woman said she had voted for Birch Bayh. "Why?" asked the reporter. "Well," said the woman, "I read the column in the paper one day where Birch Bayh had gotten up about dawn and went hard all day and about twelve o'clock somebody handed him a sandwich and he took a couple of bites of it, and by one-thirty he still hadn't finished his sandwich. And Capehart, on that same day, well, he sat down and he had a great big lunch. So I just decided Birch Bayh wanted it more." We laughed and laughed. "So much for the issues, for all those people who believed in what you can do," I teased Birch.

But as the election became national news—Walter Cronkite called it the "political upset of the year"—we became more and more overwhelmed by the debt of gratitude we owed to those people on our "team," those energetic members of the women's division, those who donated money, those who persuaded their Rotary Clubs or farmers' organizations to let us speak, those who invited their friends and neighbors into their homes for the innumerable "coffees" and "teas" in our behalf. I remembered the similar sensations I'd had back in Girls' State, which seemed a hundred years ago—the awe that people would work themselves to the bone because they wanted "their" candidate to win.

On November 11, we flew into Washington for a two-day whirlwind of meeting the President and the press, and finding a house. As we rode down Pennsylvania Avenue to the Capitol, where

Birch was to hold a press conference in Senator Vance Hartke's office, I turned to Birch. "I feel as if I'm in a movie," I told him. "I can't believe this is really happening to me."

It was happening to him, of course. But Birch had made me such a partner in that campaign that I saw the victory as ours. And he told the press as much. And when President Kennedy received us in the Oval Office, at the end of our twenty-five-minute visit, he turned to me. "I want you to meet my sister-in-law, Joan. I think you'll find that you have a lot in common." Then he leaned back in that high-backed rocking chair. "I understand that you've been active in the campaign—I hear that you're a better speaker than Birch," he said. I began to protest, but Birch put an arm around me. "That's very obviously so," he said. "I couldn't have won without her." That was reward enough for the long hours I had put in, I thought. I had been Birch's partner during the campaign, I would be his partner in Washington.

That afternoon I went househunting. My only criteria were that we have enough space for Evan and Duffy, the collie he'd won, and that we be close to a good school. I knew nothing of big-city living, of commuting distances, of Washington neighborhoods—I only knew I had two days in which to choose a home. We'd have to sell our house in Terre Haute for a down payment. At the end of the day, I joined Birch in the Vice President's office in the Capitol. I felt immediately at home with Lyndon Johnson. The cadence of his Texas voice sounded like that of my own Oklahoma friends. His expansiveness and expressiveness were familiar—he had grown up with plenty of space around him, like the Herns. In the middle of the conversation, he suddenly said, "Come on home and have dinner with me. Bird is gone to New York, but we'll find something."

The chauffeur drove us to a lovely brick home, surrounded by elms, in Washington's Spring Valley; inside all yellow and white, with French antiques, the most elegant house I'd ever seen. Allen Flory, our young campaign driver who was helping us unpack, was with us. We were served at table by the Johnsons' cook, Zephyr Wright, as if we had been expected for weeks.

Vice President Johnson took us on a tour of the house, opening doors to room after room, until, upstairs, he opened his daughter Luci's door. There she sat, a junior high student, propped up in bed studying, her hair in big pink rollers. She greeted us with a big smile, as if she were accustomed to having her bedroom door thrust open to admit strangers. Later, as we had coffee in the living room, the Vice President talked so warmly about the Senate, about how it operated and how the senators managed to work together, that I had the distinct feeling that he would like to change places with Birch—to be starting in the Senate again.

He gave Birch some strong advice: "Hire the best staff, the best brains you can possibly find. Your staff can make you—or break you. And, remember this," he said, "it is more important that they have good minds and experience than that they come from Indiana." (I would remember those words later on, when some of Johnson's staff caused him grief—and even later, when some of Birch's caused me grief.) The next piece of advice was aimed at me, too. "Buy the most expensive house you can squeeze out to afford," he said, "because chances are, when your days in the Senate are finished, about the only money you'll have been able to save will be what you were forced to put into your house." ("How can that be?" I thought. "We'll save money. Birch will be making $22,500 a year and I'm very thrifty!") He couldn't have been more gracious to us, making a call to a real-estate friend, even taking us out househunting himself, in his limousine, in neighborhoods near his own.

The next day was our last in Washington; Attorney General Robert F. Kennedy and his wife, Ethel, had us to lunch in their home, Hickory Hill, out in McLean, Virginia. (I was wearing a nondescript black dress, I remember, a campaign necessity. It made me feel out-of-place among those glamorous women.) Once more, the conversation centered on "how on earth did you win?" I had no idea that Indiana politics were being watched so closely in Washington. They told us how much we would enjoy their brother, Teddy, who, at thirty, would be the only senator younger than Birch. They were cordial to us, but I was overawed by the Eastern finesse of the Kennedys. I remember sitting very straight, hoping I wouldn't "say the wrong thing," whatever that might be, and in the manner of most rural people, wanting not to be taken for a "hick." Bobby Kennedy took us househunting, too, driving us through two neighborhoods around his in Virginia.

We bought a house late that afternoon, a not-quite-finished brick split-level in the Chesterbrook development of similar homes in suburban McLean, Virginia, near "good" schools, but not much else. It was a forty-five-minute drive to the Capitol.

We moved in December, in the middle of a blizzard; for a

while we slept on mattresses on the floor, and slipped and slid up our steep driveway, scattering groceries in the snow. When Evan saw blankets on our windows, he said, "Just think, we have to put up with this for six years." It was not until Christmas, our new house still bare of curtains and sparse of furniture, that the emotional high of victory, with all the false energy it had generated, finally came crashing down. My parents were there for the holiday, along with Daddy Bayh and Mary Alice, and Birch had dressed himself up in his Santa suit, as he always did. At Daddy Bayh's house, where we had Christmas dinner, I fled upstairs to the bathroom, where nobody could hear me. I couldn't stop crying.

I hadn't realized that I had been operating under a double dose of stress: first the intense, exhausting campaign, then the move to a different part of the country. There is a great deal of strain involved in such "routine" tasks as finding the nearest grocery store, figuring out where to buy a mousetrap or a carpet, learning how to maneuver a car in big-city traffic, getting hopelessly lost, and dealing with a homesick little boy who said, "I wish Daddy had lost by two votes. Then he wouldn't have felt bad about losing and I wouldn't have to leave my friends."

I had told my mother, "I can't wait until we're settled in Washington, so we can begin to live a normal life again, with Birch home for dinner, and maybe an occasional movie." But from the first, I began to sense that my concept of "normal" was not going to hold in Washington. My partner was down at the Capitol every day, interviewing prospective staff, learning the routines of the Senate, already separated from all the annoying domestic problems of settling into a new community. Home, I discovered, was to be my bailiwick, the office was to be his, in a sharper division of responsibility than we had ever had before. And yet there were still mountains of unanswered mail, addressed to us or, because I was identified as his partner, just to me.

In addition, the young Bayhs and their political upset seemed to have captured the attention of the press. CBS was doing a documentary, "The Senator from Shirkieville," for which Charles Collingwood and camera crew lived with us during our move and first gropings in Washington. They were with me in Terre Haute when I cleaned out our attic, their cameras freezing in the subzero weather every time we walked out of the house; they were with us in McLean, as we tried to settle Evan and Duffy, and in Washington as we went from office to office. It would be the first of many weeks of "living with the press." We were on the "Today" show. There were AP, UPI, the *New York Times, Washington Post, Washington Daily News,* and *Washington Star, Life, Ladies' Home Journal, Time, Redbook,* all wanting individual interviews—and we received them because we were thrilled—but they kept me onstage and dressed up at a time when I just wanted to find the box in which I'd packed Evan's socks.

So on that Christmas Day, I broke down and cried with fatigue and frustration that my body just wasn't holding up to transform us into this mythical "normal" life. The double vision and neckaches had continued to plague me. "Now," I told Birch, "I feel like the wind is blowing right through the skin on my elbows. I am so taut I wish that I could unfasten my tongue at its base." Birch checked in with the Senate physician, who recommended a gynecologist. Soon I was on estrogen shots again, Birch learning how to give them because I didn't have the time to drive to the doctor's office once a week. The doctor also gave me a prescription for tranquilizers.

My parents stayed with us through Birch's swearing-in, on January 9, 1963, the opening day of the 88th Congress. We watched from the gallery as the forty-one new and reelected senators took the oath from Vice President Johnson. Birch's father was there, and his sister Mary Alice, fresh from her cross-country tour as an actress in *Auntie Mame,* and our bored, squirmy little Evan, who "itched" in his new suit, and, of course, had to go to the bathroom. Tears welled up in my eyes, tears of joy, wonder, and pride for Birch. Afterward, Birch introduced us to his new friends in the "freshman class," in which he was 100th—last—in seniority: Ted Kennedy of Massachusetts, George McGovern of South Dakota, Gaylord Nelson of Wisconsin, and Thomas McIntyre of New Hampshire, Daniel Inouye of Hawaii, Abe Ribicoff of Connecticut, Danny Brewster of Maryland. We then entered into a twenty-four-hour marathon of celebration—a reception for 3,000 people in the new Senate Office Building hosted by Governor Matt Welsh, dinner at Senator Vance Hartke's house, and a mammoth buffet luncheon across the hall from the Senate chamber, also given by Senator Hartke, which included the Vice President, cabinet officers, and hundreds of Hoosiers who had chartered a plane for the occasion.

It was Birch's moment of glory, and it was marred by my

father, carrying on drunk outside, on the street corner in front of the Senate Office Building. He was argumentative, obnoxious, and he finally drove off, alone, to McLean. I was so embarrassed, so apologetic to Birch, so afraid Daddy would have a wreck. "But he doesn't drink," I cried. "Only that once in Terre Haute." Birch looked at me. "Oh, yes, he does," he said quietly. "I've been carrying out empty vodka bottles with the trash ever since they've been here."

I confronted Mother the next day. "Does Daddy have a drinking problem?"

"Yes, he does," she finally admitted.

"Was he drinking when he took that bottle of aspirin last summer?"

"Yes."

"Why wasn't I told?" I began to feel the old anger at my mother's habit of keeping things to herself.

"Because I didn't want to worry you."

"How long has this been going on?" I demanded. "How long has he been drinking like this?"

"Ever since you left home," she said.

It was not an accusation, nor was it meant to be. I realized that my mother had tried to shield me, for more than ten years, from any sense of responsibility for my father's feelings. She knew how I idolized him. Bearing the burden of his drinking, alone, was her way of protecting me.

As I look back, there were many clues, but I was blind to them. My mind was awhirl with questions: Was it an accident that these eruptions coincided with Birch's moments of public success? Was Daddy, as the Menninger doctor had suggested, reaching out to me in some bizarre way? Was he trying to punish me for having left home? Was the loss of his daughter, in whom he had invested his dreams, enough to cause this senseless drinking, all day in secret, at night in exhibition? I was angry, and ashamed. Of course, I thought, that sudden affair of his, which I'd never mentioned to Mother, was because of his drinking. And what else? "Has it been awful?" I asked my mother. "It has," she said. "And if it doesn't stop he's going to lose everything we have."

We talked to my father, my husband and I, about our fears for him. We told him we were afraid for Evan, we were afraid he might hurt somebody while driving, we were afraid for Mother's health. Daddy cried, and he promised he would stop, because he loved us. I worried about them, as they drove off for Oklahoma that January. But I was getting settled into a new, challenging, exciting, not-knowing-what-to-expect life in Washington, and they were going back to their own little house in Oklahoma, to real problems. While my world was expanding, theirs was closing in. Yet I still needed the emotional support of my parents, though I wasn't sure they still had it to give. I knew I had to get hold of myself. I wanted too much to embrace Washington, to enjoy my new career as a senator's wife—I thought of it as a career—to be a support and asset to my husband, to learn everything I possibly could about government, national politics, foreign policy. I determined not to let my tired body or my nerves or my worry about my father deter me from that. There was so much I wanted to learn!

Chapter 5

Washington, in the glamorous days of John and Jacqueline Kennedy, was like a smörgasbord with exquisite food from all over the world—and I could not get enough of it.

In the first six weeks, I found myself at home for only two full days. Katie Louchheim had a Sunday brunch in our honor, where Hubert Humphrey kept us laughing, telling about his 1960 campaign for the Democratic nomination. "You can't imagine how many precious campaign hours I lost sitting around airports waiting for commercial flights, while Jack Kennedy's private jet would swoop in and fly him off on a minute-to-minute schedule," he said, without rancor.

I was in awe of Katie, the hostess, vice-chairman of the Democratic party. She had all the style, flair, and polish of a well-to-do Eastern background. In her Georgetown home, she had blended beautiful antiques, Oriental art, and contemporary paintings with a connoisseur's hand. A poet and journalist, well traveled, keenly intelligent, she gathered stimulating people and deftly directed the most mind-expanding conversation around her table. But she was warm and witty, talking to me as if I were her equal, and I was thrilled that she'd remembered me in the play she'd written back in our Indiana law school days. At Katie Louchheim's luncheon that day, Birch and I took a big first bite of the intellectual diet that would soon be our fare at the Washington smörgasbord.

There was a party given by philanthropist Mary Lasker, where I sat between Ted Kennedy and Walter Lippmann and tried to remember every quip to share with Birch. That night I danced with

Senator William Fulbright, a longtime hero of mine, and Adlai Stevenson, and Secretary of Labor Willard Wirtz. Then the night before my birthday, February 13, we were invited to the Vice President's home, to a small dinner party, at which Lyndon Johnson made a dinner toast to me—and sang "Happy Birthday." There, once more, I felt at ease—Lady Bird Johnson was the most gracious, kind, unpretentious woman I had ever met, I thought, and very elegant in her formal, French-decorated home. (That night I called Mama, afloat in excitement: "You'll never *guess* who sang 'Happy Birthday' to me tonight.")

I went to a tea at Ethel Kennedy's, where she asked me to pour, and then to an ice-skating party given by Ted and Bob Kennedy for the New Frontier crowd, where Birch played a fierce hockey game with a broom, winning the respect of the competitive Kennedys.

We went to a small buffet dinner at the Embassy of Luxembourg, and to another at the Russian Embassy (where I developed an immediate taste for caviar) to watch motion pictures of the new Russian cosmonauts. The embassies were so exotic that they whetted my long-suppressed appetite to see Europe. One evening we had accepted an invitation to a small dinner at the Norwegian Embassy, to which I had especially looked forward because of my mother's ancestry. The afternoon of the dinner, we had a call from the White House, inviting us to drop by for a movie that night. "What shall we do?" I asked Birch. He called the Protocol Office. We sent our regrets to the Embassy. In Washington, a White House invitation was a command, we learned.

This was my first visit to the Mansion itself. We drove in through the gate on the majestic south lawn and entered on the ground floor through the Diplomatic Reception Room, where we were escorted by an usher to an elevator, which let us off upstairs at the family quarters. It was like an elegant private house, with a wide hall that was used as a sitting room, filled with antique furniture. Jacqueline Kennedy herself met us at the door of the large oval drawing room. We had cocktails in that lovely yellow room with its Louis XIV furnishings, along with a small group that included Senator Gale McGee of Wyoming and his wife Loraine. And then we took the elevator again to the ground floor, where we entered a large blue room that was set up as a movie theater. We watched *The Ugly American*, which the President seemed to enjoy, propped up in a bedlike chair to ease the discomfort in his back. Afterward,

John Kennedy told his wife that I had beaten Birch in a speech contest. "Does that make you nervous?" she asked Birch in her soft, whispery voice. "I'm glad it's not today, she'd run circles around me," he replied gallantly. It was a grand evening, I thought. I remembered sitting in our little living room in Enid during the 1960 Democratic Convention, thinking the Kennedys were the very epitome of glamor and sophistication, never dreaming that I'd know them on a social basis.

Oh, those first heady months. I accepted every invitation—I thought that we were supposed to. Besides, I didn't want to miss anything!

And yet, I was seized with terror at the thought that I'd soon have to reciprocate some of those invitations. Jackie Kennedy set the tone for Washington entertaining, which, in those days, meant intimate seated dinners with silver gleaming under candlelight, fresh flowers, French cuisine, and a formal progression of events, from pre-dinner cocktails to place cards to salad-after-the-main-course to segregation of the sexes for after-dinner coffee (or cigars and brandy).

In all the years from Lahoma to Washington, I'd never had a chance to learn about entertaining. Fried chicken on Sunday or a baked-bean supper for a few friends was just about the extent of my experience. I'd never even lived in Indianapolis! In those glittering Kennedy days of little black-tie dinners and formal embassy affairs, suddenly we were faced with what seemed like a forest of silverware at tables, confronting that great enigma, the fingerbowl. I had confessed to Lady Bird Johnson that Birch and I were babes at sea, and she gave that time-honored piece of advice, "Just keep an eye on your hostess, and follow her lead." Birch came home from a luncheon one day. "Now what do I do?" he asked. "I was seated between the Chief of Protocol and the President of the United States. You told me to watch the leader if I didn't know what to use, right?"

"That's right," I nodded.

"Well, one picked up his fork to eat his first course, and the other picked up his spoon!"

The right fork or spoon, the correct way to answer an invitation, the right dress to wear—all of those details seemed so important to me, back then. I was always calling the Protocol Office with questions: "What do you say when you're introduced to a grand duchess?" "What does it mean when an invitation is marked 'in-formal'?" (I'm glad I asked that one. I had slacks in mind. The officer answered, however, that "informal" meant dressy, but not black tie.) "I don't know a thing about protocol," I confessed to Mrs. Johnson. "Oh, my dear, most of that died with the Second World War," she said, soothingly, laughing at the old custom of new Congressional wives running all over Washington to drop en-graved calling cards at the door of just about everybody who had seniority, from the White House on down. Yes, a lot of the formality was gone, but a good bit still remained: Husbands preceded their wives in reception lines, for example, and "ranking" guests always left the party first, I noticed. But what I really wanted to know was what was expected of me, as a Senate wife.

On the advice of Mary Day, who worked in Birch's office, I enrolled in Mrs. Gladstone Williams' ten-week course on protocol, which included veritable Emily Post lessons in entertaining. At the beginning of the course, I wrote in my diary, "Am terrified at repay-ing dinners to these people who are so proper."

But before I could entertain, I had to get our house in order. Through our real-estate agent I met Bea Keller, a decorator. I was determined to learn about colors, periods of furniture, tones, hues, accessories—to make a cheerful, comfortable home without bilious green sofas and gray-and-purple chairs. For weeks Bea guided me, tactfully pointing out why I'd soon get tired of that lamp I'd bought on impulse, or why the material I liked for a living-room chair would be more suitable in a bedroom. It was the course in decorating that I never got around to taking during my brief fling as a home ec major—only this was more fun. Bea pulled together my house, and, in the process, became my friend. The result, once the interminable wait for furniture was over, the draperies delivered in the right size, and I'd returned somebody else's rug (thus introducing me to one of the "joys" of Washington—the impossible services in a transient city), was a muted traditional effect in yellows, white, and blue, in the French style I had come to admire.

Before I could think about entertaining I'd have to pull myself together, too. I knew I'd need new clothes in Washington—those few packable, crushable, unobtrusive candidate's-wife dresses were worn out from the campaign—and I didn't own a long dress. In Terre Haute, I'd bought a "formal" for Washington evenings, a gold-trimmed ivory satin gown. At its first wearing, a dinner for the new

Congress at the National Press Club, I saw very quickly that I was overdressed. Mine was a ball gown. Some unspoken signal seemed to be going around: one kind of dress for Saturday nights, another for midweek; some people's dinner parties were "dressier" than others. I was spending far too much time worrying about what to wear. I needed help.

Dorothy Stead, who owned a dress shop in Georgetown, had sent a welcome-to-Washington note to all the new Congressional wives. "I have been in Washington a long time. Come around and let me advise you on your wardrobe," she wrote. Rather timidly, I took her up on it, and soon had my entire closetful of clothes spread around her shop. "This is worn out, this is too dated, this can be livened by a scarf, this needs to be shortened, this can be remade, this can go to a luncheon at the White House, this to a five-to-seven reception. . . ." Like a wizard, she flipped through my sparse Terre Haute/Bloomington collection, and then told me what gaps needed filling. "A good, all-around coat is very important here," she began. Of course, I couldn't afford a new wardrobe, but as the year wore on, as I could, I'd buy a new dress from Dorothy Stead. Dorothy, like Bea Keller, soon became a trusted personal friend.

In the protocol class, I learned more than who sits on whose right, and how to decline an invitation. "I'm just a plain, ordinary cook," I confessed to Mrs. Williams. "I'm afraid I'd be in the kitchen all night long—even if I served a four-course meal rather than a full formal dinner." "Very few of us in Washington are lucky enough to have the time to spend in the kitchen, even if we have the ability," she answered. "Catering is a very honorable profession here." Bob Keefe, Birch's new assistant, introduced me to a wonderful caterer, Willie Mae Carter, and a butler, Norwood Williams, who served at the White House, and Mabel Taylor, who served at table. "They will come into your home," Mrs. Williams told me, "prepare dinner, and leave you time for conversation with your guests."

Conversation was the one area, I discovered, in which I did *not* feel woefully inadequate. I had worried about what people were going to talk about during those fabled Washington dinner parties. Art? Ballet? The latest European philosophers? I envisioned enrolling in classes (and still would like to!) on those subjects which had not turned up in my curriculum or my experience. What a happy surprise, from the very first, to hear familiar words being tossed around a table: "Medicare," "Peace Corps," "civil rights," "Nuclear Test Ban Treaty"— and, of course, "Cuba." Washington is a "company town." Most conversations center on the political issues being debated in Congress—in 1963 those issues I had studied so hard for Birch's and my speeches during the campaign. I had no trouble holding up my end of the conversation during a dinner party—in fact, I found these evenings of informal political discussion so informative that when two invitations would arrive for the same evening, I wanted to go to both. (An evening with statesman Averell Harriman, for example, was almost a graduate course in Western Civilization.) I went often to the Senate galleries to hear debate, and continued my clipping service for Birch, becoming almost a *Reader's Digest* of events and opinion that might help him in his work. As I look back, if I hadn't had the experience of campaign partnership, studying the issues so closely, I'd have been 100 percent overwhelmed by this complex capital city, rather than 75 percent overwhelmed.

One strong support system for me and the other new Senate wives was the Tuesday meetings of the Senate Ladies Red Cross group. Since World War I, this group had met to roll bandages for servicemen or, in peacetime, for local hospitals. Those women, of both parties, were sources of much-needed information—the best dentist or dry cleaner, for example—and supportive sympathy to a newcomer. It was there I first came to know Joan Kennedy, who was so much more worldly and sophisticated in many ways, but in others, as lost and timid as I. We worried about our husbands' health holding out, at the frantic pace they were keeping. We worried about raising our children alone. Joan was open, vulnerable, and very, very sweet, I thought. Through her easy acceptance of me, I began to relax around the awesome Kennedys and to look on them as individuals, with flaws and foibles like my own.

But it was the Vice President's wife, presiding over the Senate Ladies group, who was most instrumental in giving me guidance and the assurance that a country-born, small-town girl like me could survive in the heady sophistication of Washington. Mrs. Johnson never ceased to amaze me. I would read that she was in Texas or Norway on Sunday or Monday, but on Tuesday, jet lag or not, there she would be at Red Cross. Lady Bird Johnson took me "under her wing"; she included me in family gatherings, at poolside, sometimes with her daughters Luci and Lynda; she and the Vice President invited Birch and me to a musicale at the Mexican Embassy in the Johnsons' honor, and for a memorable evening drifting slowly down the Potomac River to Mount Vernon and back on the President's yacht, the *Honey Fitz*. How could I ever hope to reciprocate an evening like that, I worried. (Fortunately, I didn't have to worry just yet. The furniture I had ordered in January still hadn't been delivered by late spring.)

Birch left early every morning for the long drive to the Senate Office Building, totally wrapped up in organizing his staff, learning how the Senate works, finding his way among the labyrinths of the Capitol. At home, a kind woman from Indiana, Bea Smith, was helping me battle my new house, along with her own homesickness, and taking care of Evan while Birch and I sampled Washington's giant smörgasbord in the evenings.

That enchanted spring of 1963 reinforced my feeling that I was in the middle of a dream. I'd always had a pang of homesickness in the springtime. But spring in Washington is a fairyland of cherry blossoms, not just around the Tidal Basin, but also in the family neighborhoods. Then come the bright burst of azaleas, the proud stands of tulips, the greening of a thousand trees. I'd pack Evan in the back seat and drive round and round, discovering a new world of color and life. We had lots of company, old friends from Indiana whom I proudly took sightseeing. Springtime in Washington made the connection: This was my home, and I loved it. Grandma Hern would have felt the same way, I thought. I shared it with my mother as best I could, writing every week, phoning to describe our latest adventures. I could hear in her voice the vicarious pleasure she took in our trip on the *Honey Fitz*, our evening at an embassy, Birch's "maiden" speech in the Senate. We had become close friends by then, my mother and I. "How is Daddy?" I'd ask. "How is he, really?" "Oh, things are better," she'd say, but I could tell by her voice that they weren't.

Spring, of course, is the traditional period for Democratic fund-raisers which, in 1963, happily coincided with the President's birthday. It was "John F. Kennedy's Birthday Party" in New York, a thousand-dollar-a-plate banquet, at which I was told I'd meet the "fat cats." Never having heard that term before, I thought it funny, picturing a roomful of animals at the Waldorf-Astoria. It was my first trip to New York, and the city performed at its springtime best. I was wide-eyed at the live entertainment—Carol Channing,

Jimmy Durante, Ed Sullivan, Louis Armstrong, Henry Fonda, among others. I was seated at a table near the front, a ringside seat. When President Kennedy came by, he spotted me, and stopped to say hello. A few minutes later, Vice President Johnson walked by, and as I was in the line of traffic, he stopped with a big kiss on the cheek for me.

"Well, are we impressed," teased the people at my table. They were strong Kennedy supporters, the Milton Gilberts and Nathan Kalikows, and that night we added some New Yorkers to our burgeoning list of new friends.

Among the rites every spring are the Senate Ladies' luncheon at the Capitol honoring the First Lady, the Congressional Reception at the White House, and then the First Lady's luncheon at the White House for the Senate wives. In 1963, however, the First Lady didn't appear at the first two affairs because she was pregnant.

For the Senate wives' luncheon, I had a new dress, and a tiny little hat in which I felt very silly, because I didn't wear hats. But Jackie's pillbox hat had set a fashion, and after all, I was going to Jackie's house. At that time, the doctor had me on a combination of medication, which at that time I didn't even question—thyroid to juice me up, and then some little purple pills to calm me down. I walked into the Oval Diplomatic Reception Room at the White House that day, nervous in my new dress and new hat, clutching a new patent-leather handbag. Suddenly the clasp on my purse popped open, and out spilled the contents, all over the floor. The bottle of medicine hit the fireplace, broke, and little purple pills rolled out in every direction. Immediately one of those terrific White House aides, military men who are skilled in diplomacy, was at my feet, helping me scoop up everything and pull myself back together. I was shattered. As we walked out of the room, headed upstairs to the State Dining Room, I glanced back over my shoulder at the site of Franklin D. Roosevelt's fireside chats. There in the fireplace, tucked away in the corner, were two little purple pills. How significant, I thought. Some women have calling cards, but I leave my tranquilizers.

In the dining room, Mrs. Johnson was receiving, as Mrs. Kennedy was upstairs, not feeling well. I was seated between Mrs. Wayne Morse of Oregon and Mrs. Lister Hill from Alabama. In Birmingham that day, police had turned fire hoses and dogs on civil rights demonstrators, including children; Mrs. Hill seemed ill at ease. Within weeks of that luncheon, our husbands had become adversaries on President Kennedy's bill to combat discrimination in public accommodations, schools, jobs, and voting. I soon learned, through the bipartisan Senate wives' group, how Senate wives managed to remain friends even though their husbands could be locked in what seemed like mortal combat.

My husband's duties were prescribed by the Constitution: to consider and enact federal law; to ratify or reject treaties with other countries; to confirm or reject presidential appointments to federal administrative, judicial, and military offices. Moreover, he and his colleagues have the power to levy taxes, borrow money, regulate trade between the United States and foreign countries. As a member of Congress he would also share the responsibility of maintaining military forces, and of controlling industry and labor involved in interstate commerce. And, of course, the Congress alone has the power to declare war. When we considered those duties during the campaign, the responsibility had seemed awesome. Birch took his new job very seriously, studying so hard he even took a course in speed-reading to help him deal with the volume of background material he needed to get through for each day's work. What we soon learned was that the Constitution did not really spell out the nature of the job—the homework in committee, for example, where bills are first shaped and debated, and sometimes die; the intricate parliamentary maneuvering that can help or hurt a bill. Birch knew, of course, from his Indiana experience, a great deal about legislative politicking: trade-offs, adversary relationships, compromises. What he had to learn was how ninety-nine other men had voted in the past, or how they might be inclined to vote. And as the 100th in seniority, how he might be effective through his committee assignments. He was assigned to Judiciary, at first, and then Public Works.

Nor did the Constitution mention the time that would be involved in "case work"—representing individual citizens or concerns in Indiana with particular needs involving the federal government—from tracking down a missing Social Security check to finding a new industry when Studebaker shut down its automobile assembly plant in South Bend. In addition, because of the spate of publicity that accompanied our moving to Washington, Birch was suddenly a hot commodity for the Democratic National Committee. He was flooded with requests to speak at Democratic functions all over the country.

When Congress was in session, Birch would be at the office

at eight, dealing with requests, constituents, the press, mail. At ten he'd go into a committee meeting, until noon, when the Senate convenes, then back and forth from the floor to committee meetings all afternoon, then back at the office for staff work and correspondence—until about 6 P.M. Often the Senate would stay in session on some crucial vote until late at night.

All through the spring and summer Birch worked and worked, writing and rewriting what would be his "maiden" speech on the Senate floor, concerning the importance of education. A first speech is usually of earthshaking impact only to the new senator and his family. Normally, the Vice President rarely sits in his own chair to preside over the session. But on our momentous occasion, shortly after Birch began to speak, Lyndon Johnson slipped into the chamber and into his chair on the platform, looked up into the gallery where Daddy Bayh and I were sitting, gave me a nod, and then turned his attention to Birch for the duration of the entire speech. And then he slipped out again. Birch was touched by that gesture of thoughtfulness from one who knew what it felt like to be a new senator.

Being a new senator had its drawbacks, we were to discover. Our new home was so far out in the suburbs that those late homecomings from the Capitol altered what had been a pattern in our lives prior to the Senate campaign. Evan and I learned to have supper without Daddy. If we were going out in the evening, I'd sit with Evan while he ate, or read to him, then throw a fresh shirt or tuxedo in the car for Birch, and meet him at the reception or the dinner party—sometimes he'd change in the office, sometimes in the car.

There were other domestic changes. On the farm there had been a clear delineation of roles. Birch was responsible for everything outside the house, I was in charge of the house itself—until something broke, of course. Then Birch, like most farmers, would fix it. I'd never had to call a repairman on the farm. Now, I was surprised to find myself in charge of repairs, the yard, the car. Birch simply didn't have the time.

What I hadn't learned about Washington, during all those weeks of eager study, was what heavy demands a senator's job would place on our family life—and just how lonely it was going to be, much of the time. For I had not counted on Birch continuing his campaign in Indiana for six more years.

True, our margin of victory had been very slim, and Indiana is a "swing" state, as likely to vote Republican as Democratic, very conscientious about keeping an eye on its elected officials. Birch was back in Indiana just about every weekend, mending political fences, finding out how folks at home felt about what he was voting on—in other words, paying attention to the fact that he was an elected representative for that state. But as the summer wore on, and I began to miss his easy laugh, his arms at night, his sharing the burden of disciplining Evan (I had become the "heavy"), I began to wish he were senator from Alaska—which was too far away to go home every weekend. (One far-western senator told me his constituents didn't expect him to come home so often. But Birch's did, and he did what they expected.)

On weekdays during those periods when the Senate wasn't in session, it wasn't so bad—I had my various clubs and luncheons, Evan had school. But it was those weekends, those lonely suburban weekends, that were hell for a thirty-year-old and still-in-love woman who couldn't afford to fly out with him. I came to dread those Saturdays and Sundays alone out in McLean, Virginia, even though Evan and I would use them to explore the Smithsonian and the playgrounds. We found friends in the neighborhood, and Birch would phone us every night, from wherever he might be.

Without Birch's father, Evan and I would have been lost. Daddy Bayh was discreet about not wanting to "intrude" in our family life, realizing how little time we actually had together. And yet he was always willing and available to stand in when Birch was out of town, helping me with birthday parties or an important Cub Scout meeting. In the summertime, he raised vegetables out in his back yard in suburban Maryland, and brought them over by the armload for Indiana-style Sunday suppers. Together, we commiserated about the way Birch was driving himself; together we conspired to find ways to slow him down.

The Congress was working on tax reform (isn't it always?), on aid to education, on mental health aid, on farm aid, on a "domestic Peace Corps," on unemployment, on foreign aid, on civil rights, on legislation to improve the U.S. balance of payments abroad. My job, as I saw it, was to help him keep abreast of all those issues, by reading, underlining, and clipping for him articles, editorials, and essays in the three Washington newspapers and in *Time* and *Newsweek* as well. Three hours of my reading time could reduce his to thirty minutes. He said he appreciated my "digest" because I knew him so well that I could quickly pick out salient points that he would need to know. Those same points helped me, too, because I was also asked to make speeches. I spoke mostly in Indiana (and every summer at Girls' State there), but also occasionally in other states—on volunteerism or life as a senator's wife.

(Gone were the days of extemporaneous speaking. Writing speeches is not a task I enjoy—I get them ready weeks in advance, because I can't sleep until they are written. I keep an "idea file," with a big box of quotes, or thoughts, or newspaper clippings about a particular subject. You'd think there were two or three people in the room, because of all the talk as I write. What reads well sometimes doesn't speak well, and so I have to hear myself out loud as the speech takes shape. For me, it's an ordeal, but I can't rest until it's finished, typed, and filed in a drawer awaiting that speaking date. It is the speaking itself, the contact with an audience, that I like.)

One speech I particularly enjoyed that year was in May at an Oklahoma State College speech awards banquet. Birch was invited, too, and he spoke to the school convocation. Afterward, my parents gave a royal reception for us in Enid, at the American Legion Hall, for 300 people. My mother had borrowed silver candelabra and a punch bowl, their friends the Coulters and Carltons assisted, and some of my old high-school buddies provided music. It seemed as if my parents couldn't do enough for us. Mama showed me a speech she had prepared for her Toastmistress group, in which she wrote of the sacrifices she had made for me. But, she said, "My daughter has returned my investment a thousandfold." I was very moved. I looked at her face, aged beyond her years from hard work and worry and ill health, as she proudly shared us with her old friends and mine. There was so much I wanted to do for her. Next time she comes to Washington, I thought, I'm going to entertain her royally. Just wait until I finish that protocol course.

A month later I was back in Enid again, after having been made an honorary Indian princess of the Kiowa tribe at Andarko, and having delivered the commencement address at Oklahoma College for Women. I arrived full of good news: Birch had been named by the Washington press corps as one of the "ten most promising men" in Congress—and Vice President Johnson had selected him as one of the twelve senators to attend—with their wives—the NATO Conference in Paris in the fall. And my house, after all this time, was finally in shape. After "Aunt Bea" Smith succumbed to home-sickness and returned to Indiana, we had hired a wonderful new live-in helper, a wise and witty sixty-two-year-old West Virginian named Macel Nuckels, whom Evan loved, and so did I. I planned to invite my parents for Thanksgiving or Christmas.

However, I was distressed to find my father drinking again, so heavily it was frightening. Here it was harvest time, and he could barely attend to the crop. Mother was afraid he would harm himself on the machinery. She had taken refuge in Al-Anon, the supportive group for families of alcoholics. "Please, Daddy, join AA," I begged him. "They can help you."

"I don't have time," he mumbled. "Have to get in the harvest. Crops are so bad this year I don't know how we're going to survive." Mama, who had left her job in the assessor's office to help us move to Washington, had to look for work, to put food on the table.

Evan and I flew back to Washington. I began to have trouble sleeping, in contrast to the happy picture of me that appeared in *Life* magazine on July 25. President Kennedy wrote me a lovely, complimentary note about the piece. I wondered what he or Jane Howard, the reporter, would think if they saw me taking estrogen shots, thyroid medicine, the purple tranquilizers, and now, out of desperation, sometimes sleeping pills.

On August 1, we were at a dinner party at the home of the senator from Alaska. Charming old Senator Gruening had been a pioneer there, not too many years after my grandparents in Oklahoma. I was seated next to Estes Kefauver of Tennessee, who had held me and most of the nation spellbound during his crime hearings in 1951, who had been my candidate for the Democratic presidential nomination in 1952 (although Birch later converted me to Adlai Stevenson), and who had been my candidate for Vice President in 1956. He had finished his first course when he looked over and spied some fish still on my plate. "Aren't you going to eat that?" he asked. "No," I said, and he reached over and started eating right off my plate. It was exactly the kind of thing my Uncle Oren or any others of my family might have done, a "waste not, want not" generation dispensing with formal manners.

Birch was in fine form that night, accepting congratulations from senators right and left about his spectacular performance at the Democrats vs. Republicans baseball game the night before. The day after that party, when he was mowing the steep incline in our front yard, he slipped, cutting off half his big toe and fracturing two more. That put him into Sibley Hospital for two weeks in excruciating pain, and effectively halted his baseball career.

I remember flying to Indiana to make a speech for him, hating all the while to leave him. When I returned, I learned that my mother was in the hospital with nervous exhaustion, and much as I wanted to, I couldn't leave Birch to go to her.

It all seemed to be going by so fast, I couldn't take time to assess my situation or my parents', or to gather strength or to savor what goodness there was in life. Days marched by in staccato: Birch was on crutches. Daddy was worse. Senator Kefauver had died, he who had so recently been my dinner partner. Birch spoke in South Bend, at Purdue, in Rapid City, in Columbia City, in Gary, in Mount Vernon. I spoke in Akron, in Louisville. Birch co-sponsored the Freedom of Information bill. Thousands massed at the Lincoln Memorial to hear Dr. Martin Luther King, Jr.: "I have a dream. . . ." Birch was named to the subcommittee that handled civil rights legislation. We met the king of Afghanistan at an embassy reception. Birch was named chairman of the Constitutional Amendments Subcommittee, which Estes Kefauver had chaired, because nobody else on Judiciary seemed to want it. We celebrated Daddy Bayh's seventieth birthday. Birch got word that Studebaker was closing their South Bend plant, that thousands would be unemployed. I talked with my father almost every night, pleading with him to stop drinking. There was not even ten minutes a day to rest. I began counting the hours until Birch and I could go off to Paris for the NATO meeting.

On October 31, I was all packed and ready. There was a snag, however. The Senate was hung up in debate over the foreign aid bill. An Air Force plane was standing by to ferry the eleven senators and their wives and staff, another for the nine representatives and their entourage.

At departure time, the Senate was still in session. Myrtle McIntyre and I were waiting at home with our suitcases packed when our husbands called. "Just go ahead on the plane with the representatives," Birch said. "We'll join you tomorrow." I was a little relieved. With Evan only seven, I had been a bit nervous about Birch and me taking our first trip overseas together on the same plane.

At nine the next morning, I looked out over the red rooftops of Paris, gleaming in the sunshine. French food! (Was there ever anything so delectable as a first Paris breakfast—flaky croissants, hard rolls, sweet butter, strawberry preserves?) Paris traffic! (I thought Washington traffic was bad, but it can't compare with this. No wonder they drive little cars!) Versailles—beyond description, so ornate, lavish, the Palace of Louis XIV, the Sun King. Down the Seine in a glassed-in boat. Embassy parties! I wanted to see and savor everything; I could hardly wait until Birch got there. Every day, we were told that our husbands would arrive the next day. But none of them did, as the Senate was still debating. Myrtle and I were horrified. We were paying our own expenses, of course, but would we be accused of "junketing"? We went to the head of the House delegation, Congressman Wayne Hays of Ohio. "At this point, it will cause less furor if you stay here with us," he advised. Myrtle and I tried to be as inconspicuous as possible—we met the NATO delegates, went to tea at Ambassador Charles Bohlen's house, showed up at the official receptions that were expected of us, and went to dinner at Ambassador Finletter's, our ambassador to NATO, where I sat next to Congressman John Lindsay from New York ("He should be a Democrat," I wrote).

I was wide-eyed, soaking in everything I could. I memorized every detail of this childhood dream come true, to share with my parents.

We returned via a short stop in London, which I drank in with as much zest as I had Paris. That trip, with all its new experiences, was better medicine for me than all the potions in my handbag. Though it was a change of place, and not necessarily of pace, it made me realize the relentless pressures we had put ourselves under. There must now be time for ourselves, I told Birch. He promised to join me in Paris on a real vacation. Someday.

Meanwhile, Birch was up to his neck in the Studebaker situation. Since September, we had lived, breathed, eaten, slept, dreamed Studebaker. I had associated it with Indiana ever since Birch proudly drove me around the Chicago lakeshore in that funny little blue car that looked the same coming and going. ("It's made in Indiana," he announced. "And what runs it is made in Oklahoma," I retorted.) Now Studebaker was closing down its American operation entirely, because it was losing money, and its move to Canada was throwing the northern Indiana economy into a tailspin, not to mention the families of the 7,000 workers. Birch had been all over the country seeking help. Delegations of concerned Hoosiers poured into Washington; Birch and John Brademas met with government officials around the clock. Hobbling to the White House on crutches, Birch had asked President Kennedy to help.

Today, November 22, Birch had asked Teddy Kennedy to fill in for him presiding over the Senate. While he was in Texas campaigning with the President, the Vice President had asked Birch to preside, as junior senators are often asked to do, but Birch had to go to Chicago to talk to another company about moving into the Studebaker plant. He flew out of National Airport at about 12:30 P.M.

I had said goodbye at his office, where I was working on correspondence addressed to us. At about 1:30, one of Birch's assistants ran in, crying that the President and Vice President, and Governor Connally, had been shot in Dallas. As I drove home down Constitution Avenue, I looked up at the White House, to see the flag still flying, full mast. I ran into the house, crying, to meet Evan. The phone rang. Birch, from Chicago. The pilot had waited until wheels touched runway to announce the news. There was no way we could speak to each other of how we felt. We were both weeping. I blurted out the first thing that came to mind. "Why is it you are always gone when there's a crisis and I need you?"

The horror, the heartbreak of those days in Washington has been told and retold. It does not dim with memory. Driving over to Bobby Kennedy's that night, finding only the children there. Standing in the White House, looking at the flag-draped coffin in the East Room, where John and Jacqueline Kennedy had danced. Driving to Ted and Joan's, then to the Johnsons', to leave a letter. The new President welcomed us, invited us in. Lady Bird came downstairs, wearing her robe, holding out her arms to me. "It's been a year since yesterday morning," she said.

We left, and on the way home we clung to each other, weeping still. My parents called me. "Life is so short," I said. "I know," said my mother.

Chapter 6

I shall remember, always, General De Gaulle's face on that clear, still day. It stands out among those images ever imprinted on my mind—the high-spirited horse, the empty saddle, the tall, shiny black boots turned backwards in the stirrups; Ted and Bob walking alongside the President's young widow, tears streaming down Ted's face, Bob looking lost and bitter. Willy Brandt stood there, Chancellor Erhard, the Duke of Edinburgh, Haile Selassie, Eamon De Valera, the blind President of Ireland, and the others, and I felt sorry for the whole world. De Gaulle was bigger than I'd ever realized, towering above the others, every muscle of his face under control, like a tall granite statue. Yet, as Jacqueline Kennedy knelt to light the eternal flame, his eyes came alive with the agony and sorrow we all felt.

We buried President Kennedy that day, and with him that part of us that celebrated youth and the sense of immortality and invincibility which was the spirit of the New Frontier.

An Indiana politician stood next to Birch at the ceremony, "You are the only one with the Kennedy-type charisma," he whispered. "You owe it to your country to reach for higher things." We were appalled.

The next weeks went by in a daze. Birch was still scouring the country, trying to get another manufacturer to come into South Bend. There were pitiful letters from workers, fearful for their families as the Christmas holidays approached, yet expressing their grief over the death of the President. Everyone we'd ever known, it seemed, called or wrote to share their sorrow.

During the period of eulogies in the Senate, Ted and Joan

invited us to dinner on December 11, together with the McGoverns. It was a quiet, subdued evening in their Georgetown house, under the shadow of the assassination. Ted and Joan were trying hard to carry on, reaching out quietly for friendship. They seemed as they'd been before, warm and close to each other—there was just less teasing, less of the unrestrained spirit we'd known. Joan took me up to their bedroom, so pretty and lived-in, with piles of magazines here and there, on her way to tuck in the children. The cook served buffet, very informal and relaxed, and the six of us talked about the many strengths of President Johnson, and the worry in everyone's mind that there was now no Vice President.

Speaker McCormack, seventy-two, and Senate President Pro Tem Carl Hayden, eighty-six, were next in line for the presidency. Kefauver's Judiciary Subcommittee on Constitutional Amendments had passed on to Birch in September, and now he was working on the draft of a presidential succession bill, a constitutional amendment that would allow the President to appoint a Vice President should the need arise again.

We women entered into the conversation, Joan and Eleanor and I, with our "what if's"—"What if a President should become mentally ill?" "What if something should happen to a Vice President?"—none of us imagining how the spectre of the presidency would enter each of our homes, in its own way, during the coming years.

The next day, Birch phoned me from the office to read me his eulogy for President Kennedy that he planned to deliver to the Senate, and he wept as he read it. Someone had said to one of John Kennedy's aides, "We'll never laugh again." The aide replied, "Yes, we'll laugh. But we'll never be young again."

We had invited both Kennedy couples out to our house for dinner on December 16, but someone from Bob's office called to say that he and Ethel couldn't come, not until after the first of the year. Then Joan called to say that ABC television had produced a program, "Making of a President," which was being premiered for the family at Jackie's house. That's why Bob couldn't come, since Jackie had invited them for dinner beforehand. Could we join them there, Joan asked, after they had dinner with us? I ran like a house afire all day. By the time Ted and Joan arrived, I was in order, but barely, with stroganoff in the pot and chilled strawberries in the bowl.

After dinner, we raced in to Georgetown, to Jackie's, arriving only ten minutes after the film had started. Franklin D. Roosevelt, Jr., was there, and Ambassador David Ormsby-Gore of Great Britain, and JFK aides Sorenson, O'Donnell, and the others, watching the screen as the Kennedy-Nixon debates were replayed. The "clan," including Jackie and the hard-hit Bobby, cheered like football fans whenever JFK scored a good point against Nixon. And they laughed. But it seemed as though a decade had passed, instead of a year, when we first went to Bobby's house, and to the Oval Office. I thought of the last time I'd watched a movie with the Kennedys, with John Kennedy lounging on his couch in the White House theater, Jackie laughing at Birch. I felt so very much older.

As Christmas approached, my sadness grew. Every year of my life, except for the year Evan was born, I had shared Christmas with my parents. Now, however, the situation with my father was so tense that I could not face him. His drinking had become such a burden to Mother, she told me in November, she could take it no longer. Now, at fifty-five, she felt, for her own health, she must leave him. "Please, please give him one more chance," I begged.

"I have tried everything," she said. "He promises each time to stop, but he just won't." Birch and I had both pleaded with him, too, to no avail. Then would come the next letter from Mother. In September, when she was hospitalized with exhaustion, I realized the heavy weight of what she'd been keeping from me ever since I left home.

With each letter the news was worse. Each farm was mortgaged to the point where there were no more loans. Mama got a job as a telephone operator at Vance Air Base, to put groceries on the table. In desperation, she had Daddy sign a paper, to put control of the finances in her hands. She wrote all the checks now; he had to come to her for pocket money. And I begged her not to divorce him, which was a grave mistake on my part. I could not bear to think of the home breaking up, and the two of them apart. My home sustained me.

I wanted *her* to come for Christmas, but I knew it would break his heart if I invited her alone. I had never really thought of them individually. Yet, I was afraid for him to come. Afraid he would get drunk and frighten Evan; afraid he would drive the car while drunk and kill somebody; afraid he would embarrass Birch. I was ashamed of him, this slovenly, loudmouthed, ranting drunk named Delbert Hern, and I am ashamed, now, that I was ashamed.

"We can't come to Oklahoma for Christmas," I told Mama. "We just can't afford the trip this year." I knew she and Daddy couldn't afford the trip to Washington. "Evan and I will be there in the summer," I said.

Christmas was a flurry. Our first real entertaining, for which I had prepared all year, was scheduled for this December. At last I had gathered enough courage—and equipment—to try out the procedures learned in Mrs. Gladstone Williams' protocol class. My guests were Gaylord and Carrie Lee Nelson of Wisconsin, Bethine and Frank Church of Idaho, Becky and Paul Rogers of Florida, and Sherrye and Bill Henry, chairman of the Federal Communications Commission. Willie Mae Carter catered, preparing everything in our home. We had fabulous hot and cold hors d'oeuvres in the basement rec room, around a big fire. Then we went upstairs for buffet: chicken breasts (bone removed) under wine sauce, green beans with almonds. biscuits, wild rice. We were served the rest—tossed salad, apricot soufflé with sauce, and champagne from France. Four of us ate in the living room, six at the dining table. We dined by candlelight, accenting my gold-and-white color scheme. Then we had our after-dinner coffee and drinks in the living room. I was so excited by the perfect evening that I awoke at 4 A.M. and couldn't go back to sleep.

And then we entertained the Fulbrights, Greens, and McGoverns on the 20th, starting late because the Senate stayed in session on foreign aid (Wayne Morse holding forth), with Birch running down for a live quorum call at 3:45 A.M. The next night we had a group of neighbors over. We spent Christmas Eve at home, with Evan, Daddy Bayh, and Mary Alice, and then were off to West Virginia where Birch and Evan skied and I wrote a speech. Even there, Birch was on the phone trying to deal with the Studebaker plant employment problem. We were back for New Year's Eve with the Howars, our new Washington friends. Ed, a builder about Birch's age, was a sturdy, charming fellow. Barbara, his wife, was a lively southerner. Barbara sat on the floor and told funny jokes, and served pheasant for dinner. My folks called. They wanted to be with us, so badly. I missed them.

The Senate session had been the longest in history, dealing with the railroad strike, civil rights, and the nuclear test ban treaty. And now, Birch's subcommittee hearings on presidential disability and succession were to begin. On January 23, the day after he turned thirty-six, he introduced his "Senate Judiciary Resolution #139" with two senior senators, Edward Long of Missouri and Jacob Javits of New York, as co-sponsors. It provided that if the President dies, resigns, or is removed from office, the Vice President would immediately become President, and would nominate a new Vice President within thirty days. The new Vice President would take office after confirmation by a majority of both houses of Congress. In the event that the Vice President died, resigned, or was removed from office, within thirty days the President would nominate a successor, who had to be confirmed by Congress. (There were also specific methods by which a President could be declared disabled.) We spent nearly every minute talking about the bill, whether at home or on our long drives to and from McLean.

After the intense two days of hearings, we were on a plane to California, where Birch was to receive a JayCees award as one of the "Ten Outstanding Young Men of America." *

"What do you think of your young man?" he asked.

"John Kennedy was a recipient, and Bobby. But then, so was Billie Sol Estes," I teased. We held hands on the plane, and laughed, and it seemed the year might be off to a good start. He jotted down on a little pink slip his notes for the acceptance speech: "So long as there are those in this country who are said to be of the wrong color—or church—or from the wrong country of origin—all the frontiers of America have not been conquered." He'd just turned thirty-six, and I couldn't have been more proud. (Just to keep him humble, of course, the zipper on his pants broke, and his first California speech was delivered with a strategically held suit jacket.)

On the way back, I stopped in Oklahoma for a day with my parents. Daddy looked pitiful, his eyelids puffy, his whole face swollen. He seemed despondent, but he said he'd stopped drinking. "For good." I was relieved that my mother seemed to be so much better, although she was smoking heavily.

"Why can't you stay a little longer?" she asked, as she always did.

---

* Others were Zbigniew Brzezinski; Ted Yates, TV producer; Jerome Cavanaugh, mayor of Detroit; George Stevens of USIA; John Mack Carter, then editor of *McCall's*; Representatives Edgar Foreman and James Whitaker; FTC Commissioner A. Leon Higginbotham, Jr.; and Texas engineer Thomas Mackey.

"President and Mrs. Johnson have invited us to dinner. My first dinner at the White House. I just wouldn't want to miss that," I replied. "Oh, by all means, you must go," she said. "And I want to know everything that happens. Every detail." We said goodbye, promising to count the days until summer, when Evan and I would return.

The new President was holding three working dinners for senators and their wives, a smart and unique political move to gain support in those tense days of transition. As we entered the White House to the music of the Marine Band, we were greeted warmly by Lynda Bird and by President and Mrs. Johnson. We Senate wives soon parted company with our husbands, President Johnson shepherding them downstairs for a briefing by Secretary of Defense McNamara and Secretary of State Rusk on the situation arising in Vietnam. Lady Bird and Lynda took the women upstairs for a tour of the family quarters.

Mrs. Johnson, lovely in her soft white wool dress, took us through the guest chambers—the room used by five queens, the Lincoln bedroom—and then, to our surprise, their own rooms. Everything was carpeted, even the bathrooms, and there were fresh flowers everywhere. I noticed a table at the foot of the President's bed, with eight different newspapers. On a table in their sitting room was a letter that Thomas Jefferson had written ten years after he had left office, a letter pointing out that a former President has no power at all. "Lyndon likes to keep this out in view," she said.

When we joined the men downstairs for dinner, there were about seventy of us in the State Dining Room, at round tables for eight, and to my surprise I was seated at the President's table. There also were Senators Maurine Neuberger, Ed Muskie, and Philip Hart, J. Caleb Boggs from Delaware, and Betty Talmadge from Georgia, and Joan Kennedy. The President talked with us about the coming campaign, about the popularity polls—which showed him well ahead of Rockefeller—and about his wife and daughters. After dinner, when he stood to speak, he said, "We are enjoying living in *your* house." Then we all walked over to the East Room, most of us very aware that the last time we had been there was to view President Kennedy's coffin. Now, here we were dancing to the Marine Band, and during the second dance, Lyndon Johnson cut in on Birch. I felt quite at ease with him, and in the White House this evening—and I suddenly realized why: There was a warm, western, homey feeling, with which I was very familiar. Lyndon Johnson, with the plain sound of his Texas voice, his strength and assurance, reminded me of my father, the way he was when I was a girl. As we walked off the dance floor, he turned to the group standing with Birch. "Have you ever heard Marvella give a speech?" he asked. "She's tremendous." (I was standing on a cloud for days.)

My speech, the next day in Terre Haute, was to the House-wives Effort for Local Progress—or H.E.L.P.—an organization that was attempting to solve local problems in the areas of education, legislation, health, sewer service, juvenile problems, and gambling, and working with specific public service projects. It always pleased me to talk to such a group of women activists, because I know women *care*. I knew they responded to my concerns, and I felt that if my words propelled even one of those women to run for public office herself—or simply to support the programs we were trying to work on in Washington, such as the "war on poverty" the President had declared in his State of the Union message—then I would be rewarded.

From that exhortation to action, my next stop was at another level of political action: a giant "birthday party" for Birch at Indianapolis' Cadle Tabernacle, which was really a fundraiser for additional office expenses. Birch, of course, was not up for election in 1964, but part of any politician's obligation is to his party. In this case it was a grand party—7,000 people paid good money to see entertainers Janet Leigh, Barry Sullivan, Vic Damone, and my husband.

Back in Washington, I unpacked our suitcase and repacked another. Senator Fulbright had invited Birch to be one of four senators, along with four members of the House, to represent this country at the Interparliamentary Union Conference in Bermuda. It was one of the most educational trips we'd ever made, for it gave us the opportunity to know and understand the British Labour party as we never had before, even though they were not in power then.

Patrick Gordon Walker, with whom Birch played tennis practically every afternoon, gave us his view that his country was opposed to entering the Common Market because they were afraid doing so would loosen their ties with the U.S.—and all the while I thought that De Gaulle had kept them out. At dinner, we grabbed Walker, Denis Healy, and Sir Edward Boyle to go out and celebrate my thirty-first birthday. I sat between Senator Fulbright and Patrick Gordon Walker, and Senator Fulbright offered me a bite of his steak. "I can't believe it," I wrote in my diary. "Here I am eating out of Mr. Fulbright's plate! I have admired him for such a long time."

The desk was piled high when we returned home—and so was the snow. We rushed through February—lunch at the Indian Embassy, then Senate Red Cross, then a dinner party at my house for fourteen—the largest number I'd ever entertained (I had to order more silver and then borrow some)—the Martin Agronskys, the Hubert Humphreys, the John McClellans, Katie and Walter Louchheim, Bess and Tyler Abell, Scooter and Dale Miller. The stalwart Democratic crowd all made it through the snow. Late that evening, Birch flew to California for air pollution hearings, and while he was out there, President Johnson asked him to head the national Young Citizens for Johnson. I wondered where Birch's energy and time would come from. Not from Evan, I hoped.

Making jack o'lanterns, attending Evan's ball games, teaching him how to pitch and catch, Birch tried to spend as much time as he could with Evan. But he wasn't there very often for the day-to-day "no, you can't go to Steven's house now," or "why didn't you call me when you were going to be an hour late getting home," or the homework discipline, the fevers, the broken bones. There were piano recitals, Cub Scout banquets, Walt Disney movies, and home-work in his eight-year-old world, which were far more important to him than Young Citizens or presidential succession.

A group of constituents arrived the day Birch came home, and I took them down to Birch's subcommittee hearings, where former Vice President Nixon testified on the presidential succession bill.

Life was a rush from meeting to meeting to meeting. Demo-cratic Women's Club. Congressional Club. International Club. Senate Ladies Red Cross. Joan Kennedy asked me to sit beside her at lunch there, one day in March. My heart went out to her—she confessed to feeling as listless as I did. She was on thyroid medica-tion, as I was, and she told me how much she wanted to have an-other child. Our lives were much alike: so many requests; so many luncheons, dinner parties, meetings and modeling, chauffeuring our children, running, running, running.

We also took our youth and seized what fun we could during those hectic days. One night soon after, we had Ted and Joan to dinner at our house, with a group of vivacious new friends—Fred Harris, senator from Oklahoma, and LaDonna; Admiral Tazewell Shepard, President Kennedy's naval advisor, and Jan; Frank and Bethine Church, from Idaho; Jim Symington, congressman from Missouri, and Sylvia; the Howars, and the Henrys. Jim Symington played Birch's guitar and sang; Sylvia played the piano, and so did Joan Kennedy. Some played Ping-Pong. I played our campaign record. The Howars and Henrys brought records, and Barbara Howar tried to teach us to dance "Can Your Monkey Do the Dog?" We all talked about astronaut John Glenn running for the Senate. "I hope I acted all right and said the right things," I worried to my diary. Birch left home at 12:45 A.M. to fly to Indiana for four and a half days.

I felt as though I were on a speeding train rushing through beautiful countryside. I loved it, but wished I could slow it down a little. My diary for March 17 reflects those days—"Birch left for Indiana this morning. I love him so. I'm the luckiest girl in the entire world!"

My mother was thrilled when I called on her birthday to tell her I'd been chosen Indiana's Woman of the Year by the state's women journalists. There would be a banquet in my honor.

"This is the best birthday present you could give me," she said. "How I wish that I could be there." But she was working, trying to make ends meet at home. We were two adults now, and friends, but she was still my mother, with whom I could be unabashedly immodest.

After the "Woman of the Year" award, in Indianapolis, I packed up my press clippings in a letter to Mama, and wrote her how I was "counting the days" until Evan and I could come to Enid for a visit. A week later, on April 18, Evan, at the breakfast table, suddenly spoke up: "Mom, let's call Gran." Evan could stretch out the word "Gra-an" with a voice full of love. Those two were pals, my mother with her big purse full of treasures for him, her letters and phone calls as much a treat for Evan as they were for me. But he'd never asked, just out of the blue, to call her before.

"Let's wait until tonight," I said. "It won't cost so much after six." But then I was busy getting ready to go out, and forgot his request to call my mother.

That evening, Birch and I were at Bill and Sherrye Henry's

in Washington. We'd just finished dinner, and the men and women separated for coffee in different rooms. Someone knocked on the door. Sherrye turned to me. "There is an emergency call for Birch to call your home." "I'll take it," I said. We didn't have an unlisted phone then, and were forever getting "emergency" calls from constituents in the middle of the night, very few of them even sober. I dialed our number in Virginia. "What's the matter, Macel?"

"Marvella, come home."

"Is something the matter with Evan?" He was sick with measles, but the doctor had said it was only the three-day variety.

"No, it's not Evan. He's fine. Please, just come home."

"Macel, for heaven's sake, you've got to tell me what is wrong." I was beginning to get worried. "Is somebody *dead* or something?"

"Yes," she said. "Your mother."

I screamed. Then I began to cry, and cry, and cry.

It was her heart, they said. All the strain finally had been too much for her. On the plane to Oklahoma, I was numb, filled with remorse. If only I'd called her that morning when Evan suggested it. Why hadn't I gone home at Christmas? Why had I begged her not to leave Daddy? I had thought of me, of my feelings, and not hers. I thought of Lady Bird Johnson, only a few years younger than Mama, how beautiful and serene she was. In contrast, I thought of my mother's life, of how she had worked so hard, done without so much, suffered such pain, looked so much older. How she lived her life through me.

We walked into the house, our little home at 2024 West Oklahoma that I loved so, my basketball goal still beside the driveway. There was the rabbit Mama had fried for supper, still in the refrigerator, and the bowl of Jell-O salad she'd made. On the dining-room table was a sack with the cotton dress she'd bought the morning she died. There was the Kleenex on the dresser where she had blotted her lipstick, the mark of her lips on it. Everything was the same, but Mother wasn't there.

We went to the funeral home. I remember arranging her hair. Then I held her arm, held on to it until it was warm. Aunty took me away.

We buried my mother on a warm, sunny day, when the lilacs were blooming. They sang "Rock of Ages" for her, and read the quote from Dag Hammarskjöld that Mother had kept in her Bible:

"The day you were born, everyone laughed. You cried alone. So live your life that the day you die everyone else weeps, and you alone are happy."

"When sorrows come," Shakespeare wrote, "they come . . . in battalions." I could not know, of course, that my sorrow for my mother was but the first that year. Birch stayed with me in Oklahoma for awhile, and then he went back to Indiana. He shared my grief, for he had buried his mother, too. My cousin Maxine, and Aunty and Aunt Lavern, stayed with me for a week while I cleaned the house, sorting through all Mother's treasures and her clothes. Each thing of hers I touched, I ached for her. I felt lost, cut adrift. I hired a cleaning woman to come in once a week for Daddy, and asked all the neighbors to invite him to come by for dinner. I worried so about leaving him there alone.

I found a hundred and eighty dollars in twenty-dollar bills in her purse, and a will in her handwriting dated November 29, 1963, leaving her half of the property to me. I handed them to my father. He had left the house, briefly, to place a long-distance call from the drugstore. I verified the charge, but thought nothing about it. He drove me to the airport, and I flew to Washington. The next day I took Evan to his piano lesson, and while he was playing, I placed a call to my father. He'd looked so sad, so alone at the airport. There was no answer. I tried for twenty-four hours and there was still no answer. I was in a panic. I called my cousin Bill. "Where is Daddy? I've been calling morning, noon, and night."

They found him in Tennessee. He had caught the next plane after mine, to go to a woman two years younger than I. He was in love, he said. She was the same woman he had wanted to marry in 1960.

My Aunty, Mother's sister, then told me bitterly how my mother had lived in fear. He had beaten her, broken her ribs, and she never told me, not even when she'd said she wanted a divorce. She'd never told me that she knew Daddy was having an affair. (She had not told her sister, either. Only after my mother's death did a nurse tell Aunty that one day, when Mama was in the hospital for "nervous exhaustion," she found her in tears. "Can you tell me what is the matter?" the nurse asked. "Oh, so many heartaches and troubles," my mother replied. And finally: "I have to tell someone. My husband is in love with another woman." But then she made the woman promise not to tell Aunty, or anyone else.) She'd bottled it all up inside her. And now, a week after we buried her, he'd run off with that other woman. I could tell he was drinking when I talked to him, in Tennessee. I thought he'd gone berserk with grief. I pleaded. I offered to go to him. Five weeks later, he married her, and brought her home to my mother's house.

There was no time to mourn for my mother, or the desecration of her memory. Neither did I take time to analyze why I didn't stop to mourn. My grief was great, my energy depleted, but I charged on, to a Senate Ladies' luncheon at the White House; lunch at the Moroccan Embassy; more evening receptions; Evan to the dentist; Evan to Little League. Running to the Senate to watch Birch preside over the civil rights debate, where Senator Long and Senator Talmadge were filibustering; running to Indiana, where Ted Kennedy came, at Birch's request, to speak to the Democrats on Jefferson-Jackson Day; running back to Washington to speak to an audience of physicians' wives at a medical convention ("I like to be a part of Birch's political activity," I told them. "One of the advantages of our life, as I see it, is that it is something a wife and husband can share so completely"); running back to Indiana to speak to a sisterhood luncheon at the Indianapolis Hebrew Congregation; to New York for a presidential rally at Madison Square Garden; to Missouri to speak at William Woods College commencement; to Indianapolis for the "500" race with Birch and guests; running back so that Birch could vote for cloture to end the civil rights filibuster.

Birch came home and announced that he couldn't go to the state convention in Indiana because he had to vote on the civil rights bill. I had to go and represent him—back to Indiana to read Birch's statement, where I was mobbed, and in one day juggled three TV interviews and three radio interviews. All this and more in the two months after my mother's funeral. I was exhausted, yet I couldn't sleep. Birch was my anchor, my greatest help. He listened. For weeks I was like a pitcher, pouring out all my memories of Mama, talking every evening about her. He was gentle, listening quietly, until the pitcher ran dry.

From our Oklahoma attic, I had brought home my mother's girlhood diaries, and a bundle of her and Daddy's love letters mailed from Drummond to Enid during the year before they married. "Why are you reading those, if it causes you such pain?" Macel would ask. "I have to," I said. I read them, the innocent young letters of an Oklahoma girl and boy in love, and I burned them. As each letter hit flame, I became more distressed that this hopeful young love had ended so tragically. Where had it gone so wrong? There were the letters of condolence from friends and acquaintances, writing me about how wonderful my mother had been, which made me feel all over again that she had been betrayed.

Every time I closed my eyes, there would be my father's face. I had been hearing from old friends and neighbors in Enid; my father's behavior, his remarriage, was an affront to my mother's memory. The community had turned its back on him. And so, I decided, must I.

On June 13, I sat down to type him a Father's Day letter. It would be my last:

> . . . I have never known a father and daughter to have any finer
> relationship than we had. Many people commented upon it. It
> stood the test of many strains through the years, especially the last
> few years. During my growing up years, you were a fine father
> to me, and for that you have told me yourself that I have fulfilled
> your dreams and have more than repaid you. You said I have
> brought you much happiness and also how happy you were to have
> a son-in-law like Birch. I have written at least once a week, kept
> in touch in every way and tried to show my love for my parents.
> You often called me when you were "down" and I did everything
> to cheer you. I have told you over and over that it made no
> difference what kind of home you lived in or other material things.
> I have told you many times so that so long as you were good,
> moral and honest, I did not care if you lived in a tent. You were
> my father, and I was proud of you.

I recounted the events that had distressed me so, his drinking, his brutal treatment of Mother, her death.

". . . You promised me by Mother's open coffin that you would never drink again," I wrote.

> . . . My heart was heavy for you. Then you flew to Memphis to
> see Pat. . . . I pleaded with you not to throw away all that was
> decent. My mother had not yet been buried one week.
> . . . You had turned your back so quickly on the world of which
> I was a part. No one would have minded you marrying again.
> In fact, at your age it would rather have been expected, but not
> like this, with no decent respect for my mother, or the rest of the

family. You took our relationship and threw it in the gutter. When someone you love is in trouble, one wants to run to them and help. I have done this with you over and over. This time you turned your back. I could not help. You shut me out. Words mean nothing to you. You used your God-given ability with words to say what others want to hear, and then in the next breath say and do differently. Your actions do not correspond to what you often say. No one can really believe you. One has to wait and see what your actions turn out to be. So sad, and absolutely heartbreaking, but true.

So now we come to today. I am what I always have been. I have not changed my way of life. You have no idea the embarrassment you have caused me in the last few months, the heartache, the tears, the sleepless nights. But this is not all. If you continue as you are, the worst embarrassment is yet to come. You have turned your back on me and all that has ever been important, dear, upright, and honorable. You make your own life. The way you are going now you have left no room for me in it. You knew this when you made your decision. You are not worth the shaking, trembling hands you have caused me. I try to forget, but there are the nights. But I tell you this, I will forget. I will make myself do it. This is what you have done to me. So, this is my Father's Day letter to you. The future is in your hands. What do you choose? As of right now, if you continue, you must forget I exist. Do not mention my name. If you decide to be the type of person you once were, and the father I loved and knew and admired, then you know my telephone number. It is your decision. I love and cherish my memories of what you were. I hope I have made myself very clear. You cannot have both lives at once.

Goodbye.

I read the letter, weeping, and I mailed it, along with the last of the thank-yous for Mother's funeral flowers.

⁓

The Friday before Father's Day, June 19, we were scheduled to fly to Massachusetts with Ted Kennedy. Birch was to be the keynote speaker at the Massachusetts Democratic Convention in Springfield, where Ted was to be renominated for the Senate by acclamation. Afterward, they had invited us for the weekend at Hyannis Port. I was looking forward to a rest and a long visit with

Joan. She had been a wonderful friend to me, sending me clippings and a note when I was Indiana "Woman of the Year," calling about my mother, and visiting often, by telephone, from her bedside. She had been so happy about her pregnancy, although she was confined to bed. When she'd lost her baby two weeks ago, I had felt so sorry for her. What a brave soldier she was, trudging off to the state convention so soon after her loss, also taking no time to mourn. I just wanted to be with her. She had called as I was finishing the last of the thank-you notes for my mother's funeral flowers, to ask me to fly up with her on the Kennedy family plane, the *Caroline*. I was tempted, but I wanted to stay and watch the Senate vote on the civil rights bill. It would be one of the most historic days in Washington, the 101st anniversary of the Emancipation Proclamation. The bill would enforce the right of Americans, of whatever color or creed, to use public accommodations and receive equal employment at equal pay. Birch had worked long and hard in support of this bill, and the vote was expected to come up in the afternoon. I sat in the gallery with Myrtle McIntyre and Bethine Church, checking my watch, as the opponents presented their stalls and delays—Senators Stennis, Russell, Hickenlooper, and Tower delivering dire predictions. Evening approached as Senator Dirksen took the floor. Ted told Birch, who sent a note to me, that if they didn't vote by 8:30 at the latest, there'd be no use in our going. But Joan was waiting for us at the convention, and the suspense of an important vote might keep the delegates there.

The eloquent Everett Dirksen talked on and on, full of the privilege of closing the civil rights debate. Finally, well after eight, they cast the historic vote, 73 to 27 for passage of the bill. Ted, Birch, and I dashed for National Airport.

A twin-engine Aero Commander, a seven-seat plane belonging to Ted's friend Daniel Hogan, was waiting for us. Hogan usually piloted the plane himself, with Ted as copilot, but tonight he was attending a Yale reunion. He had hired Edwin Zimny, a veteran pilot, to take us to West Springfield to an airport fifteen minutes from the convention. As we boarded the plane, Edward Moss, Ted's aide and good friend, stood aside so Ted could take his usual place up front beside the pilot. "I'll sit back with the Bayhs tonight," Ted said, "so we can talk and work on our speeches." Moss climbed into the copilot seat.

We took off at 8:39 P.M., strapped into our seats, Ted with

his back to the pilot, munching on a sandwich and sipping chocolate milk. Hanging on the wall behind me was my standby turquoise dress, the one I'd worn to my mother's reception for us in Enid, the one I'd worn to Sherrye Henry's the night my mother died. I kicked off my shoes and looked out the window at the clear, starry night as Ted and Birch began to work on their speeches. I noticed the Emergency Exit sign next to me. "We'll arrive at the airport at five minutes after ten," Ed Moss called out. Cars were waiting to speed us to the Coliseum, where we'd be royally escorted to the center of the convention. After Birch and Ted finished their speech work, we tried to talk over the roar of the engines—Birch unfastening his seat belt to lean across to hear Ted. "Bob is thinking about running for the Senate from New York," Ted said, "but he hasn't made a decision yet." Then he laughed. "He's always after me to lose weight. I just don't understand how he does it. He can eat anything without gaining a pound, and I weigh two-fifteen." I looked out the window again, and the stars had disappeared. There were clouds and an occasional flash of lightning. Ted spoke occasionally with the men in the cockpit. I noticed that his watch read 10:20. "We're going to be awfully late," I said. "We've had to fly a hundred miles out of our way because of bad weather," Ted replied.

Then we really got into the weather. The plane began to bounce and lift and drop in the wind. I'd never been afraid of flying—anything with wings was all right with me—but now I was scared. Ted turned around to talk to the pilot. It was the roughest weather I'd ever seen. I said to Birch. "We're in trouble, aren't we?"

"No, no, everything will be fine," he said. Birch fastened his safety belt and took my hand. "Hasn't your old Dad always taken care of you?"

"You've never gotten me out of a plane before," I whispered.

"You've never asked me to take you out of a plane!"

A clap of thunder, and the plane shook like a rag doll. Ted reached over to switch off the light. "Let's give this pilot every opportunity we can to come in for a landing," he said.

It was pitch black. Then CRACK! A loud noise, an incredible jolt, and the next minute we were all crumpled up.

There was sudden, total silence. It was like being in a vacuum. My seat was thrust forward, my lower back felt as if there were a knife in it, but I was conscious. I screamed for Birch. He didn't answer. I was terrified. I screamed again, and this time he did answer. The breath had been knocked out of him. "Let's get out of here," he said. He called to Ted. He did not answer.

The plane was leaning over on the side where the door was, but the impact had knocked out the little emergency window to my right. Behind my seat, the jolt had flipped on an emergency flashlight. When it came on, giving us a thread of light in the blackness, I had a sudden thought that God surely must be looking out for us. I crawled out the window over the torn wing and the dangling motor, Birch behind me, still calling for Ted. We dropped through thick fog into tall, wet grass. We had crashed in an apple orchard, a mile from the end of the runway, in the black, dead silence. Nothing moved except the red light on top of the plane, which whirled round and round. There was a strong smell of gasoline. The front of the plane had plunged into the earth, its nose smashed and the cockpit peeled off. "It's going to explode!" I cried. Birch took the flashlight and looked up front, into what had been the cockpit. "Oh, my God," he said. "We've got to go for help." He took a few steps away from the plane. The smell of gasoline was overwhelming. "I can't leave Ted," he said. "We must make an attempt to get him out of there."

It's going to catch on fire, I thought. Evan will be an orphan. We climbed back up to the hole from which we'd escaped and both called to Ted again. With the flashlight we could see him lying on the floor. This time, Ted mumbled.

"Ted, you have got to get up and get out of here," Birch yelled. "Come on, now, you've got to do it."

Ted was barely conscious, but he began to try to move. "My back," he moaned. We both knew that a person with a spinal injury should not be moved. But the fumes made it imperative.

Birch crawled back in. They locked fingers, and Birch managed to get him over the seat, through the window, and over the motor. "You've got to catch his feet," Birch said to me. I held out my arms, praying that I could catch him. His feet hit, thud, on my arms, and went right through them. Birch pulled him over in the wet grass, far enough from the plane to escape the flames if they came. "Get something to put under his head," Birch said to me. I reached back through the window for my turquoise dress, and rolled the unlucky garment into a pillow for Ted's head. Then we covered him with my raincoat. Birch leaned over him. "We're going to get help," he said.

"What about Moss? Zimny?" Ted asked.

Birch hesitated. "We'll have to get help. Are you all right? Is there anything else we can do before we go?"

And Ted said, "Oh, Birch, if you could just get this wet grass out of my face."

We took the flashlight and walked—I was limping barefoot— down through the apple orchard to a back road. A car slowed down. We hollered and waved our arms. A woman, alone, rolled her window down a slight way but she kept moving, slowly. "A plane crash! There's been a plane crash," Birch screamed. "Help us!" She drove on, afraid. (I didn't really blame her. It was a dark, lonely road. We could have been thugs.)

A second car approached, driven by a man who'd come to investigate the noise. He took us to his house about half a mile away, called the ambulance, fire department, and police, brought blankets, and then drove us back to the plane. We were near Southampton, he told us, only a little over a mile from Westfield Airport. I could no longer walk. People began to arrive. "Is that really Teddy Kennedy?" they kept saying.

The pilot had been killed, instantly, but Ed Moss was still breathing. They had to use crowbars to get him out of the plane. Ted was lifted into one ambulance and Moss into the other, with me on a stretcher beside him and Birch in front with the driver. Through the fog, slowly, we drove to the hospital in Northampton, Ed Moss beside me, his breath labored, guttural. His arm fell over on me, and I thought, he is dying.

He died seven hours later at Cooley-Dickenson Hospital, of massive brain injuries.

Ted's back was broken. He had fractured two ribs and three lumbar vertebrae. At first they feared he wouldn't live; he had no pulse, and had to have three blood transfusions. They didn't know if he would ever walk again. We were all humbled, shaken, wondering what quirk of fate had decreed that the children orphaned that night were named Moss and Zimny, and not Bayh and Kennedy.

Richard Nixon wrote Birch that "anyone who comes out of an airplane accident alive must have a charmed life." I didn't feel charmed. I felt awed. Awed that death had come so close, and had spared me. We were both in pain; I with coccyxodermia—hairline cracks in my coccyx—Birch with torn muscles in his right hip and stomach; and we were hospitalized for ten days. But our pain was nothing compared to the devastation of the families of the two men who were killed.

In those first days in the hospital, when the shock set in, I kept remembering the Oklahoma hospital, after the car wreck when my mother was with me. She always took care of me when I needed her. I missed her now. The hospital bent its rules to let Birch and me share a room.

Compared to Ted's, our injuries were minor. Ted, who was in excruciating pain, also grieved over the loss of the Moss and Zimny families. And Joan, who had just lost her baby, and who had been waiting for us to come to the convention, had heard the news flash on TV, and not known if Ted were dead or alive. Now, no one knew if he would ever walk again. How could I help her in this terrible time of strain?

It was she who helped me. Joan came to see me every day while she stayed with Ted. She went out and bought clippies for my hair, and arranged for somebody to come in and shampoo it as I lay in bed. "You're so far away from home," she said. "Let me be your family." Ted was in the hospital for eight months, and Joan went out to campaign for him, all over the state.

The telegrams poured in from all over the country, and from all the senators, thanking God for our deliverance from death. President and Mrs. Johnson called, and sent us a profusion of flowers. (The President sent two neurosurgeons from Walter Reed Hospital for Ted as soon as he heard of the crash.) Jackie came, and Bobby, and Mike Mansfield, the majority leader. My father did not call, and I did not call him, although I ached to do so. Father's Day was the Sunday after we crashed; I knew he'd be in pain, reading my letter, but I had cut my ties. I tried to keep my resolve.

They flew us home on the Kennedy plane, me on a stretcher because I couldn't yet sit up. Evan met us at the airport, sturdy little crew-cut Evan with his bright smile. "I'm so glad you're okay," he said. "I missed you." Birch's father had been there every day to help Macel with him.

In the weeks following, we tried to make life normal for Evan, taking him to the World's Fair. I went through the motions, but my mind was absorbed. Later, I remember taking a walk in the woods, looking at the dull sky, and all I could think about was death.

I looked at nature and I couldn't see the bright green leaves of summer. I saw only dead leaves on the ground.

But on July 27, I got all dressed up to go to the White House. President Tsirianana of the Malagasy Republic was being honored with a State dinner. Birch called to say he'd have to be late. The Senate was voting on the Ethics Committee bill—a law designed to prevent any more Bobby Baker messes. Could I please bring his tuxedo down to the office? Betty Kuchel from California and I rode down to the White House without our husbands. To pump up my spirits, I'd had my hair done in Georgetown by Jackie Kennedy's hairdresser, Jean-Paul Amsellem, and treated myself to a new mint-green formal. As we entered the Diplomatic Reception Room, a Colonel Fowler took my arm and handed me a card stating that I'd be seated at the head table. In the East Room, where we had cocktails, Adlai Stevenson rushed up to welcome me back, followed by many others. Then the Marine Band struck up "Hail to the Chief." In the welcoming line, both Johnsons received me warmly with a kiss, Luci and Lynda with big hugs. Birch arrived just then, taking me outside to the Rose Garden, where formal tables with gold-braided tablecloths stood in rows, with Japanese lanterns swinging overhead. On opposite sides of the head table, with President Monroe's lovely vermeil centerpiece between them, sat President and Mrs. Johnson. I was placed between the Ambassador of Malagasy to the U.S. (who spoke English) and the Prime Minister (who did not). With interpreters hovering behind us, we carried on a marvelous conversation. There was entertainment after dinner, on a stage set up on the south lawn. As the curtain parted, a big, full, yellow moon rose over the garden, while the opening bars of the music, quite suddenly, brought magic to me:

"*Ooooo-kla-homa, where the wind comes sweepin' down the plain—*"

My throat caught. I could see that wind, that plain, the bright golden haze on Grandma Hern's meadow, my mother running out to the clothesline where the wind kicked up red dirt on her wet white sheets, the chicks all a-scurry as she shooed them. Shirley Jones and that Broadway cast on the White House lawn were singing just to me.

"*We know we belong to the land, and the land we belong to is grand—*"

The floodlit fountains sparkled with the music. Behind them, the Washington Monument, the Jefferson Memorial glowed in the night. Suddenly I knew that Marvella Hern, of Oklahoma, was going to be "okay." On the way home I said to my husband, "I'm doing fine, Birch. I'm okay."

"Do you know what President Johnson said to me?" he replied.

"What?"

"He asked about you. He said, 'She's going to make you President someday.' "

Chapter 7

My new friend Jane Sinnenberg, who lived on the next street in McLean, once said that "Trying to live up to someone's expectations is an act of love in itself." Birch's expectations of me were never stated outright, as my parents' had been. In retrospect, I can see that I was trying to live up to what I *perceived* were his expectations. It was I who conjured up the model of what I thought he wanted and needed, and who worried constantly that I wouldn't be able to live up to it. He rewarded my efforts with loving appreciation, with a telegram wherever I was making a speech, with showers of compliments on how I looked in my new hairdo, with those funny little notes around the house ("You don't need this to get me to stick around" taped on my can of hairspray) like fan letters from an appreciative audience. And yet our actual time alone together was becoming so limited that I began keeping two lists: "Things I must talk to Birch about," and "Things I need to talk to Birch about." Needless to say, the latter list stretched on to infinity.

I worried about his health. He was zooming around the country organizing Young Citizens for Johnson, spending more time in Indiana than in Washington, it seemed; on those rare weekends home he was working all day at his desk on the presidential succession bill he had introduced to the Judiciary Committee, glad to get four and a half hours sleep a night. On the evenings in between, it never occurred to either of us to say "no" to social obligations and try to spend what little time we had alone together. All those obligations, I felt, were "expected" of me. We had been told that the social contacts were very important for Birch's work. Indeed, Birch found that he could more easily seek out a cabinet member, or another senator, or somebody from the President's staff, at a dinner party. "More is accomplished in Washington after five than before five," a columnist once wrote, and that verges on truth.

I hoped that plunging into the festivities leading up to the 1964 Democratic Convention would ease the pain of the loss of my mother, and take my mind off my father. But the deeper I plunged, the worse my body seemed to feel. I remember rushing from a luncheon at Mary Ellen Monroney's for a group of ambassadors' wives to a fitting for a costume to wear to Lynda Bird Johnson's party at the White House, and home to dress for the President's Salute to Congress. I was again on the White House lawn where only last month I had felt so Oklahoma-okay, but when Mrs. Johnson asked us in for "a bite to eat," I was terrified that somebody would see how badly my hand was shaking. The President put his arm around Birch, complimenting him on the job he was doing for Young Citizens for Johnson, and I told him what great campaigners his own daughters had turned out to be. "If they can do as well as you, that will be tremendous," he said, and I prayed that I would be able to hold out through the convention. Birch had two speeches to make there, and we had more invitations than I could juggle.

How could I let Birch down by falling apart? I vowed to control that shaking left hand at all costs, to get over my terror about airplanes, to conquer that insomnia. The next day, I pulled myself together and danced my heels off at Lynda Bird's White House costume party. Birch, in his gray top hat, sideburns, and ruffled shirt, was President William Henry Harrison (the Indiana Territory governor whose untimely death brought about the first example of presidential succession). In my rosy pink taffeta empire dress, carrying a fan, I was his Anna. Lynda, as the "Yellow Rose of Texas," and her father cornered Birch, there on the White House roof, to talk about Young Citizens and the convention. The Marine Band played, and we did the frug until after 2 A.M.

The next day, of course, we were off to Atlantic City for the convention. It was to have been a gala time, staying with the Henrys and the Rogerses at the Howars' summer house in Ventnor (where the men all sat around working on Birch's speech), gadding about the Perle Mesta party, modeling in the style show for the "Today" TV program, basking in the audience during Birch's speech to the convention, enjoying the big rally for Young Democrats on which Birch had worked so hard, and, finally, celebrating our twelfth wedding anniversary with our friends. Instead, I dragged about, plagued by headaches and double vision, freezing my face into a smile so there'd be no place for tears to squeeze out, being marched up to the highest rafters of the auditorium to watch Birch, a tiny speck, make the speech we had labored over (later I discovered that I had been invited to sit with Lady Bird in her box), until on Wednesday night, after the President selected Senator Humphrey, I slipped out of the convention hall and collapsed. Our friends stayed the weekend, dancing until 3 A.M., they told me, to celebrate our anniversary. Birch drove home to Washington with me lying in the back seat, his last weekend at home until after the November election.

That first morning home, the phone woke me with a threatening crank call from a stranger. I couldn't decide whether to feel annoyed or sorry for the woman or fearful at the madness her call symbolized. Later that day, my heart began to race, over 115 beats per minute. Birch drove me to the doctor. Estrogen didn't seem to help. Insomnia—waking at 3:30 A.M., and then getting up with Evan at 7—was draining me. Dr. Brill examined me. "Is something the matter emotionally?" he asked. "Yes, I hate my father," I said, suddenly weeping. He made an appointment for me to see a psychiatrist, Dr. John Francis, the following day.

It took three visits to Dr. Francis for me to spill out everything I had been trying to handle: the emptiness where my mother had been; my feelings of guilt that she had sacrificed so much for me, and I had not done enough for her; the feelings of anguish about my father, despite my resolve to cut him out of my life; the fear of Birch getting into an airplane; my feelings of inadequacy as I tried to improve myself; my frustration at feeling sick all the time, at not being able to sleep.

The doctor's voice was comforting as he summed up my problems. "You are expecting too much of yourself. You are trying to be everything to everybody," he said. "No wonder your body is in rebellion. It takes at least a year to get over the shock of death." Dr. Francis talked with me about grief, about the way we subvert our troubling emotions by not recognizing them, about the effect of impossible expectations upon our physical health. And he invited me to come back, whenever I needed him. But I never returned, thinking I could handle it. I should have stopped, then and there, to examine what "expecting too much of myself" really meant. But no, I thought that this kind of professional help was too time-consuming, too much of an expense. Our expenses—including now a private school for Evan—had been far heavier than we had expected. I didn't think I should pay somebody to help me deal with my grief now that I knew it was normal, and would come to an end in time.

I had always been taught that to wallow in grief was a weakness. My mother would have wanted me to keep on doing the things that would make her proud of me, I thought. And yet I did not make the connection that because she, herself, had tried to bear up under more than she could take, she had died at age fifty-six, almost literally, of a broken heart. I still did not take "a time to mourn," as it tells us in the Bible. I took comfort only in being able to label what was wrong with me: Grief.

I continued to rush helter-skelter into the demands of a presidential election year. And just as my insomnia began to improve for the first time since Mother's death, the phone calls from Oklahoma started again. This time it was the neighbors, calling to complain about Daddy's drunken behavior. "He's backed over my yard in his car," said one. "I'm afraid he'll hit a child." "The noise over there is more than we can stand," said another. "I thought you might be able to do something about it."

Our lawyer in Enid, Earl Mitchell, wrote that there was "not one of his old friends and associates, neighbors and acquaintances who does not avoid him and shun him," because he had "violated and flaunted standards of common decency," and advised me, "as difficult as I know it is, I believe you owe it to yourself, your good husband and your good name, and especially so in view of your position, to sever your relations with him, at least and until there are some drastic changes in the situation." But Daddy's neighbors did not know that I had already severed relations with him. Not realizing that I had tried, and failed, they thought I could influence him. According to Aunty, nobody could influence him. He had changed in other ways that I could not accept. He had a new hobby: bear hunting in Colorado. He who had advised his daughter, and later his grandson, "Never kill for sport. Never kill a living thing."

I was ashamed of him, embarrassed by him, wounded and angry with him. And I went to bed worrying that my physical problems, the headaches and lack of energy, and my family's problems, especially any publicity about my father, might be detriments to Birch's career.

I was so proud of Birch. I "basked," as someone wrote of a politician's wife, "in reflected glory." It was true. In that fall of 1964, I felt that Birch's political star was beginning to rise. He had been lucky, as freshman senator, to inherit Senator Kefauver's Constitutional Amendments Subcommittee. For the country now lacked a Vice President, and it was Birch who introduced the bill that would insure that wouldn't happen again. On September 27, Birch's office told me the presidential succession bill was scheduled to be introduced on the floor of the Senate that afternoon. I called my friends Barbara Howar and Sherrye Henry, and we rushed down to the Capitol to hear the debate between Birch and the other senators, Bible, Javits, Church, Monroney, Ervin. I marveled at how skillfully Birch was able to keep the debate on the right track. "S J 139" passed the Senate by unanimous voice vote. It provided that the President nominate a person to fill the office of Vice President, if a vacancy occurred; and that if the President is unable to discharge the powers and duties of his office, the Vice President shall become President. I was thrilled beyond description. Birch came up to the "family" gallery, where we were looking down on the discussions, and I kissed him. "I'm about to become a father," he beamed, as the bill, passed by roll call vote of 65–0 on September 29, would be his first major legislation.

I was equally proud that Birch's efforts to find a manufacturer to replace Studebaker in South Bend had paid off with the opening of a Kaiser Jeep factory in the old Studebaker plant. As chairman of Young Citizens for Johnson-Humphrey, he was flying all over the country with Lynda and Luci Johnson, staging barbecues to raise money and enthusiasm for the upcoming election. I yearned to be with him. And on October 8, Lyndon Johnson had flown into Indianapolis to campaign, telling a throng of 40,000 Hoosiers to "Watch Birch Bayh—he's going on to even higher things."

During the debate on Birch's presidential succession bill, I had received a call from the Democratic National Committee. Would I join a group of Cabinet wives who were going on a "Flying Caravan" campaign trip? I accepted, then prayed my health would hold. My insomnia had taken a new turn: awake at 4:30 A.M.

"I wouldn't change my life for anything," I told *Cosmopolitan* magazine that year, and I'm sure I thought it was true. The more successes that Birch piled up, the more I identified with his feeling of accomplishment—yet the more I feared that some act of mine was going to cause him trouble.

There were sixteen of us that October, Washington wives who flew out across the country in teams of two to campaign for Johnson and Humphrey. Jane Celebrezze, wife of the Secretary of HEW, and I were assigned to the Far West: Salt Lake City, Boise, Spokane, and Seattle. Two days later, with Betty Furness and Jane Freeman, wife of the Secretary of Agriculture, we went on to Florida. It was a chance to learn national politics in an efficient, superbly organized presidential campaign, with speeches, press conferences, meetings, coffee, teas—the whole campaign rigamarole, standing in line pumping hands, smiling at faces we'd never see again. "We're like the song-and-dance team that never had a chance to rehearse," Mrs. Celebrezze whispered to me, but we managed to glean publicity, and polished off our campaign speeches like seasoned "pols." Our days began at six; by noon we had made four appearances, by midnight we were winding up our tenth. Between times, television interviewers were pummeling us with questions about Bobby Baker and Walter Jenkins, one former and one current assistant of Lyndon Johnson's, who had caused great embarrassment to the President. As we fielded questions, I couldn't help but remember Lyndon Johnson's words when he advised Birch to "select the strongest staff you can find." Those who surround one—staff, friends, wife—have to appear as perfect as the politician himself.

From Florida I went on alone to Allentown, Pennsylvania, stopping at Washington's National Airport long enough to grab a change of clothes (for the icy fall weather), as I changed planes, and then flew straight to East Chicago, Hammond, and Gary, for a speech in each city. While in Chicago, I received an invitation to join Mrs. Johnson in Little Rock, on the last leg of the Lady Bird Special "Flying Whistle Stop."

She must have been exhausted, this woman who had become something of an idol to me. After thousands of miles on trains, buses, vans, and planes with an entourage of what she called "women doers," staff, and press, Lady Bird Johnson was winding up her considerable role in her husband's campaign. As she stepped off the Braniff plane leased for her "whistle stop," she gave me a big hug. She was wearing a red suit, with a mink hat perched on the back of her head, and except for her tired eyes, looked bandbox fresh. But when she turned to the crowd, she radiated such warmth and enthusiasm that the tired Arkansans seemed to forget they had waited so long.

I was impressed with the superb organization that put wings on the "Lady Bird Special." The front part of the plane was partitioned off, containing press people and Mrs. Johnson's staff. The back part was for Lady Bird to relax or work with those of us traveling with her. It was obvious that she was able to do the great volume of work because of the attention to detail of the people around her. Liz Carpenter drafted her speeches, and took care of the press; Bess Abell, her social secretary, was the "idea" person, as well as the efficient "oiler" of all the cogs in the political machinery; "Scooter" Miller was her close friend and protector, the one who thought of "Bird's" needs while the rest were concentrating on logistics; Dr. Janet Travell took care of her health, as well as that of everybody on board, and Helen Williams took care of Lady Bird's clothes. Each person had clearly in mind the importance of the mindless mechanics of getting a complicated function together, nobody seemed to think any task was "beneath" her, and they all had an unspoken solidarity in purpose, goals, and procedures. I took careful note of their attitude and efficiency, hoping to translate it to our next Senate campaign.

President Johnson joined us in Evansville, touching down in his great silver Air Force One, and spoke to our Indiana crowd of 15,000. Lady Bird went on with him for their final week of campaigning together.

On October 29, I made my last out-of-town campaign trip, to Pennsylvania, a demanding, Mack Sennett movie of a day. My appearance was delayed, but at 11 P.M. I finally began speaking, and I held that crowd. After all the back-and-forth of the day, out of somewhere came an extra burst of Girls' Nation-Farm Bureau Contest oratory, and I came home at 1 A.M., not really tired or suffering from the insomnia, the backaches, the headaches, the total exhaustion of most of my Washington days.

I returned to find Evan in terrific shape—well-adjusted to his new school, involved in serious detective work with his best friend Steve Sinnenberg, and generally thriving under the care of his "substitute grandmother," Macel Nuckels, and Martha Swanson from Birch's office, who volunteered her weekend time. With her earthy, West Virginia wisdom and calm, simple faith, Macel seemed to be intent on taking care of me. It was a joy to take her on family trips, to do those things I had hoped to do with my mother. I only wished that I had more time to enjoy her. With Evan she was a steady, loving, religious presence, providing exactly the same kind of experience Grandma Hern had given me. She and Evan talked politics, sports, Cub Scouts, music, like two old friends. We all loved Macel, and were hopelessly addicted to her delicious homemade bread, no-nonsense American cooking, and spectacular birthday cakes in the form of rabbits, Santa Clauses, boats. It was gratifying to return from a long trip and find Evan in good spirits and good hands, growing into a sturdy, playful nearly-nine-year-old, a nonstop talker like his mother, and almost, just almost, as smooth a politician as his dad.

By election day, however, I felt a letdown. Birch and I watched the returns of the Johnson-Humphrey landslide at a party at the Henrys—and went home to the biggest fight we had ever had. One of the guests mentioned that somebody in Birch's office had declined an invitation to a party for us, and that was the first I had heard about the invitation. I had returned home from the campaign to mail addressed to me, personally, because the writers "haven't been able to get a reply from the senator's office." We found one secretary had about a thousand unanswered letters—six months' worth—stashed away. Of course, Birch had been busy with Young Citizens, but I complained that he should "run a tighter ship." He retorted that his office was not my business, which of course it wasn't, but I said that it became my business when the complaints were addressed to me. And now, someone on the staff was even declining our personal invitations. And so on and so on until we were shouting at each other. This woke up Evan, which mortified both of us.

We patched up our quarrel, both full of remorse, but it had brought to a head something that had been bothering me almost since we moved to Washington. We had been such *partners* during the campaign. I had looked forward to feeling the same sense of partnership when we came to Washington. But what, exactly, was my role as a senator's wife? Where did I fit in?

I still clipped the newspapers for him, still answered the mail, but his "quality time" was taken up in conferences with those people down at his office. I was jealous of his staff. (I would later learn that a common "staff syndrome" is to be jealous of wives, too, both fighting for the same person's time.) I was angry when some of them operated at less than maximum efficiency. I had been concentrating on running a "shipshape" house, on ferrying Evan thither and yon, on keeping myself hairdo-ed and hemlined to the standard of good grooming and public demeanor I thought was expected of me, and trying to appear bright-eyed and alert at every single social function I could crowd into my day or evening. When Birch's staff made me feel unwelcome, my headaches came rushing back with a vengeance, and a series of low-grade infections followed.

The brightest event of the new year, 1965, was Teddy Kennedy's return to Washington. It had been a full six months before he could walk—and we were overjoyed to see him make his way down the aisle of the Senate.

He and Joan were coming to our house for dinner on January 31; I wanted everything to be perfect. I'd hoped to spend the week getting ready for the party. But it didn't work out that way, and though the party itself went well, the mischances, changes of guests, back problems, and a defective furnace nearly defeated me.

The headaches grew worse, and my neck was constantly "out," with visits to my osteopathic doctor, Dr. John Cifala, now a part of my weekly routine. At the end of every day I was so exhausted I was near tears. I tried to convince myself that the compensations were worth the expenditure of energy. Look "how far I had come" in two years, I kept telling myself. I was hungry for education, for experience. I had traveled in Europe, talked to ambassadors, danced with my President. I was even wearing a dressmaker's copies of exclusive designer clothes that two years ago I'd never even heard about. At formal dinners, I was entertaining people who'd been born to luxury or whom I'd held in awe, when two years ago I didn't know a fish fork from a finger bowl. And yet I seemed further and further away from the "ideal" Senate wife I was hoping to become. How could I be when I was physically ill most of the time? (If there was one thing I coveted, it was Ethel Kennedy's energy.) And my temper, held in tight check during my "public" moments, began erupting at little things—at a staff member who'd promised to pick me up at the airport after an Indiana speech, and didn't show; at a tailor who'd promised alterations on Birch's trousers, and didn't deliver; at anybody, for any reason, who had "let me down."

"But I wouldn't change it for anything," I had told that Business and Professional Women's group in Portland, Indiana. "It's like a giant smörgasbord—"

I would have changed it for one thing. There was a gaping hole in my life where my mother and father had been. Although there were now others who also seemed parents to me, not all of Macel's earthy kindness nor Aunty's love nor Daddy Bayh's quiet pride nor Gladys and Mike Sperling's generous spirit and counsel, nor my hero-worship for Lady Bird and Lyndon Johnson, could touch that void. At night, when the sleep I longed for and that my body so needed stubbornly eluded me, I writhed with guilt, anger, fear, shame—all the darker emotions I tried to bury by day. How had I let my parents down? Why had my mother been taken? Why had Daddy let me down by becoming a drunk?

I worried incessantly about appearing to others as "imperfect" as I saw myself to be. I wanted to be like Lady Bird Johnson. I marveled at her—her intelligence, her tact, her warmth, her calm, even her down-to-the-last-button, every-hair-in-place appearance. I wanted her to like me. And when she showed that she did, I clung to each shred of her approval as an affirmation that I might be "all right." I loved her daughters, different from each other as night and day. I saw them as the sisters I might have had. Invitations to the Johnson White House came frequently in those days. I felt that they were more than political, that Birch and I had become real friends to these homey Texans I so admired. Those invitations were treasures, each one pasted into my scrapbook with a host of memories that kept me fueled despite my aches and pains. What I missed most was to call my mother with a "Guess what the President said to me. . . ."

The President. Lyndon Johnson was not "bigger than life," as some have described him; to me he *was* life, real as life as I had known it growing up in Oklahoma. Those long-legged strides of his had covered lots of flat, dusty earth. The wide sweep of his arms as he told a story had described the size of many a cow at an auction. And his barnyard stories, which shocked some people, reminded me of my dad's in happier days, and of Grandma Hern's. He, too, had come from a place where everybody had a touch of manure on his boots, and where outhouses were funny. I felt comfortable around him. He was down-to-earth, the earth I had known, and he was commanding. He demanded perfection from his staff, as fine a performance as he demanded of himself.

On March 1, 1965, the President called Birch over to the White House for a half hour's conversation, the gist of which was to ask him if he felt inclined to speak out for him on Vietnam. Birch came home and asked my opinion. I felt then that I knew little about this war that Lyndon Johnson had inherited, and I thought he must be pursuing the wisest course.

Then, on February 18, we were invited to the White House with a group of twenty-five Senate couples, and the President, Bob McNamara, Hubert Humphrey, and Dean Rusk briefed the men on Vietnam. It began as a social evening, with cocktails in the East Room, and then the men went to the Blue Room for their briefing, and we wives went downstairs to the theater for a movie on the history of paintings in the White House. After the film, Lady Bird said, "Marvella, will you tell us one of your experiences in the White House?" So I told about my purple pills in the fireplace, which seemed so long ago. Ellen Proxmire of Wisconsin told a story and then the curator of the White House, Jim Ketchum, told us a host of anecdotes about the families who had lived there. Vietnam was a world away. A couple of days later, I was at the French Embassy for dinner, seated between the Ambassador and Ben Bradlee, then Washington bureau chief of *Newsweek*. I listened intently to their conversation about Vietnam, noting that the French, who had lost a war there, wanted us to negotiate.

On March 13 we were invited back to the White House again, for an "unofficial" dinner party with a group of friends, including the McGees and Coopers from the Senate, to say goodbye to Angie and Robin Duke, the chief of protocol who had been named ambassador to Spain. Though it was a personal, not-covered-by-press party, it followed the Johnsons' style of entertaining—cocktails and hors d'oeuvres in the Blue Room and East Room, then dinner in the State Dining Room at round tables for eight. "Guess what?" I actually wrote in my diary. "I was at the President's table again. Wow!" (I would have told Mama that Mrs. Vanderbilt and Mrs. Astor were both there, too.) The President was in great form, I remember. "I have just spent three and a half hours with Governor Wallace today," he said, "and I feel I've made progress." I was elated. Birch had been spending sleepless nights about the senseless killings of civil rights demonstrators in Alabama. We had pledged solid support for the President's voting rights bill. Mr. Johnson toasted the Dukes, Angie toasted the President, and Mrs. Johnson spoke. Then the President started teasing his "Bird" with a story from his Senate days. It seems old Senator Theodore Francis Green from Rhode

Island had asked Johnson to sponsor a bill he favored, and see it through—which Johnson did. "I got home too late to keep a dinner appointment and Bird was fit to be tied," the President told us. " 'I'd *promised* the old man,' I told her. 'Well, even Senator Green made it to the party,' Bird said. Now that's what I call efficient management." After dinner there was dancing in the East Room. Lee Udall and I excused ourselves and made our way upstairs (I was surprised to find that there isn't a restroom on the State Floor of the White House), to the family floor, where we found ourselves in the President's bathroom. It was. carpeted in blue, and there was a massage table. He used Ipana toothpaste, I noted.

Just before we left the party, Birch told President Johnson he was going to speak out Tuesday, on Vietnam.

Meanwhile, I was beginning to listen to some of the voices raised against the war, especially those of mothers. Evan and Steve Sinnenberg played for hours with their toy soldiers. After seeing Vietnam on the news every evening, I began to hope that Evan's make-believe wars would be all he'd ever have to face, that his biggest battles would be those of his Little League baseball team. Some Senate wives, such as Janey Hart, had spoken publicly against the war. Others of us just spoke to each other. On July 14, I talked to Bethine Church, and later wrote in my diary:

> She's almost physically sick over Vietnam. We keep sending more and more troops. Now our boys are having to kill women. Now Vietcong women are fighting alongside the men. I personally don't think we're doing right. But just don't know.
>
> July 20—Met Carol Brewster for lunch. We discussed Vietnam. We're both against the military build-up there—of course, we wouldn't say anything publicly. So worried about it.
>
> July 23—Went to small party at Sen. Joe Clark's. All there but Birch were "doves" on Vietnam. They call the rest "War Hawks."

In early June, while accompanying Birch to Purdue to receive his honorary doctorate there, I had slipped on a marble step, cutting a deep gash on my shin bone. There had been a blood clot; it was taking forever to heal. I was doubly annoyed because I was beginning to enjoy traveling around to make speeches in behalf of Mrs. Johnson's beautification bill. On July 24 I limped to the phone. "The White House is calling . . ." It was Lady Bird Johnson. "It's been so long since we've seen you," she said. "Could you and Birch come up to Camp David to have dinner with us tomorrow evening?" Birch had left for Indiana, for a weekend of speaking. He was in the air, I explained, and I asked for a rain check. I felt like soaking my head, as well as my leg. But Birch phoned from Dayton. "Call her right back," he insisted. "Of course, I'll fly home."

It was evening before I could get through to her. When the call from Camp David finally came, they tracked me down at the Embassy of Kuwait. The noise of the party was deafening; I took the phone into the little bathroom. I told Mrs. Johnson that Birch had called, and said he'd come back—but that we would understand if she had already invited someone else. I was embarrassed. She was the soul of tact. "Well, you just tell Birch to go right ahead and make his speech." ("She said it in a nice way," I wrote, "and I don't think—I pray—she wasn't offended.") But then she said, "Just a minute . . ." and a man's voice came on the line: "Hello, honey." I thought it might be Jack Valenti, the President's assistant. The noise of the Kuwaiti party was coming right through the door of the john. "Hello there, honey," he repeated.

"Who is this?" I said.

"Lyndon Johnson."

"Oh, Mr. President. . . ." He told me to bring our hiking boots, swim trunks, and shorts, and for Birch to "call my people at the White House as soon as he can get back, and a White House car will bring you to Camp David."

Birch flew back from Indiana in a small National Guard jet; we met on a Saturday afternoon at the nearly deserted White House and went in a White House car to the Naval Observatory, where we picked up the McNamaras and the Clark Cliffords. We flew over the green Pennsylvania countryside to the Maryland mountain retreat in an eleven-passenger Presidential helicopter. Bob McNamara, just back from Vietnam, was poring over maps and papers of Vietnam, which he spread out for Birch in the chopper. It was to be a working weekend for him.

As we landed, the President drove up to meet us in a light blue convertible, looking much the country gentleman in tan slacks and light brown jacket. Lady Bird, also wearing slacks, came bubbling out of the car with "Him," the ever-present beagle.

It was so peaceful there, surrounded by tall trees and quiet. You could stand still and not hear a sound. The cabins were rustic, but comfortable, with beds that folded up into the walls. The Mc-Namaras brought their fifteen-year-old son; the Jack Valentis brought their little daughter, Courtney Lynda. The Arthur Goldbergs were there—he had just stepped down from the Supreme Court to replace the late Adlai Stevenson at the United Nations.

We all went to the bowling alley—which, I discovered, was the one building without air-conditioning. President and Mrs. Johnson and Horace Busby gave me lessons, but to little avail. My score was 67. Birch, who hadn't bowled in three years, wound up scoring over 200, beating the President, which we supposed he shouldn't have done.

At about 9 P.M. we went to supper in Aspen, the main lodge, as informal as if we were at summer camp. There were two tables of us, all wearing slacks, all very comfortable, served by the Navy stewards who man Camp David. Just after the President asked Mrs. Johnson to say grace, "Him" and Jack Valenti's beagle got into a dogfight underneath our table. My first concern was my injured, bandaged leg—I pulled up my feet. Mrs. McNamara scrambled down underneath the table on all fours, to pull the dogs apart.

The President was drinking diet root beer—I noticed he'd put on quite a bit of weight around the middle—he was as relaxed as anybody around Grandma Hern's harvest board, eating with both elbows on the table, lifting the small dessert dish up close to his mouth. I smiled, remembering how terrified I'd been about minding my table manners. This was just like homefolks. He picked up the Valentis' baby in his lap, hugging her until she squealed. We all talked and laughed, and politics was never mentioned. Birch walked me back to the cabin at 11:30, and then went back to Aspen to visit with the President and his assistants.

Sunday morning, we were up at nine—"Sleep as late as you want to," Lady Bird had said. "Call for juice or coffee, or a car, if you'd like." On our doorstep were copies of the *New York Times*, the *Washington Post*, and the *Washington Star*. Birch went out to play tennis with Jack Valenti; I joined the others at Aspen for a huge breakfast, hotcakes with molasses and syrup, fried and scrambled eggs, grits, bacon, and link sausages. "We've got to get some country sausage up here," the President said, but he ate everything. Luci, who had joined us the evening before with her friend Pat Nugent, said she couldn't eat anything before going to communion.

Her father teased her about Catholicism. "Say hello to the Pope for me," he said. "Yes, sir," said Luci.

We went to church services in the theater, at 12:15. John Chancellor, who would be the new director of Voice of America, and his wife joined us there to hear Mrs. Johnson's Episcopal minister's sermon. The service, also, was very informal—the Valenti dog inside, "Him" outside the door whining to get in. The gist of the sermon appealed to me—that you don't have to go to church to be a good Christian. Since moving from Terre Haute, I had rather drifted away from the church. I hadn't quite sorted out my feelings about religion. I was in a questioning period.

Unable to go into the water because of my leg, I sat at the pool and watched Mrs. Johnson swim. I apologized for being such a poor athlete. "You're like Luci," she said. "She wouldn't touch anything athletic." She told me how she missed Senate Ladies Red Cross, that it had been a "quiet time" for her. "And there are so few quiet times now," she said wistfully. The President was taking a nap.

Lunch was served at four, buffet outside. I spoke to Justice Goldberg. "Wouldn't it be good if we could bring the Vietnam problem into the U.N.?" I asked him. He agreed. "The U.N. has to be preserved," he said, "and the confidence in it restored. It's really on a dying path at this time." He told me how he hated to leave the Supreme Court—it was the ideal spot, he said, his dream of a lifetime. "But if I said no to the President, and the United Nations failed, I would hate myself," he said. And in the next breath, "we've got to restore the President's confidence in the U.N."

As we were finishing lunch, the President came to get Goldberg and they walked and talked privately on the "green" in front of us. The President had a meeting inside the main lodge with McNamara and Clifford, and the top assistants. Birch was not included. Not realizing, I burst in right in the middle, to get my purse.

Lynda had been away on a six-week camping trip. After dinner Sunday, Mrs. Johnson phoned her at the White House, asking her to join us at Camp David. No, she was "just dead." Lady Bird called her husband to the phone, to welcome Lynda home. "I'll go back now and welcome her back," Mrs. Johnson said, and she kissed the President goodbye. They were easily, openly affectionate with each other, I noticed.

But something came up. Within five minutes the President

decided we would all return. Like a double-time movie, we sped out of Camp David and back to the White House, helicopters moving as in a field evacuation. As we stepped down onto the White House lawn, I told the President what a marvelous time we'd had. He kissed me on the cheek and said, "Don't tell anyone about it and we'll do it again sometime." And he razzed Birch even more about his bowling ability.

We came home to house guests, Bob Rock, who was now lieutenant governor of Indiana, and his wife Mary Jo, whom we entertained by taking them to hear Peter, Paul, and Mary and Peter Nero in concert at the Carter Barron theater. Later that evening at our house Mary Travers predicted that "the Democrats will lose in 1968 if we don't get out of Vietnam."

The next day, July 28, the President announced that an additional 50,000 men were being sent to Vietnam, bringing our commitment there to 125,000 troops—and the monthly draft was increased from 17,000 to 35,000. That was also the day he appointed Abe Fortas associate justice of the Supreme Court, in Goldberg's place—and the day, I recall, that our basement flooded almost knee-deep.

Washington itself was knee-deep in dissension about Vietnam. This was the one issue, I discovered, in which I could not follow Lyndon Johnson. It was the first serious political issue on which Birch and I would differ.

Adlai Stevenson once described Washington as a sedate town that ran on "alcohol, protocol, and Geritol." It was not so in the sixties. Hawks and Doves eventually almost stopped speaking to one another; relations became very strained between the southerners who had befriended us and other friends who had championed civil rights in the Senate. And with the situation in the Middle East heating up, we were torn between the views of our cherished Jewish friends, such as the Sperlings, and those of our delightful new Arab friends, Talat and Bessima Al-Ghoussein of Kuwait.

And nowhere, that summer, did I feel the strain on the tightrope more acutely than in our relationships with the Johnsons and the Kennedys. Barbara Howar, whose political antennae were always out, was the first to mention it, back in the spring: "You're going to have to choose between the Kennedys and the Johnsons. This town is dividing up between the two camps and you can't be a friend to both." People were predicting that Bobby Kennedy, now senator from New York, would run against the President in 1968.

In truth, I still felt rather uncomfortable around Bobby Kennedy, as if we weren't on the same wavelength. But Ted and Joan were another matter. I adored them. Birch and Ted were friends, colleagues, political allies in the Senate. They had started out together as the two youngest senators. Joan and I were close friends, with much in common in those days. To choose between them and the Johnsons would have been painful.

Joan and Ted had invited us to join them for a weekend at Hyannis Port, in August. To say I was thrilled was an understatement. On August 20, Evan left for Rehoboth Beach with his grandfather Bayh and Aunt Mary Alice, who had now moved to Washington. I met Birch at National Airport, where we boarded the *Caroline*. We were guests of Ted and Joan; Fred and LaDonna Harris were guests of Bobby and Ethel. Mary McGrory, the columnist, was there, as was cartoonist Charles Addams. After stopping in New York to pick up Jean Smith and her family, we arrived at the Hyannis Port airport, and were met by Bobby and Ethel, Peter Lawford, Joan and her children—and a crowd of tourists snapping pictures and trying to shake everybody's hand. We piled into Ted's convertible, and he drove up lickety-split to the Kennedy "compound," where little John, Jr., ran out to greet us. Three large white frame houses, the Joseph Kennedys', Jean Smith's, and Bobby's, stood near the ocean, sharing a common lawn. Out a way was the Sargent Shrivers' house, more rustic than the rest, and high on a hill overlooking Hyannis Port was Ted and Joan's, with its own private beach at the bottom of the hill.

It was away from the others, and quiet, with a breathtaking view of the sea from their bedroom and sun porch. This was a house of the sea, I thought, decorated in cool shades of blues, greens, and white. In the big bay window of the living room stood an immense ship model, a wedding present from Bob and Ethel; on the coffee table lay a cigarette box from President Kennedy inscribed "To Joan Bennett Kennedy—too beautiful to use." In straw baskets in every room Joan had placed bunches of fresh flowers. The house was streamlined, and childproof, it seemed. Joan had a staff of three—a cook, a governess, and a housekeeper. Kara and Teddy were bouncing about happily, in and out of antics with their crew of cousins.

We all gathered at Bobby and Ethel's for dinner. Bobby had to show me how to eat the steamed clams and lobster—and we laughed together. "There goes my diet," I moaned. "I diet all week long and lose four pounds just so I can gain it all back here on the weekends," Ted laughed.

We all went sailing the next morning, with the sun sparkling on the sea. The two family captains, Ted and Bob, raced each other —Bob in his sleek, elegant new boat and Teddy in the old family boat, the one in which Jack had learned to sail. Poor Ted had as his only crew Fred Harris and Birch, who had never sailed before, and Joan, who was taking lessons, and me. (I added nothing but my weight, I'm afraid.) Bob had as his crew the best sailor in all of New England. Ted won. A photographer following the Teddy Kennedy family that day shouted to us, laughing, "I can prove it, he really did win."

In the Sunday *Boston Globe* that day was a Ted Kennedy family picture, accompanying a story about Joan; in the *New York Times Magazine*, Bob and Ted's picture was on the cover, with a long article about Ted inside. I scanned the stories while the others went swimming (I still kept out of the water). Then we had lunch on Ted and Joan's terrace and in the afternoon, the sailors raced again. Excursion boats jammed with tourists passed close by. "That's Teddy Kennedy sailing that boat," we heard over its loudspeaker. This time, Bobby won.

There were cocktails at the Shrivers' for everybody, followed by dinner, for the eight of us from the Senate, at Ted's. Ted broiled steaks on the grill, with Bobby kibitzing. "You're ruining them," he teased. "They're burned to a crisp," he announced to us. They weren't. There was corn on the cob, green beans, green salad—our favorite Indiana meal. Long into the night, we sat around and talked politics. Bobby was warmer, more relaxed than I'd ever seen him. Perhaps I had been wrong, I thought.

Even though it was raining, Birch and Ted went out to sail in the Sunday race. Joan went for a swim; I took a long nap. Dinner that evening was at the Steve Smiths', the oldest house in Hyannis Port, they told me, built thirty years before the Revolution. Jackie came by for cocktails, the first time I'd seen her all weekend, and left before dinner. Ted told a funny joke after dinner, so dramatic that he leaped up on a chair in front of the crackling fire. I wish I could remember the joke—what I do recall is how he put his arm

The Hern family in Oklahoma in 1898. The two children
are my uncles Orville and Otis, with Grandma Hern.

My mother and I when I was four weeks
old, at our farmhouse.

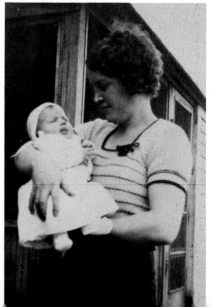

Four generations: at left is Grandma Hern (65 years
old); seated, her father Thomas Jefferson Murphy (93);
and my father (23) at right, holding me in his arms—a
seven-month-old baby.

The fat little girl at the right of the wedding picture is me just before I went on the diet.

Delbert and Bernett and Marvella Hern (six years old).

Driving the tractor at harvest time (I'm second from right).

Mother, Marvella, and Daddy—1947.

Marvella at left; Beverly Smith at right. My song was "The Man Who Paints the Rainbow in the Sky."

June, 1950: left to right, Gloria Fowler, Veldena Jonas, Joanne Pendergraft, Nancy Green. Enid town officials are at the right.

MARVELLA HERN
NEWLY ELECTED
GOVERNOR
of GIRLS STATE

I am sworn in as President
of Girls' Nation.

Sally McTague and I present President Harry Truman
with a Special Citation from Girls' Nation.

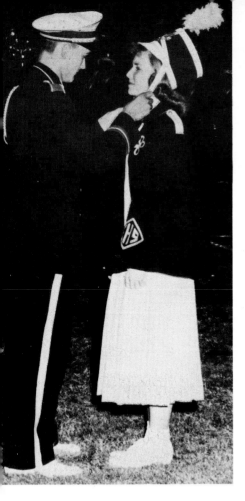

Birch makes his speech for the Farm Bureau contest semi-finals in Chicago, December 10, 1951, the day we met.

Band Queen.

In January, Birch came to visit me in Enid.

In April, Birch invited me to Purdue for Junior Prom.

On August 24, 1952, we were married.

At Indiana State in 1954, just before the car crash.

Marvella and son, Evan, in 1956.

Birch playing on the red tarp with Debbie Vaughan,
Ellen Vaughan, and Evan.

Birch is sworn in as Speaker of the House of the Indiana Legislature in 1959.

Birch graduates from law school,
Marvella from college,
on June 6, 1960; Indiana University.

JFK campaigns for Birch Bayh in 1962.

Elected!

Calling on JFK after the Senate election.

June 19, 1964—the plane crash.

August, 1964—Lynda Bird's costume party at the
White House. Birch and I dressed as Mr. and Mrs.
Benjamin Harrison, Lynda Bird as the Yellow Rose of
Texas.

November, 1965—our trip to South America.

In January, 1967, Lyndon Johnson offered me a job—which I had to turn down.

Birch's second Senate campaign; Joan Kennedy helped us.

Birch and his father, who lived in Washington (1968).

On October 5, the night before I went into the hospital for breast surgery, I danced in a show given by the Women's National Democratic Club.

Women's Wear Daily interviewed us in 1971, when Birch planned to run for President.

Abigail Van Buren ("Dear Abby") helped me campaign for Birch's third Senate term in 1974.

Jane Sinnenberg—closest and most loyal of friends.

Travel! (Here it's Morocco.)

Birch announced he was a candidate for the presidency on October 21, 1975, at our farm near Shirkieville, Indiana.

Speaking for the
American Cancer Society.

With Mrs. Papanicolaou in the East Room of the White
House on May 18, 1978.

Evan and Marvella, November, 1978.

My Aunty Lillian.

Birch and Taze Shepard's birthday, January 22, 1978;
the Shepards are at left and the Rogerses in the middle.

around his wife, before we turned in, and tousled her hair, calling her "Joansie."

We were to get up at 5:30 on Monday morning, breakfast at 6:30, leave for the plane at 6:45. I awoke at three, and never went back to sleep. When we got to the *Caroline*, we discovered we'd left the keys to the trunk of the car—where all our luggage was—back at the house. While Ted raced back to get the keys, they left me on the plane as proof that our group had arrived on time. I'd just lowered my seat back to rest when Bobby came aboard. "You know, there's a bed in the next compartment," he said, and walked with me to the back of the plane. He saw that I was comfortable, reached up to get a blanket, and covered me with it. (I would long remember that gesture, solicitous and almost tender. He really does have warmth, I thought.) I slept almost all the way to Washington, arriving at about 10:30 Monday morning.

Birch (who had caught a dreadful cold after Sunday's drenching race) was called to the White House almost immediately, to have his picture made with the President signing the National American Legion Baseball Week proclamation. Mr. Johnson called him aside. "We missed you this weekend," the President said. "We wanted you to go down the river with us on the *Sequoia* Sunday night." Then he asked, "Did you have a nice time at Hyannis Port?"

It wasn't that the President was clairvoyant; Evan, answering the telephone Sunday night, had reported on our whereabouts.

We returned from Hyannis to celebrate our thirteenth wedding anniversary. It seemed that so much had been crammed into those thirteen years—finishing college . . . law school . . . Evan . . . eight years in the legislature . . . already three years in the Senate. Birch had promised me a quiet date to celebrate, to reflect a bit on our lives. We had reservations at the Talleyrand for dinner and dancing. For two. As I was dressing, a basket of flowers arrived, from the White House. "How did they know it was our anniversary?" I asked Birch.

"I've asked Bill and Judith Moyers to join us tonight," he said. I'd hoped that we would be alone. He started driving toward the White House, to pick up Bill. Judith would join us there, he said. When we pulled up to the gate, there sat Sherrye Henry, in her car. "Birch, the guard won't let me in. Will you identify me?" I wondered what she was doing there.

"Let's go inside," Birch said. "I'll just wait in the car," I said. "But Bill has just decorated his office," he argued. "You'll hurt his feelings if you don't come in to see it." So I walked in. Lloyd Hand walked in with a big gift-wrapped box—and Jack Valenti apologized for not being able to go with us. Then Danny Brewster, the senator from Maryland, and Carol, arrived. "What's going on?" I asked Birch.

"Well, I've just invited a few friends. We're all going to the Talleyrand." But I couldn't figure out why we were meeting at the White House.

"We're meeting in the Diplomatic Reception Room," Vicki Mc-Cammon announced. The room was full—the Howars, the Rogerses, Harry MacPherson, all our friends. Then the big limousines began pulling up to the door. "We're going to the *Sequoia*," Bill Moyers announced.

The big yacht was moored down on the Potomac, on this balmy, moonlit night. Luci came aboard, with Pat Nugent in tow. Her mother and sister were in Texas, she explained. We had drinks, and stood around a bit. The hour was getting later, and I was getting hungry. I whispered to Birch, "Why don't we push off and get started?"

"We're waiting for somebody," he said. About that time, the big black White House limousine pulled up. Out stepped Lyndon Johnson. The whole thing, I found out later, was his idea, even to suggesting some of the guests. I was so excited. I kept wondering if this really could be happening. We cruised down the river that night, stopping only to let Bill Moyers off so he could go back to work. And then the President said, "Let's cruise for another hour," and on we sailed. He was wearing loafers, slacks, and a sport jacket, and sat in the big easy chair set up on the deck just for him. We watched the eleven o'clock news on the boat's television set. Los Angeles, a large chunk of it, was in ruins. Ironically, the Watts riots began just after passage of the President's hard-fought civil rights bill. "Could that happen in Washington? That we could have riots here?" I asked the President.

"I'm sure we could," he replied. "That's why I am pushing so hard for home rule."

Meanwhile, the tightwire stretched tauter. A Washington society columnist reported that we were one of the "few couples close to both the Johnsons and the Kennedys." That was okay, I supposed.

But then Drew Pearson reported on the radio that "the Birch Bayhs tried to sneak away to Hyannis Port with the Ted Kennedys," but that President Johnson had tracked us down via our nine-year-old son.

We continued to be invited for private evenings at the White House—and once after dinner, when the President took the men away for Vietnam briefings that lasted well past midnight, Birch said the Vice President fell asleep and actually snored. Another time, at ten of eight, Lyndon Johnson called, "Come on over for supper" (we'd just finished but would willingly eat again). When we couldn't find a sitter, he insisted that we "bring the boy along." Evan, all dressed up in his gray flannel slacks, was thrilled, though cautioned to behave and advised not to tell his friends, and when we arrived, he was entertained royally by Mrs. Johnson. We also continued to be friends with Luci and Lynda, through both of their weddings (we kept some of Luci's wedding party at our house) and afterward. We also continued to see Ted and Joan Kennedy, at our house or theirs, to talk on the phone, to be friends.

In the midst of it all, we had fun. We tasted every bite of the lighter side of the sixties. We sang all the folk songs—Birch played his guitar—I danced the frug and watusi, pinned a "fall" in my hair, and paid serious attention to shorter and shorter skirts. We cherished the evenings of laughter with our friends.

Washington has been described as a transient city, where friendships are ephemeral, of the moment—not of the bedrock quality of, say, those in Indiana. That is only partially true. We formed lasting personal friendships here, with people of our own age and interests, who could laugh together at the world and at each other. There was a clutch of us—five couples at first—who got together to celebrate birthdays and anniversaries, to take a once-a-year trip to New York, or occasionally to escape to the Greenbrier resort in West Virginia. They happened to be Democrats, naturally. But politics was not what bound us. They were lively, attractive, smart, "savvy," competent—but mostly fun. The men were all in positions where they could flex their ability: Bill Henry, Taze Shepard, Ed Howar, and Paul Rogers. The women were "belles"—some by name (Becky Bell, Marvella Belle) and some by nature. Sherrye Henry was a tall, willowy beauty from Tennessee. Jan Shepard, daughter of Senator Sparkman of Alabama, was also tall, brunet, calm and easygoing. Barbara Howar had a great sense of style, and a natural gift of wit that kept all of us in stitches. Becky Rogers, a striking brunet, was a new bride when we met, whose outgoing nature, warmth, and understanding reached out to me in low periods in my life. We called them our "couples" friends in those days, the "tight ten." After divorce (Howars, Henrys) reduced us to six, we continued our tradition of celebrating important occasions together, the Rogerses, Shepards, and Bayhs (we've survived the years). It gave me a sense of "family" in Washington—and still does.

Without the sustenance of such friendships, I don't think I could have survived the blows that life was to deal me in the years ahead. I certainly could not have done without Jane Sinnenberg. Jane and I moved into McLean, Virginia, at the same time, sharing the same problems of finding a pediatrician, a dry cleaner, a plumber, and the quickest route to Washington. Her husband, Bob, was a successful businessman, not involved in politics.

Our sons were our first link to each other; Steven and Evan were inseparable. They were always staying overnight at one house or the other, and whenever either set of parents took off for a week, we could count on the other to put up a little boy. That's how it began. But as the years went by, Jane and I developed a bond between us that grew stronger. As I once told Birch, "There are two people in this world I can absolutely count on. If I ever decided to do you in, my Aunty in Oklahoma would say, 'Well, dear, I know you must have had a reason.' And Jane would say, 'Quick, I'll help you get rid of the fingerprints.'"

Friends kept me from going absolutely berserk in those crazy days when I was putting so much pressure on myself. Now that I was thirty-two, my body went into even deeper rebellion against the demands I placed on it. Whenever my neck would go "out," the excruciating pain returned. That leg took forever to heal. My hormones were helter-skelter; I'd go on a crying jag for the least reason. Add shots of B-12 to estrogen and thyroid, tranquilizers, and the occasional sleeping pill.

But then there were the rewards. Birch had been appointed to the congressional delegation to the Interparliamentary Union and the North Atlantic Treaty Organization conferences, and wives were invited to both. For Birch, those trips involved hard work. They expanded and enriched my life.

Sometimes the trips were fact-finding expeditions. Sometimes they were dangerous. For three weeks in November, 1965, we went with Fred and LaDonna Harris to look at some of the Peace Corps and foreign-aid work in South America. Until then the term "population explosion" had seemed abstract to me. I came back committed to help, in some way, with the need for birth-control education. We walked through the wretched, teeming slums of the cities. We talked with university students, we met with dedicated Peace Corps workers in the high outreaches of the Andes. We flew in an old World War II amphibian plane deep into the Amazon jungle, where we were met by the students, young Indian girls with rings in their noses and designs painted on their faces, who wanted to show us their educational projects with the native tribes out in the jungle. We flew deeper in, landing on a river, and then hiked a mile through the jungle to a primitive native village. But when it was time to leave, the plane couldn't take off, first because it was stuck in the mud, and then because it was nighttime and there were no landing lights. In the plane were hard wooden benches. I stretched out on one of those, Birch stretched out on the floor, and still caked in mud from the jungle downpour, we wrapped ourselves in mosquito netting. Finally, we did go to sleep and Birch said that the next morning what woke him up was hearing the mosquitoes inside the netting trying to get away from him.

This was a hard trip, one I'm glad I took but which I wouldn't want to repeat. Those Peace Corps volunteers haunted me. What was I doing to add my two cents to solving the vast problems confronting this world of ours? I was trying to keep a home together for a United States senator. But was that enough? After all the activities with which I kept pace, I was feeling frustration, an emptiness inside. I felt I had accomplished so little.

There was so much happening at home, too: Vista, Model Cities programs, the real brigades of the War on Poverty. We believed the dream was possible. I remember going to Indianapolis in January, 1966, to visit a Head Start center there. There was a little girl who had never seen an egg before, whose mother could neither read nor write; nineteen parents had gone back to elementary school after their children enrolled in Head Start. I began to study day care for children, to speak about Head Start.

Evan was doing well in school, his days running smoothly, and there was a new presence in our home, Lachina Morrison, a pretty

Scottish lass of twenty-one, who could drive a car. (Macel had to go home to West Virginia.) I seemed to have organized my life as efficiently as possible, considering the unpredictability of my husband's schedule. I felt that the speeches I was writing and delivering were meaningful. But something was missing.

In April, 1966, I was invited to make a speech at Oklahoma State College in Stillwater. I accepted, with misgivings—it would be my first trip home since Mother's death. I worried about seeing my father. I didn't want to meet his wife. We had been under family strain at home. Birch's sister was in a severe emotional crisis; his father had suffered a serious heart attack. Birch was deeply worried about both of them. I had night-after-night insomnia, dreading to go to Enid.

I stayed in Aunty's house, feeling so odd not to be driving down our old street, so sad at not being met by my mother. I took flowers to the cemetery. There was a double headstone, with my parents' names on it. My father had had mother's grave moved thirteen inches to the north, to make a space for his new wife on the other side. He had ordered a new headstone, with both women's pictures on it. It struck me as more than bizarre, especially since his wife was younger than I.

Daddy came out to Aunty's to see me, all dressed up in his best brown suit that Mother had bought him, wearing a necktie I had given him. He was thicker around the middle, his eyes puffy. His wife was in Tennessee, he said. After lunch, Aunty left us alone. "You look just like my little girl again," he said. He had put me through so much, and here he was just standing quietly, asking for my love.

"To say I'm sorry sounds so little," he said. "But I am sorry." Seeing him standing there so meekly, with love in his eyes, was a comfort, but it wasn't easy. And yet, he was still my father, despite everything. I loved him, felt sorry for him.

From my own dilemma as a daughter, I went to Stillwater, to give a speech at a conference entitled "Action—the Association of Women Students." It was the strongest I had ever made. Influenced by a book I had just read (long after most of my friends did, I am sorry to say), Betty Friedan's *The Feminine Mystique*, I spoke on the importance of defining new roles for women in modern society, of the women's revolution, of the possibilities of combining a career with marriage. Reading *The Feminine Mystique* was one of those compass-point experiences for me. I recognized myself in its pages. It put my thinking into focus.

Gladys Sperling called me that spring. Muriel Humphrey had told her I looked "awfully tired." Would Birch and I come down to Miami to join her and Mike for a week's rest? Would we! We stayed in their suite in the Eden Roc, sleeping late and trying to unwind in the sun. It was to be a quiet time together, with no conferences to attend, no paperwork at night. However, it seemed that our major conflicts always erupted on vacation. We both knew why: at home there was never any time for a personal discussion, never time to iron out the day-to-day difficulties that arise in any marriage. They got packed away in our suitcases with our bathing suits, to come up the first time we were alone together, the very times we were supposed to be resting and forgetting our troubles, on vacation.

It erupted in Miami, all the vague dissatisfaction that had been building up since we entered this hectic life in Washington. I tried to explain to him why I was unhappy, why I didn't feel fulfilled in my life. He didn't understand. In fact, he was shocked. We sat up half the night, talking. Finally, he asked, in exasperation, "But what do you *want*? What is it that I haven't given you?"

"What I want isn't yours to give," I tried to tell him. The education, the experiences that being married to a senator had given me had carried me to heights beyond my wildest dreams—to heights from which I could see that my ability to make a contribution *in my own right* had never been tested. "But you have made a contribution, an enormous contribution to my career," he said.

I remember replying to him, "Look. If you were married to a rich woman like Barbara Hutton, and she could keep you in luxury, even, and have you lie on the French Riviera and sip champagne and go to parties all the time, would you feel that *your* life was making a contribution? That you were doing something?"

I could see his wheels turning. Though the analogy was not an exact one, he could suddenly see a glimmer of what I was trying to tell him. "I must work, Birch," I said. "I must have my own work. I am busy all the time, but my life is not fulfilling."

We went back to our whirlwind with the seed planted, but the discussion unresolved. He was busy with electoral college reform and with a special investigation into foreign countries that were profiteering on steel sales to Vietnam. He was debating Senator Dirksen on the prayer amendment. Or flying off to Indiana to make a speech. He does not understand my need, I thought. I went to the Senate to watch him preside over a civil rights bill debate. He wrote me a note. "Hi, Beautiful. Like your hairdo."

As when I entered college, there was nobody to give me direction. But unlike the ill-suited young home ec student that I had been, I began to search for a direction. What do I want to do? To work. To really work, and earn money.

But then Birch interjected: "I'm up for reelection in 'sixty-eight. I need you to help campaign. After that you can do anything."

⁀

On September 2, at Becky Rogers' birthday party, Paul kept talking about how we ought to start laying the groundwork now for Birch to be President someday. I laughed. "It looks as if the Kennedys are going to be around for a long time. There's Bobby and Teddy, and then Bobby's son, Joseph third, and then John-John. . . ."

"We ought to be able to slip a Bayh in there somewhere," Paul said. I thought we both were joking.

That fall, after Evan entered school, I was asked by the Democratic National Committee Women's Speakers' Bureau to travel again, speaking in behalf of the Democratic congressional candidates. I agreed. Birch was in Indiana every weekend all autumn, campaigning for Democrats there. I was lonesome. That was the fall, I recall, that I read *Gone With the Wind* aloud to Evan.

So in October I went out on the "Flying Caravan" again, this time with Jocelyn Monroney, pushing political candidates, giving speeches on inflation, education, highway safety, and conservation—in Boise, Spokane, Salt Lake City. The questions by reporters, and from the audiences, were more pointed and issue-directed than in previous trips. I was glad I had done my homework—glad to see that women speakers were being taken seriously.

I came back exhilarated. I wondered how I could spend the same amount of energy househunting, taking care of termites, shut-off water, broken washing machines, helping Evan with homework, dressing for an embassy—and drop from exhaustion. My father was drinking again, and crying to me about trouble with his wife.

It was a blessed escape, after the November, 1966, elections, to join Birch on a trip to the NATO conference in Paris. I went with the delegation to Rome and Lisbon, and unwound into history.

We talked about what we would do if we lost the '68 election. Birch said he might like journalism. I might like journalism, too, I thought. If I were a journalist, I would certainly know how to look underneath the facade of a political wife. Take me, for example.

I have a reasonably good set of brains, and, since childhood, I have been highly motivated; I was ambitious. After all, weren't those among the components for achieving the American dream? In 1966, however, I would never have dared state those qualities publicly. Women were taught that to do so, even if it meant assessing themselves honestly, was overly aggressive, not ladylike. Pushy.

I also tend to be strong-willed, short-tempered, and rather emotional. Never could I admit publicly to those dubious qualities, either, because as a politician's wife I should strive to be perfect, above criticism. After all, ten minutes in a no-parking zone, and somebody writes a letter to the editor of the *Indianapolis Star*. I should be serene, well-groomed, polite, diplomatic, unassuming, and sweet. If I just happened to be articulate, or talented, or intelligent, those would be extra assets. To further my husband's career, that is.

When I thought of all the information and experience that I had amassed during these four years in Washington, I wanted to *use* that education. As my mother told me, to "put back in this world some of what you have taken out."

We had decided to build a house in the District of Columbia. Commuting to McLean was consuming too much of our precious time. Building this house, making all the tiny decisions involved in such a project, was consuming too much of my own time. I was going over plans with the builder on January 7, 1967, when Birch called. "The President wants to see us *both* down at the White House at three P.M.," he said.

We appeared at the Oval Office, not knowing what to expect. President Johnson sat us down on the couch, and pulled his rocker over close to me. He showed us some papers—statistics proving he had come much closer than the last two Presidents in predicting the budget. "So you see, there is no credibility gap," he said. "But I can't make up my mind whether or not to run again—I'll make that decision in 'sixty-eight." He talked on, not much like a candidate, we thought. He talked about the "Georgetown crowd" being "down on him"—said he didn't know what they meant when they criticized his "style." "I'm just an Okie, a Texan, a Hoosier, just an American doing his best," he said. "There's no way I can be Ivy League." My heart went out to him. I knew how he felt.

Then his voice changed, down to business: "We need to give the Democratic National Committee a new image. We need somebody on the Committee who is Christian, young, sexy, and can talk to the Luci Johnsons of this country." He turned to Birch. "I want your wife to be vice-chairman of the Democratic National Committee."

I went numb. I'd thought he was leading up to asking Birch something.

He went on, looking at me—"You'd be your own boss. If Evan has the measles you can stay home. But you'd have a staff and an office at Democratic National Headquarters—and a good salary so you can buy pretty clothes and travel all around all over the country. . . ."

My mouth must have dropped open, because he said, "Now I realize you have to talk this over. Will you give me your answer in three days?" We talked for an hour and a half.

We went out, speechless, to McLean. I could feel the wanting in my stomach. I wanted that job more than I had ever wanted anything in my life.

Birch was not sure. He called the top men from his staff—I called them his "henchmen"—to come out to our house in McLean. The big decision was not what was right for Marvella, but how this would affect the 1968 Senate campaign. They were very clear in their opinions. "This will cost Birch votes in Indiana." It would be, they said, "very unwise politics" for me to be on the payroll of the DNC, for me to be publicly that close to the President.

I remember walking the floor as they talked, looking out the window, and crying. Katie Louchheim had held that job, when I first met her. Katie, whom I so admired, who was now Ambassador to UNESCO. Margaret Price had it this year, but the President wanted to appoint her to another position, he told us. For me, this had been like offering candy to a starving baby. A top position, with a staff and big salary would be heady stuff to anybody, but put that offer in the Oval Office of the White House and have the President of the United States look at you and say, "I need you. You are the best person in this country for this job." It was more than just a job offer to me. It was the culmination of dreams. It could be the beginning of a career of my own, one I had been postponing for so long.

Birch never told me, "You can't take this job." He knew better than that. But the advisors talked on. It was implied that if he ran and lost, even by a little bit, I would be blamed.

After the two advisors left, I was still walking the floor. Birch almost got mad at the President. "He really has put us in a dilemma. He has put us in a box by offering you this job."

I couldn't answer. I could tell that he wished it had never happened. To me, it was crystal clear: This was the job for which I had spent my life preparing.

I went to Dr. Stafford Hawken for a physical. (This new doctor, an obstetrician-gynecologist, had stopped the estrogen shots and put me on estrogen pills—and stopped the purple tranquilizers.) Perhaps, with my sorry health, I couldn't stand up to the job. It was his opinion that I could. "If it were my wife, I don't feel that I could stand in her way for a minute," he said.

We lost a week talking it over, back and forth, back and forth. My efforts in Indiana could "make the difference" in his upcoming Senate race, Birch and his staff aides insisted: "Look how much 'Marvella's last-minute appeal' had helped in 'sixty-two."

Finally, on Friday the thirteenth of January, we walked into the President's office again.

"Mr. President, I need her in Indiana," Birch said, and spelled out his reasons why.

Lyndon Johnson understood, he said. "What is most important is for you to be reelected, Birch. Even if you have to campaign against me. Even if you have to speak out against me." (That, I thought, was a great and generous spirit.)

It is a hard business for anybody to say no to the President of the United States when he offers you a job or says he needs you—even if you are president of the Bendix Corporation, or a Supreme Court justice like Arthur Goldberg. When you take a girl who has always wanted something, has had nothing this important in her own life since being president of Girls' Nation, and you put her here in the Oval Office with the President, to say no, against every yearning that is within her, it is almost unbearable.

I told him that it was the greatest honor I had ever received, that his confidence in me meant more than he would ever know. But that my first duty was to my husband and marriage.

"Well, of course I understand," he said. "Mrs. Johnson has been the greatest political asset to me. But I know that you could have done a great job for us here as well, Marvella."

Outside, as we drove out the White House gates, Birch reached over and took my hand. "I know how much you wanted that job. I'll never forget what you gave up for me."

I couldn't answer. There was no voice in my throat.

He said in later years that it was the worst mistake he had ever made.

Chapter 8

During the two months since turning down President Johnson's job offer, I had vowed to get in high gear for Birch's 1968 campaign. Already, Helen Ryan had filmed a half-hour campaign piece in Washington, "The Senator's Lady," to be shown throughout the state. Now, with these initial speeches to women's groups, my trips back to Indiana would be more frequent, more focused on getting Birch reelected. Between speeches came interviews. Ann Cologne, a television interviewer in Indianapolis, asked a tough question.

"Do you have any political ambitions for yourself?"

"Oh, no," I answered sweetly. "One politician in the family is enough."

That had been our decision; we would abide by it. I knew I would have to summon all the forces within me to battle a sense of regret.

The evening before the interview, Agnes Woolery, the state Democratic vice-chairman, briefed me on political realities in Indiana. Birch's advisors had been right on one score—that Johnson was unpopular in Indiana was an understatement. The conservatives were up in the air about the war against poverty, the liberals about the war in Vietnam. The Republicans were denouncing the Job Corps as yet another "dole to eat up tax dollars." The Democrats were outraged that the busy President "didn't even say hello" to the Indiana county chairman when they visited the White House.

Back home in Washington, we held our first strategy session with Birch's staff, at our house. It would be a very different campaign from 1962's; there would have to be more advance scheduling, more organized fundraising. And with the Senate likely to be in session right up to the end, all of Birch's speech acceptances in Indiana would carry a "conditional" clause so that people back home would understand if it "becomes necessary to call and cancel at the last minute because of Senate votes. In that case, Mrs. Bayh would substitute for the Senator." In addition to her own speaking schedule.

I remember baking a chocolate cake for that meeting, and feeling a surge of importance at my role. I was needed in a way that I hadn't been in six years. I would be a partner again.

A few days later, Katie Louchheim invited me to lunch, along with Jane Wirtz, Loraine McGee, Jean Kinter—all women who had been involved in Democratic campaigning. We talked mostly about equal rights for women, about women's groups, and about how to tap the vast resources of women's unused talent in this country. "The President is disappointed to find that so few 'qualified' women are available for top jobs," Katie related. "He said he's found that if they are married, they can't move to Washington because of *his* job. They always have to do what their husbands want them to."

"I find that hard to believe," one of the other women said.

I don't, I thought to myself.

I had to hurry home. Birch and Evan were taking me out to supper and then to the airport. I had to make a speech to the Business and Professional Women in Indianapolis, another at a tea in Martinsville, then back to Indianapolis for a television interview (I was asked my views on fashions) and for a speech at Beth El Temple.

On May 10, 1967, the day after I got home, President Johnson called Birch to his office for a talk. Among other things, Birch said, the President told him, "You concentrate on being the politician this year. And tell Marvella to work real hard at getting you elected—and afterwards, I'll have a job for her." (And then he said, "I cannot sleep, worrying about Vietnam.")

Johnson's promise of a job gave me a hope that fueled me throughout the beginning days of the campaign. Partners with Birch now, when I am needed; and after our house is built, after Evan is ensconced in St. Albans School, after the 1968 election—I might be able to have a career of my own.

Birch and I talked long into the night. His perceptions about women were changing, slowly, as were mine. He was such a champion of equal opportunity, of equal rights for Americans, and yet he just had never really thought about women as lacking in those opportunities. It seemed logical to wonder: If I, who had been so blessed in so many ways, felt "unfinished," how must the woman feel who had not been so lucky, who had to earn a living and who had not been prepared for it? In the investigations of Operation Head Start I had made, I found out that the vast majority of working mothers worked, not for "fulfillment," but for economic survival. They *had* to work. How many of those were in "dead end" jobs, with no hope for advancement or development? Perhaps he should look into the problems of being a woman in our society, I suggested.

The conversation came back to Us. "You've always said that I was your career," Birch said.

"So long as I feel I'm contributing something, you are," I answered. "But if I feel less than a full partner, then I feel that I am not fully utilizing the gifts God gave me. Do you remember the story of the 'talents' in the Bible, where the man hid his talent under the bushel, and it didn't multiply?"

"But you do feel fulfilled when you are a full partner?" he asked.

"Yes," I said. "Then I feel we are One, as the love song says, that I am part of a whole. But," I pointed out for perhaps the seventieth time, "I haven't felt a partnership, not really, since we moved to Washington."

I also needed a feeling of security, I explained. I kept worrying about that, especially after Mother's death and Daddy's behavior. I had a haunting fear of being left alone, and not being able to support myself if something should happen to Birch. Since the plane crash, that fear froze me every time he stepped into a small plane. I needed to know that I could put food on the table for Evan and me. Besides, I had struggled so hard to get my college education, and I wanted to use it. I wasn't doing anything concrete, anything on my own.

He still couldn't quite understand what I was talking about. But then perhaps I didn't either. Not yet.

"This is no way to live. After this election," he said, "we're going to have more time together. I promise you that. After we win this election." So much in our lives hinged upon that election.

Politics is a year-round guessing game in Washington, and, I discovered early on, the guessing is not much different from that in Terre Haute, or Des Moines, or New Orleans, or Enid.

May 18, 1967

Met Tom and Neva Wicker of the *New York Times,* for dinner at the Jockey Club. Bethine and Frank Church joined us.

Tom Wicker predicts that Rockefeller will be President. Church believes it will be Reagan. Everyone feels that Percy is the sleeper. We talked about how President Johnson does not project well on TV. He is such a great man in person. Talked about the credibility gap and how it would be to Johnson's advantage for Wallace to run on a third ticket.

Neva Wicker does not feel there will be any Negro riots in Washington this summer. I certainly hope not. We discussed the present college-age generation trying to find themselves, and doubting. We thought that our own age, perhaps, did not doubt enough.

Birch had begun a staggering schedule that spring, flying to Indiana in the evenings to speak, returning to Washington by noon the next day to vote in the Senate. I was busy writing speeches, and planning the trip to Oklahoma. Enid High School was presenting me their Pride of the Plainsmen award—as much a thrill to me as Birch's honorary doctorate at Purdue had been to him. But my emotions were so mixed about going that I felt like a too tightly wound spring.

In January I had seen Daddy at his worst. I had been home for a day, to visit Aunty and Uncle Oren on Uncle Oren's seventy-third birthday. Uncle Oren had been bitter, recounting the times my father had beaten my mother. Without a penny to lose, Daddy had been playing the stock market, and losing heavily. He and his wife had been on a week-long binge, without eating; the car had been wrecked; holes were burned in the furniture; the dog had died from not being fed. And now, Daddy was in the hospital.

I called Dr. Leroy.

"Don't go down to the hospital," he warned. "It will just tear you up."

"But will it help Daddy, my being there?" I asked.

"Only a little. And only if he recognizes you."

"I'm afraid he's going to harm somebody, or harm himself," I said. "He's destroying himself. Is there any way, any way to have him committed, until he gets well?"

"Not under Oklahoma law," Dr. Leroy answered. "He cannot be committed by anyone other than himself unless he has committed a criminal act."

I went to Memorial Hospital, wearing a scarf and dark glasses, hoping nobody would recognize me, hoping to protect Birch from any unsavory publicity—and really hoping that Daddy would be asleep. My cousin Bill Tharp waited for me in the hall.

There was a nurse beside his bed. Glucose was being fed into his veins. His face was gray and bloated, beard-stubbled and stained, his eyes swollen almost shut. He looked at me as if I were a mirage, and said, thick-tongued, "They called you!" He could not say two words without hiccupping, but he stammered out his despair about money. "My nerves, my nerves. I cannot stand it," he cried.

I was not prepared for what I saw. He had been drinking for days, not eating at all. I had never seen anybody in that condition before, let alone Daddy. It tore me to pieces.

"We've got to talk about *you*, Daddy," I said. "Surely, you realize by now that you cannot lick this illness alone. I would commit you to a hospital for treatment if I could forcibly do so, but I can't. Please, please, in the name of everything you have ever loved, will you go away for help?"

"Yes, yes, I will," he mumbled. He did not even know what he was saying.

I caught my plane and left, despairing at how he looked, feeling that my visit accomplished nothing. Through those next few months, as we were beginning Birch's campaign effort, I had waited, hoping against hope to hear that Daddy would seek treatment. I knew that I had to carry on with my life, with Birch's career. As always, I just piled on more activities—then wondered why I was always losing my temper, lashing out at the slightest offense.

Now, three months later, I was sitting in a Nashville airport on my way to Oklahoma, to accept my award, writing in my diary about my fears. I was afraid to go—irrationally afraid my father's wife would try to harm me. He had phoned, insisting that I meet her. When I arrived, my first stop was at the cemetery. He sent me a corsage of baby orchids and he phoned me at Aunty's, sounding very "down." He had lost $23,000 last year—and because of drought the wheat harvest would be almost nothing this year. He would see me at the high school, he said.

It was a morning ceremony, on a school day, the school-hall odors and class bells so familiar I was awash in sentiment. Even the students looked familiar, faces that reminded me of people who were in school there sixteen years before. D. Bruce Selby, that cheerleading principal who had prodded me to excel, shared the Pride of the Plainsmen award as did (posthumously) Governor Francis Cherry of Arkansas. I was filled with pride in my old school —they were still winning "firsts" in everything. And they handed out $100,000 in college scholarships that day.

Daddy was in the audience. He came with me to the Home Ec room, where there was a reception, and stood by very patiently and sweetly while I greeted my old friends.

Daddy and I had lunch at the Holiday Inn. "I want it to be the same again between us," he said.

I told him I loved him, that I wanted only the best for him.

"She's not in your class," he said apologetically. "Not on your intellectual level."

I didn't want to hear him talk like that. It was too demeaning for him, the pedestal too uncomfortable for me.

"Of course I'll meet her," I said. And I did, going to my mother's house for the first time since the funeral, for only a few minutes, and it was less painful than I had feared. Perhaps time is a healer, perhaps I could live with the fact that 2024 West Oklahoma and all it had meant to me no longer existed. I had discovered that I could not live with total estrangement. Now if I could somehow have a new relationship with my father, if this pretty young woman he had married could take good care of him, if he could continue without alcohol. . . .

I came back to Washington praying for a respite from his tangled life.

But I could not escape a sense of sorrow closing in that spring. Indiana mothers and fathers who had sons missing in Vietnam were calling, day and night. Compared to their loss, my own problems seemed small. We were so glad to see our friend Ted Yates return safely from his tour in Vietnam. Ted, a producer and reporter for NBC News, and his wife Mary had been our friends since 1964, when he and Birch were among the JayCees' "Ten Outstanding Young Men." We had especially enjoyed their company in Washington this spring. At the White House one night, Ted kept us spellbound with his stories of the bravery of the young American soldiers he had met in Vietnam.

Late in May, Ted went off to the Middle East, where he would film a report on the Arab-Israeli situation, which shortly thereafter erupted into the Six Day War. Ted was killed on the first day.

I felt so sick inside. The night we heard the news about Ted, June 6, we were at dinner at the Swiss Embassy. I sat between the Ambassador of Ceylon and a Swiss journalist, both of whom were proud of their neutralist countries. Both felt strongly that we should again stop the bombing in Vietnam, the bombing that had gone on for over a year now, with the exception of a few days at Christmas. "It really has not accomplished anything," said the ambassador. "More Americans were killed last week than ever before."

"The majority of the world is against you in this war," added the Swiss.

June 14, 1967

I am sick at heart. Sam Beecher, our dear friend from Terre Haute, called last night, telling us that Quentin, their only son, was missing in Vietnam. His helicopter went out over the water three days ago. Margaret could not even talk on the phone. They asked Birch to find out anything that he could. He has been up all night, trying. As Sam said, "You keep thinking about what he was like, what he did when he was five or six years old."

I went into Evan's room, my Evan at almost twelve, sound asleep in his bed. How would I feel if this were Evan? I wept for Margaret Beecher, and for Quentin's young bride, and for Mary Yates. DAMN! Will wars ever stop?

Evan was the star pitcher in Little League baseball that summer. I got glazed eyes and sunburn watching him play. Baseball, it seemed, would be with us for quite awhile. Birch came through, dropping everything to drive out to McLean to see his boy play baseball and to help coach the team. It became a bond between father and son, one that strengthened our family.

Of all times to build a house, we had to choose that year before an election. Even I, who am such a stickler for detail, got bogged down in all the details of building. It was a Williamsburg colonial on a cul-de-sac of similar homes, more compact than our McLean house, on a tiny lot. (Lyndon Johnson had been right. We were able to realize a profit on the sale of the suburban property for a down payment, and to secure what was probably Washington's last 6 percent mortgage loan for construction.) But the real saving would be in the commuting time. Evan would be a short walk from St. Albans, his new school. But Evan was miserable about moving. And each day brought some new disaster in the construction: The kitchen couldn't be installed until Sears delivered the window shutters, which took weeks longer than promised; the stairs were too close to the front door. And on and on until my mind was running over with doorknobs, bathroom fixtures, paint colors, the myriad details of starting-from-the-ground-up.

In the midst of all this Birch made a trip to Israel, and I couldn't sleep, worrying for his safety. Then we took Evan to camp at Culver Military Academy in Indiana, his first summer away from home, albeit for only seven weeks. But as I watched my young soldier, marching in his camp uniform, I could not stop thinking about Quentin Beecher. On the way back, Birch and I exchanged harsh words about Vietnam. It was a dilemma: We both felt strongly positive about Lyndon Johnson, and yet we differed about this war. Birch had served in the military and he had strong convictions about the need for our presence there; he felt that with support from the American people, the President's policies would eventually be proved right. I felt just as strongly, by now, that Birch should put all of his energies toward trying to stop the war.

Poor Birch. We exchanged harsh words about more than Vietnam. He had picked up a case of dysentery in the Middle East, and, as a result, was exceedingly cross. He had managed to be absent while we were packing up to move to Washington from McLean. Now, all of a sudden, he was joining Evan in opposing the move.

For two days we huffed and puffed. Finally I said to him, "We are acting like they did in *Divorce, American Style*." Birch started laughing, and then I started, and we threw our arms around each other and laughed until tears ran down our cheeks. The marriage was strong, and we both knew it. Like most people, however, we had let the irritants pile up.

The next three days only put into perspective for both of us just how fortunate we were. Margaret Beecher and Quentin's young bride came to Washington, still hoping against hope to find word

of Quentin; then, also from Indiana, came Ann Foltz, who had just
lost her husband at home. And Daddy called, with the sad news
that our dear Dr. Leroy had died in a plane crash.

Aug. 25, 1967

> The week that was. I could never live through it again. We
> moved into an unfinished house. Movers were late. Repairmen
> didn't show up. Refrigerator, air conditioner didn't work. Torrential
> rain, roof leaked into attic. Sod wasn't delivered. Part of kitchen
> wasn't delivered. Tile man didn't show up. Carpet man shoved
> red silk roses in front of my new white draperies, and they faded
> permanent red streaks on them. I'd work until 2 A.M., then up at
> 6 to be dressed when men arrived. 15 or 20 men in and out of
> house in one day. Finally so exhausted I would burst into tears
> when each new thing went wrong. Evan came home from Culver,
> a lieutenant, crying about new school.
>   Luncheon at White House with Mrs. Johnson. Luncheon on
> *Sequoia* with Mrs. Rusk. Off to Indiana to Democratic Editor's
> Conference. Returned to find wrong color tile had been laid.
> Wrong cabinet in basement bathroom. Birch's suit pants lost by
> cleaners. Bought $40.00 worth of groceries. Took Evan to see
> *Oklahoma*. Had wheels aligned. Had to buy 3 new tires. Birch
> left early for Indiana for 3 days. When he returns on Monday
> will go straight to office and then take Evan to baseball game.
> I won't get to see him until Tuesday morning. Went alone to
> dinner party at Sulgrave Club. Talked with many influential
> people who want to help Birch in campaign. Hope contributions
> will be sizeable. Tomorrow: electricians, plumber, yard men,
> telephone man.

Despite my plans to campaign in Indiana all that year, Evan's ad-
justment to a new neighborhood, a new school, a new house, seemed
to be paramount at that time. My campaigning in Indiana would
have to wait until spring. Picnic lunches in Rock Creek Park, going
on "nature trips," playing miniature golf, going swimming together
—Evan and I had fun that fall. He went out for the football team,
and before long, Number 86 was one of St. Albans' wildest partisans.
   The John Logans gave a fundraiser in Washington for us that
fall. I was embarrassed. Asking strangers for money for a campaign
is painful enough; asking friends is mortification. "But it is done,"
Polly Logan assured me, "all the time." To top it all, Birch arrived
an hour late, because the President had detained him with a long

talk on Vietnam. I stood in the receiving line alone until he got there. At the Logans' elegant Tudor estate, Firenze House, which is now owned by the Italian Embassy, the party included much of "Old Washington"—people who had become our friends, people who watched politicians come and go. There was Gwen Cafritz, the millionaire developer's wife, who shared honors with Perle Mesta as "hostess with the mostest."

"If we lost this election, and had no title, I wonder how many of our friends would still be around," I asked her.

"If I lost all my money I wonder who my friends would be," she replied.

Reality-facing entered into our election plans. A politician's future is so uncertain, it would be maddening not to consider alternatives. What would we do if we lost the election? My sixth-grader was on the football team, working hard at an excellent school; my house was here; the excitement of our Washington life was almost enough to sustain us through the separations. Birch was holding hearings on representation in Congress for the District of Columbia. "Have them elect one senator," I teased, "and then get elected yourself. That way you won't have to spend most of your time in the air."

Birch, however, maintained that he wasn't going to lose.

Birch's political skills, developed in the Indiana State House, were coming to the fore in the Senate. His personality, so easygoing and jovial, was perfectly suited to this forum. He could battle a senator on one bill, and seek the same man as an ally on the next. His manner concealed the fact that he was shrewd and studious and extremely hardworking, qualities that even in men are apt to provoke enmity if clearly exposed.

The Senator. His staff all called him that, and, I noticed, even I had begun to refer to him that way in my diary. He had grown, grown, grown in those six years, and my pride grew with him. On February 10, his amendment on presidential succession had been ratified by Minnesota and Nevada, leading to its inclusion as the 25th Amendment to the Constitution; my husband was the first freshman senator to accomplish this feat since the signers themselves. Now, he was working on a way to alter the archaic "electoral college" method of electing the President through direct elections, on that bill to provide representation for the District of Columbia, and, to my everlasting delight, on a bill to insure equal rights for women in this country. But I am not writing a book about my Senator. I'll leave that to the historians.

In 1968, however, I was quite ready to go to work for the re-election of this man, although I wished he would be tougher. People in Indiana were calling me to ask help in getting their letters and phone calls answered. A friend who wanted to contribute to the campaign had called the office several times, and had had no response; the staff was squabbling among itself, dividing the office up into "clods" and "kings." It was evident, I thought, from those first strategy sessions, that a few heads needed to roll. If Birch were too tenderhearted for decapitation, I told him, then he needed to hire a precision-minded, toe-the-line administrator. A campaign needs an incredible amount of selfless teamwork, not a bunch of ambitious employees jockeying for position. In those campaign meetings, I tried my best to "shape up" the office to my own perfectionist standards. It was my mistake.

I remember Christmas shopping with Evan that year. When we were in Sears buying Irish handkerchiefs for Daddy Bayh, the saleslady introduced herself to me. She was the wife of a former member of Congress who had first been elected the year we were, and then had been defeated. "I wouldn't go through another campaign for anything in this world," she said. But I wanted to. I had convinced myself that it was my career, too.

The President and the Vice President urged Birch to go to Vietnam. I didn't want him to go, nor did P. A. Mack, our "best man" and Birch's closest friend. Politically, it would portray him as too closely aligned with the Administration. My feelings were more selfish. I heard that Senator and Mrs. Percy were fired on when they went to Vietnam, and I was afraid for him. Birch went in January.

I had a card from him: "I've never been so confused in my life."

I was just glad to see him back at Dulles Airport, confused or not. His strongest impression, he told me, was of the corruption in government there. "If they've done nothing to make progress in government in six months, we should reconsider our involvement." I was glad he went, if the trip at least forced him to question the war more strongly. He told me about "our boys," how they were fighting an uphill battle, how they impressed him—boys only six years older than Evan.

War. It surrounded us. There were students chanting in the streets, burning draft cards, moving to Canada. Eartha Kitt's attack on Mrs. Johnson about the war, at the White House luncheon for "women doers," appalled me, however. It was neither the time, place, nor person to attack. At Birch's fortieth birthday party on January 28, Lynda and her bridegroom, Chuck Robb, a captain in the Marines, spoke about it.

"Whenever they attack my father, I don't pay too much attention," Lynda said, "for as Truman said, 'if you can't stand the heat, get out of the kitchen.' Dad asked for the heat by getting into politics. But my mother has never said an unkind thing. And for her to be attacked is another story." I agreed. At the party, Birch proposed a toast to the President.

Two days later, I went into Indiana on my first real campaign swing for the '68 election. It would be a tough one. The Republicans had turned out an energetic thirty-five-year-old state legislator, an excellent speaker named William Ruckelshaus, who started out by attacking the Johnson Administration.

I was shocked at the depth of the anti-Johnson feeling I found, even among our own campaign workers. One of our best supporters walked out on the State of the Union speech telecast, he said. People all over Indiana believed that Johnson was lying to them. If the people only knew the agony Johnson was going through, I thought.

On the way home from Indiana, our plane stopped at Charleston, West Virginia. I saw two coffins, wrapped in khaki, being taken from the plane. Their families were waiting for them.

Had I taken that job for President Johnson, would I have been able to tell him how I felt?

I do not know.

When the war was expanded in 1964, less than a handful of senators had opposed it. Four years later, the small Senate opposition to the war was led by the respected Senator Fulbright. Eugene McCarthy of Minnesota had gone outside the Senate to express his convictions; he provided a rallying point for dissenters throughout the country by announcing his intention to oppose Johnson for the Democratic nomination.

One of my husband's aides had to brief me carefully on Birch's position on Vietnam (Birch did not have the time, and our sessions on that subject usually led to an argument) as most of the Indiana questioners zeroed in on the subject. I had to represent his views, and not my own.

Right at campaign kickoff time, I blew another fuse at the staff. With Vietnam, inflation, our cities in flames uppermost in voters' minds, Birch's office had sent out a press release about the senator's trying to find out what kind of food could be given a turtle which was losing its toenails—just the kind of little, idiosyncratic item that could mushroom into a deciding factor in a campaign.

And we discovered that Ruckelshaus, too, had a "secret weapon." Jill Ruckelshaus was young, bright, articulate, energetic, and spoke to the issues. For the first time, I would have a counterpart, if not an "opponent." The Republicans were rolling their big guns into Indiana this election—and the local Democrats, like Democrats at the national level, were squabbling among themselves. Fence-mending would take a good part of our energy; walking a political tight-wire on Vietnam, another good part.

Chet and Tippy Huntley came down from New York to celebrate my thirty-fifth birthday on February 14. Our Evan was delighted to learn that they had named a prize bull on their ranch "Evan." Becky Rogers (Paul was in Florida) and Jan and Taze Shepard joined us for dinner at Le Provencal, hairdresser Jean-Paul's new French restaurant. Talat and Bessima Al-Ghoussein, who were dining with the Dean Rusks, would join us at our house later.

After our meal, Birch was called to the telephone. "Unwrap your gifts later; we need to get home," he told me. Chet and Tippy got into our car, Jan and Taze followed. "Follow me," Birch said to Taze.

"You're going the wrong way," I pointed out to Birch, and said to the Huntleys, "Good grief, he is gone so much he can't find his own house." Again, I did not tumble until we pulled up at the White House gate. Birch's phone call had been an invitation from the President.

Mrs. Johnson, wearing a long, gold-colored gown, invited us to join them upstairs in the family dining room while they finished dessert. The President steered me to his right, and ordered coffee for us.

He was in good spirits, but I was distressed to see how perceptibly he had aged, his hair gray now, his face lined. Twice during dessert, an aide brought in a folder of material for him to read.

Chet, who supported the President on Vietnam, couldn't resist advising him a bit: "I wish you would do more casual, relaxed TV appearances, talking just like you are tonight," rather than those stiff, looking-straight-at-the-camera speeches. So many of us wanted to help the President develop a stronger style of television delivery. The real "credibility gap" was between the powerful, persuasive man in person, and the image that people in Indiana felt was "lying" to them.

We walked out into the sitting room, where Lady Bird excused herself to go to bed. As we began saying our goodbyes, the President insisted on taking us on a tour—the Lincoln bedroom, the queens' bedroom, his own bedroom, with the photograph of little Lyn Nugent and the stacks of folders beside his bed. (Jan whispered that her father, who had been a senator for thirty to thirty-five years, and had been a candidate for Vice President, had never seen the Lincoln bedroom.) I remembered two years ago, when Mrs. Johnson had taken Evan in and sat him on Lincoln's bed. How privileged we have been by this family's friendship, I thought.

The campaign started in earnest that spring: ten months of passing Birch in midair as we shuttled back and forth to Indiana, trying to hang onto our sanity, or at least our equilibrium, and win an election during that period of unmitigated horror that swept through our country in 1968.

My speeches had to be substantive, so I tried using a speech-writer; that didn't work, for I was not comfortable unless I wrote it myself. However, I needed updated facts for these speeches, facts I didn't have time to dig up—statistics on crime, education, and so forth. In January, while Birch was in Vietnam, I had requested cards with such facts from Birch's staff. By March 1, just before my trip out, they were still not forthcoming. Then I discovered that I had not been invited to an all-day staff meeting on the campaign, which included the Indiana contingent. I was furious. It seemed they were treating me like a stepchild. The infuriating insomnia came back with a rush, that left hand started shaking again. Nineteen sixty-eight was supposed to be a great year, a year of victory. Was this any way to begin?

Chapter 9

For us, the tensions of 1968 began to build in March, after Gene McCarthy's big win in Wisconsin. Ted Kennedy called on March 25: "Bobby has decided to enter the Indiana primary. I know it's going to be difficult for you, but it could be our West Virginia." *

Birch was quiet for a moment.

"Well, Ted, we are not often on different sides, but we are this time. But I've already committed myself to the President. When it is all over, we'll be working together again." Despite pressure from Mike Sperling, our friend and supporter, whose Kennedy ties ran deep, Birch made his statement in support of Johnson the next day. In answer came a wire from a constituent: "I spent $10.00 attending your birthday gala in Indianapolis, a campaign contribution. I demand my money back."

I had to fly to Indiana on the 30th for a Jefferson-Jackson Day dinner, back home the next day, and back out again on April 3. On the first trip, I was furious at the vicious anti-Johnson attacks I heard. On March 31 at about 7 p.m. I called Marvin Watson at the White House, to ask permission to speak out at women's groups about "Lyndon Johnson as I know him"—how he likes to help Lady Bird and his daughters select their clothes, about our weekend at Camp David, about bowling—that kind of story.

"Surely," Marvin said. "Go ahead and say anything you think

---

*John F. Kennedy had won the West Virginia primary in 1960, opening his successful bid for the presidency.

will help—" and he reminded me to watch Lyndon Johnson address the nation on television at nine.

Evan and I sat in the den to watch the speech. Tears sprang to my eyes as the President announced a halt in the air and naval bombardment of North Vietnam, and invited Hanoi to the bargaining table "in a series of mutual moves toward peace." At last, I thought. At last. Because of this quest for peace, he continued, he didn't feel he should be involved in partisan politics. I thought that he was going to say he wouldn't involve himself in the primaries. Instead he said in that familiar southwestern voice, emphasizing every word, "I shall not seek, and I will not accept, the nomination of my party for another term as your President."

For a minute I thought I'd misunderstood. Then all the emotions I'd packed down began to surge. The tears burst out.

The phone rang all night: Birch, from a roadside phone booth; Mike Sperling saying "I told you so"; Ted Kennedy trying to get in touch with Birch.

I felt like my heart was lost. If only it hadn't been for that war. If only . . . I flew to Indiana the next day, in pain about Lyndon Johnson. What a tragedy for our country that Lyndon Johnson had been saddled with that war. His great interest and strength was in the domestic field. In spite of the drain of the war, he had accomplished so much for this country in civil rights, in education, in health care—and tried to lift people out of their poverty. If he had not carried that war on his back, with the drain of time and money and all that it took, just think what he could have done! I hurt for Lyndon Johnson, the man. I could identify with him, understand him. I felt toward him the way I had felt about Daddy when I was a child. I loved him.

Through the rich black soil of Indiana farmland, driving from Gary to Rensselaer to Kentland in the pouring rain, campaigning for Birch Bayh, I thought about little else but Lyndon Johnson the next few days. Speaking to a group of teenagers at Earl Park, Jr., High School gave me the kind of lift high-schoolers always seem to impart. "Will your husband run for President?" one asked. "He is a candidate for reelection to the Senate," I answered, "but of course no one knows what the future holds."

Later, after reading that President Johnson had conferred individually with Vice President Humphrey and Bobby Kennedy that same day, I began to feel among Hoosiers a kind of resentment toward Bobby Kennedy. I heard Indiana people whispering about his hair, the way they had whispered about my yellow shoes; they were astonished that he was sweeping into Indiana with half a million dollars for one month of campaigning (the presidential preference primary would be May 7), and Indiana folks don't like to make up their minds that quickly. I drove from Monticello to Lafayette to Logansport on April 4, very aware that Bobby Kennedy was campaigning in Indiana that same day. In Logansport I decided in the middle of a speech to an all-Democratic audience to tell them about Lyndon Johnson, about the time he and Mrs. Johnson asked us to the White House for dinner and I couldn't get a babysitter, how they invited Evan to join us—and I almost broke down and cried.

After the speech, as I was standing in the receiving line, someone rushed up and said, "Martin Luther King was shot and killed in Memphis." I was stunned. Numb. He was a man of peace, a follower of Gandhi. He had moved the country's conscience. On the way back to the hotel, we stopped at a gas station. "I knew somebody would kill him," the attendant said. "I couldn't do it, but you take that boy in there just back from Vietnam—he's been trained by the United States government to kill, and he wouldn't think twice about it."

Bobby Kennedy was in Indianapolis. He spoke with a sensitivity and leadership that impressed me profoundly:

"For those of you who are black, and are tempted to be filled with hatred and distrust at the injustice of such an act, I can only say I feel the same kind of feeling. I had a member of my family killed, but he was killed by a white man."

Lake County the next day had changed since the last time I campaigned there—the hatred between whites and blacks was almost palpable. At a women's meeting in Highland, I was surprised to see not one black face. It would take a Bobby Kennedy to heal the divisions among us, I thought—if it were not already too late.

In Washington, it was too late. I arrived home to find parts of my beautiful city in flames, in the wake of rioting and looting that followed news of the King assassination. Birch was out of town, as usual; I was afraid. I could hear the sirens all night long, could see the soldiers arriving the next day. Before it was over, six people were killed, 350 injured in Washington, and 125 other cities erupted, too. I watched Mrs. King on television, so strong and courageous, and thought of the country's loss, and her own. When Birch came home I clung to him, in fear for his safety. Were we living in the same country in which I had grown up so hopeful and patriotic? Was the undercurrent of violence in America so strong?

Washington was like a city after a war. Soldiers at the Capitol, curfews in the evening, the smell of buildings smoldering. Evan and I went to the Uptown Shopping Center to get groceries, and on each corner stood a soldier with a gun slung over his back. I didn't expect that in Washington, just a couple of blocks away from my house. Birch went to Dr. King's funeral, emotionally drained, but renewed in his dedication to equal rights by the moving experience of all those people marching together singing "We Shall Overcome."

During the next few days, Birch's office staff pulled together mailing lists and other Indiana information to share with Bob Kennedy. Officially, we were neutral; behind the scenes we were helping. Our next-door neighbor, Jane Suydam, was off to Indiana to help with the Kennedy campaign, armed with the names of some of our friends there. Senator Kennedy himself left a message at our home, while Birch was out of town. I returned the call to Joan. No, it wasn't Ted, he was in Alaska. I called Bob at Hickory Hill. He came to the phone, warm and friendly, to say how very much he appreciated Birch's help. "How does it look in Indiana?" he asked me.

"You'll have to get the man-in-the-street," I replied. "The party people are really sticking by Governor Branigan." Branigan had announced as a "favorite son" candidate, a stand-in for Johnson before Johnson withdrew. I told him about the acrimonious anti-black feeling I had discovered in Lake County. "What else do you hear?" he asked.

"I keep hearing people say 'they can't come in here and buy us,'" I reported, "so you'll have to spend your money, but not in a flamboyant way."

"I'll send Ethel in," he said. "Maybe she can get into places where they dislike me. Can you tell her where to go?"

"Certainly," I agreed, and we chatted a bit longer. I was struck by his personal concern, the same kind that he had shown that weekend in Hyannis Port.

On April 27, Vice President Humphrey announced his candidacy, and once again I was torn between the two "camps." All our friends from the Johnson Administration suddenly sprouted HHH

buttons. My thirteen-year-old partisan, Evan, applied HHH bumper-
stickers to his St. Albans bookbag. Friends from the Senate, the
Mondales and Harrises, began working for Humphrey.

May 5, 1968

Birch came home from two weeks in Indiana. County chairmen
urged him to come out for Governor Branigan. He and Evan
worked in the yard. We grilled hamburgers outside.

Birch had a 20-minute meeting with the President. Said the
President said he thought he could have won, again; but with
Mansfield & group giving him trouble in the Senate, and Gerald
Ford in the House, what could he have accomplished? Said he
thought we were doing right to stay neutral in Indiana, and hoped
we could survive. Said he thought Bobby Kennedy would win
the nomination, but rather thought it would be a Republican year.

Ted Kennedy called Birch to see if they needed to worry about
the election being stolen from them by rigged voting in the rural
areas. Birch answered, "No. The people out there are more
concerned about the county courthouse than the presidential
election."

Bob Kennedy won the Indiana primary, 42 percent to Gene
McCarthy's 27 percent, to Governor Branigan's 31 percent. On
May 28, McCarthy won the Oregon primary. On June 4, Robert F.
Kennedy won both the South Dakota primary and the one in
California. Jane Suydam, my next-door neighbor, told me the next
day she'd had a terrifying dream. She'd stayed awake watching TV
until she was sure Bobby Kennedy had won in California, and then
had gone to sleep. She dreamed that Birch Bayh was shot, twice, in
the head, and was in the hospital. Of course, it was Bob Kennedy
who was shot twice in the head, and who died on June 6.

How could the Kennedys bear all of this? The horror was almost too much to comprehend. Ethel's unborn baby who would
never see its father, Teddy's voice cracking at the eulogy in St.
Patrick's Cathedral, Rose Kennedy at seventy-eight, a mother's grief
on her face, her head erect, her footsteps quick. We were horrified
by the danger of crowds pushing too close to the tracks alongside
the funeral train. They saluted and waved homemade signs, "Farewell, Bobby." Little Leaguers in uniforms, classes in their graduation gowns, Cub Scout groups, bands playing hymns . . . at one

point we saw a woman's body, covered with blood, lying at the tracks.

Ethel left the family car for two hours, greeting every single person, "Thank you so much for being aboard the train." Ted, making the same trip, stopped to talk about Indiana.

Burial was at night, after the much delayed eight-hour train trip, by candlelight, a few feet from John Kennedy's grave at Arlington Cemetery.

President Johnson stood there, pain in his eyes. His administration began with a Kennedy assassination; it was ending with a Kennedy assassination. How could the country bear all of this?

There is no way to catalogue emotions at such a time. Mine tumbled all together into a hard knot of anger at the violence in our society, at the daily parade of murder on television, both in fiction and on the news. I had pleaded with Birch to come out for a strong gun-control bill; he had voted "no" to the Kennedy proposals. He was in favor of controlling only "Saturday night specials," those cheap handguns that are made with imported parts.

Birch and I argued. "I'm afraid, when people ask me about your vote on the gun bill I will have no choice but to say that 'you will have to ask my husband to explain it, because I disagree with him.'"

For the first time I dared to say that I would not give Birch's views. It was a big step. But I now feared for my husband's life, as a politician constantly surrounded by crowds of people.

I had to read in the Terre Haute newspaper that there had been a threat on Birch's life the day Bobby Kennedy died. A man had phoned him: "The Ku Klux Klan is going to kill you when you speak in Whiting." My fear and anger mingled all over again. Why had he kept it from me? Of course, he was trying to protect me, knowing how upset I was already. But I felt that he was "protecting" himself from my reaction—and I would now imagine the worst.

On June 17, Attorney General Ramsey Clark called Birch at home to persuade him to support a stronger gun-control bill in the Judiciary Committee. I let out a victory whoop when I heard Birch say that he would do so.

The state nominating convention in Indianapolis was far different from six years before. No donkeys, no Birch trees, no walkie-talkies. Birch was nominated for reelection without opposition. As

I looked at our calendars, I noted that Birch would be in Washington only three nights in August—and I'd be in Indiana for two of those.

The Sinnenbergs drove Evan and Steven out to Culver Military Academy for summer camp. When we went to visit, I could not believe that Evan had grown so tall. At dinner, the Sinnenbergs were talking about the father of one of the boys' friends, who had changed jobs. "At least his daddy won't have a job where he might be shot," Evan said.

Gladys Sperling, in Indiana, had noticed my hand shaking from tension. "You're going to take a rest," she announced, in her generous, motherly way, and she sent me to Elizabeth Arden's Maine Chance, the first week of August. I think she may have saved my life—at least through the campaign.

My body came back to normal, in six days. My headaches disappeared, my first normal menstrual period in years occurred, my weight dropped to 104—exactly where it should be. Most evenings, I took dinner on a tray in my room, watching the Republican Convention in Miami. It seemed to me that Richard Nixon said what people wanted to hear—if simple platitudes could erase the turmoil in our country.

Returning to Washington, I found the range, refrigerator, and air-conditioner not working—and a movement afoot to run my husband for Vice President.

It started after Teddy Kennedy's statement that he would not be a candidate because of family obligations. Tom McIntyre, from New Hampshire, made a speech on the floor of the Senate, calling for Birch's youth and vigor to unite the party. Next, five Indiana congressmen called a press conference to urge his selection as Vice President. Birch and I smiled at each other, noting how many men John Kennedy had "considered" for Vice President, how many had been hoping for Lyndon Johnson to nod their way. If Hubert Humphrey were to select Birch, without our having actively campaigned for him, it would be something of a miracle. Still . . . all the talk would do us no harm in Indiana.

Nat Kalikow, a friend and supporter from New York (Chairman of the N.Y. State Finance Committee and a founder of U.S. Presidents' Club), wanted to push Birch for the spot. Milton Gilbert, another New York friend who had contributed heavily to the Humphrey campaign, spoke with the Vice President about Birch's candidacy. "Go!" Humphrey told him. "Terrific. He's young, good-looking, has a wife who's an asset. . . ."

"That and thirteen hundred twelve delegates will get you nominated," I told Birch.

Milt and Nat already had a hundred trucks in Chicago with "Bayh for Vice President" on them, buttons, stationery, and a suite of rooms for the convention. In Indiana, supporting committees organized by the Henry F. Schricker Democratic Club sprang up in twenty-three counties.

On the front page of the *Washington Star* on August 16, and also on the "Huntley-Brinkley Report," was a story about Birch's turning down the "Favorite Son" opportunity to support Humphrey. Birch phoned the Vice President at his home in Waverly, Minnesota. Hubert Humphrey sounded rather emotional in gratitude. "About that other project," he said (meaning our running for Vice President). "Keep working on it."

Evan, who was now working at the Pharmacy, the HHH campaign boutique in Georgetown, couldn't have been more excited. "Can I go to Chicago if Daddy's nominated?" he kept asking me. I began to get his clothes ready, just in case.

As it happened, Evan's time during the convention was far more peaceful than ours. He stayed on a farm in Martinsville, Indiana, with Birch's cousin Bill Bayh and his wife Janie and their children, fishing, riding horses, even catching a snake in the barn. But there, too, politics finally moved in. The Indianapolis papers, with our approval, sent a photographer to follow Evan around.

Humphrey had mentioned Birch's name along with other possible vice-presidential candidates—Governor Richard Hughes of New Jersey, Mayor Joseph Alioto of San Francisco, Senator Fred Harris of Oklahoma, and Senator Ed Muskie of Maine. Just before the convention, Birch called President Johnson down in Texas, seeking advice. Nobody had discussed it with him, the President said. He didn't know what Humphrey was thinking. "But the nominee, whoever he is, will pick somebody who will help the ticket the most," Lyndon Johnson added. "I've observed that those running the hardest usually don't get it. Play cool," Mr. Johnson advised. "Just tell people you're running for reelection."

Which, of course, is what we did. We sat down to the matters at hand, Birch's speech introducing Senator Inouye as the keynoter and his attempt to get the right to vote for eighteen-year-olds into the platform.

Ted Kennedy called, back from Europe after chaperoning Jackie on a cruise on Aristotle Onassis' yacht, assuring Birch that he would not accept the nomination, that he would campaign for Birch's reelection. Joan called me, long distance, and offered to help me campaign in Indiana in October. We took off for Chicago, wrapped in friendship, expecting nothing.

We certainly didn't expect that the Democratic Convention would become an armed camp. I was sickened by the violence in the streets, the obscenities, the police brutality, the invasion of McCarthy headquarters. Inside Convention Hall, tensions ran so high, security was so tight, it seemed a parody of the democratic process. The battle line, inside the hall and outside in the streets, was Vietnam. My Birch, I am proud to say, voted for the "peace plank," the minority report that was defeated by the convention.

There in Chicago, as in most major choices during the campaign, Birch made me a full partner in his decisions. I had to battle against his staff for that status. One even wanted me to surrender my walkie-talkie, isolating me from Birch's team because I was dead-set against distributing the "Bayh for Vice President" buttons and brochures on the convention floor as the time didn't seem ripe. "There are better ways for the Senator to become better known," I told Nat Kalikow. Later, Nat said, "Marvella, you are absolutely right. We are just trying to make waves for the future."

Birch and I were relieved when Humphrey made his announcement: the choice was Ed Muskie. When it was all over, Birch came back to the hotel room, ordered a dozen scoops of chocolate ice cream, and ate all but four of them. Now we could concentrate on our Senate race.

After Chicago, I felt in my bones that it was going to be a Republican year. It would be all we could do to hang on to our Senate seat. In early September, Birch began in double-time: to bed at midnight and up at 3:30 A.M. to be at factory gates for the early morning shifts. I worried about his health; he was all of forty now, with fewer reserves of energy than he had had six years ago. Money, for us, was harder to come by in 1968—perhaps because we had a larger campaign organization to support. By mid-September I felt as if I were running as hard as I could and somebody kept saying faster, faster. I felt fragmented.

Like a race horse, all day long I ran through the Washington routine. In Indiana, there would be nerve-wracking, split-second timing, but I found campaigning exhilarating. It was fun to parry and thrust with television interviewers, wonderful to be embraced by old friends I hadn't really seen since '62, to win over an audience that eyed me suspiciously as I walked into an auditorium, to fall into the "campaign closeness" that traveling companions for two months can provide.

Gail Alexander from Birch's office traveled with me in 1968; Lane Ayres drove the car from town to town, hauling the boxes of campaign literature, pins, and bumper stickers from speech to speech, Gail setting up a table to distribute them after my speeches. Getting there was one thing, I found out, finding our way to the right place another. So many times, our local contact would say, "It's at the Elks' Club—you can't miss it." Well, of course, you can't, if you've lived there all your life. "Just take Main Street three blocks" did not apply when "main street" might be labeled "Wabash Avenue," and we'd be lost, or late for the speech. We soon learned to have a local contact meet us at the edge of town and escort us to the proper meeting place.

On October 1, Joan Kennedy came out to help me campaign, the first appearance of any Kennedy on the campaign trail since Bobby's death. "I wouldn't be here if Birch and Marvella weren't the closest of friends," she told her first press conference in Hammond. It was her first formal press conference, I discovered. She had had nightmares all summer that Ted became President, and she wasn't "mature enough" to be First Lady, she told me.

Joan was self-assured in public, however, earnest and spontaneous, saying words of admiration for Birch that we couldn't say for ourselves. She spoke of Birch's courage in 1964, saying that he risked his life to save her husband's, and she told of his work with "My Ted" on the Senate Judiciary Committee. Everywhere she went, she drew crowds, and interviewers, speaking in her honest, straightforward manner. In Gary, she kicked off her shoes because the podium was too short, and her barefoot picture was plastered all over the front of the *Indianapolis Star*. In South Bend, after shaking the hundredth hand, she turned to me: "Doesn't your face ever feel frozen?" We "powdered over the dirt" from city to city. When we got to Indianapolis, she turned on the water for a bath; instead, the shower came on and drenched her hair. Luckily she had brought a "fall" to pin on. That night, after our speeches, we shook 500 hands.

She was a trooper, enduring all that so good-naturedly, donating her energy to us. The effect of an outside celebrity to boost a candidate only works if that person has the warmth to charm the crowd. Those autumn days, Joan Kennedy had it.

The campaign was different in many ways from that of '62. Ed Ziegner, political editor of the *Indianapolis News*, wrote that "Bayh and Ruckelshaus are outstanding, even in an interesting race. It is one of those happy and really rare contests in which the people get an able man, no matter which way the election cooky crumbles." Ideologically, Birch and Ruckelshaus did not seem to be too far apart, certainly not as divergent as Birch and Capehart had been. Our strategy was not to be defensive (although the Administration was so unpopular that Humphrey made only one brief stop in Indiana), but rather to present Birch's actions in the Senate, item by item, as a proud record, and, not least, to emphasize the public works projects that had come into the state since Birch had been a member of the Public Works Committee. As election day neared, it appeared to be a close race, one that probably would be decided on "personality." We would have to match the Republicans in energy, in exposure, in television appeal, in handshaking by the thousands, and surpass them in appeal to the voters.

Both Birch and Ruckelshaus whirled about the state in helicopters, adding a Vietnam-era touch to the campaigning. I stuck to the ground, most of the time, on my speaking schedule. Birch asked for my advice on his major speeches, on television appearances. I stood in for him when he had to miss a speech. Once, when I had to rush back to Washington for minor surgery, he stood in for me.

What I did not enjoy was that I saw him so little. But we talked every day on the phone. One evening, Birch checked into his hotel, handed my schedule to his aide, and said, "Here, get Marvella on the phone for me." So the aide got me on the phone, and Birch and I were exchanging notes about what had happened that day. "By the way," Birch said, "where are you?"

"At the Airport Holiday Inn, in Indianapolis," I said. "Where are you?"

There was a long silence. "Well, where *are* you?" I repeated.

"I am at the Airport Hilton, right across the street," he said. We were there to speak before different groups. The staff had booked us into different hotels.

Our campaign organization was larger, more complex. There was more paid staff, I discovered, and fewer attempts to enlist volunteers. Campaign costs were heavy, with bigger advertising agencies, costlier air time. Communication breakdowns between parts of the organization, or between the organization and the candidate, began to occur with some frequency. I began to long for the simpler days of '62, when it was just Birch and me and that handful of volunteers.

As in the last campaign, I had written a "last-minute appeal" for television, in behalf of my husband. This year's was fifteen minutes' worth, running twice on each of Indiana's TV stations. In addition, we had spent a lot of money on a documentary film. On October 31, Mike Sperling called. "The documentary stinks. It's not worth anything," he said bluntly. I knew we needed something fresh for a closing appeal. Ruckelshaus had a thirty-minute family film all ready to go.

Thursday, October 31, 1968

I reached Senator in Lafayette, and gave him my plan: In the thirty minutes of his closing appeal, he should do five minutes to be taped on Saturday. It would be a thank-you. "I've enjoyed so much serving you as individuals, Hoosiers as a state, and the nation." He should sit on a corner of a desk, then show ten minutes of Birch's speeches, and parts showing us as a family, kissing me goodbye on the steps of the Capitol, and with his son. Then Birch would say, "I need your help so that together we can solve America's problems and build the future for ourselves and our children. Please give me your help." Birch thought my plan was pretty good, and used it.

Tuesday, November 5, 1968

Birch went to a plant gate at 5:30 A.M., back at 8:30 to pick me up. Drove together to Terre Haute, to vote, the first chance to talk uninterrupted in months. One minute we talked about winning, what changes we would make. The next minute, about losing—what alternatives we had. It sprinkled rain a little, just like six years ago. Things I cleaned out of the glove compartment: Anacin, dental floss, toothbrush, contact lens cleaner, throat lozenges, paperclips—campaign necessities. It costs only 25¢ an hour to park in Terre Haute, 75¢ in Washington. At New Goshen, there were photographers. Went to the Goodie Shop cafeteria to eat. Hardest thing about being married to Birch Bayh is that it takes thirty minutes to go half a block. Senator and I voted, my first straight ticket. Birch drove me back to Indianapolis, then was to go to Bloomington for a plant gate. He was so tired his eyes were pink and puffy. I tried to discourage him. He said he felt like a prize fighter before a big fight. He took me in his arms and said, "Shots, God has been good to us since we met each other. Win or lose, it will be fine." The day seemed 80 hours long. We had a working supper.

About 8:30 P.M., we went up to room 1206, where there were three TVs and a board listing all the counties. I wore the bracelet LBJ gave me in 1965, and mother's watch. Tony Hulman, Mike Sperling, our Senate staff, a photographer, and P. A. Mack, our "best man," from Chicago, and his wife Marian, joined us. My father had flown up from Oklahoma. There was money only for one ticket, he said. He was subdued, not quite himself, and he looked puffy, like a real alcoholic. He was wearing cowboy boots, real western garb, an Oklahoman among Hoosiers.

Early returns showed us persistently 14,000 behind. But Mike Sperling said there was nothing to worry about. When 44 percent of the vote came in, we finally took the lead by 7,000 and some. By one A.M., it was 71,000.

Wednesday, November 6, 1968

The telegram: "Jill joins me in congratulating you and Marvella on your reelection. You are a gallant and hard campaigner and our prayers go with you in your efforts to form unity in our divided country. Good luck for the next six years. Bill Ruckelshaus." The calls. From Teddy Kennedy, President and Mrs. Johnson. Paul and Becky Rogers. Our good friends from the Senate and others. The press conference. Birch spoke, then looked at me. "After sixteen years of marriage, there just aren't words to say . . ." and he couldn't finish.

Birch hasn't stopped campaigning in six years. We won't pay that price again.

Birch was the only Democrat to win statewide in Indiana. Nixon carried the state by 252,000 votes. Birch is going to see what he can do to get me the job offer again. It is probably useless, but worth a try. Evan cried himself to sleep about Humphrey. Called the Vice President at his home in Minnesota. "Just trying to pull back together," he said. There was no jolly ring in his voice this time. He said he felt especially bad because the young people were let down. It's a great loss. We hope he won't leave public life. I looked at Birch's tired face, and thought of Senator Engle from

California, the most popular politician in his state, who died at 53.
"The next six years won't be like the last six. I promise you,"
Birch said.

That turbulent year, 1968, which historians will be trying to
analyze for years to come, ended on a bittersweet note for me: the
Johnsons' last state dinner at the White House, for Sheik Sabah
al-Salim al Sabah, Emir of Kuwait. It was a cold, clear evening,
December 11, and the White House was all dressed up for Christmas; so was I, in a high-necked, long-sleeved lime green gown with
white mink cuffs and trim at the hem. The red-uniformed Marine
Band was playing lively music in the foyer. "Soak it all in, Birch,"
I said. "This will be our last White House dinner for a long, long
time."

A uniformed military aide offered me his arm. Birch followed
behind as we entered the East Room, where the crowd was gathering. At the door, another aide announced, "Senator and Mrs. Bayh."
Soon the music stopped; the four-man color guard marched in, bearing flags, and the band struck up "Ruffles and Flourishes." My throat
caught as they began to play "Hail to the Chief." President and
Mrs. Johnson and the Emir of Kuwait entered, to form a receiving
line. We had never ranked so high before—only Vice President and
Mrs. Humphrey, Secretary of State and Mrs. Rusk, Attorney General and Mrs. Clark, and Senator and Mrs. Gale McGee preceded
us. President and Mrs. Johnson both kissed me. She was wearing a
bright yellow satin gown. I noticed his hair was almost completely
white. Again, I choked up.

In the Green Room, Birch and I studied the calm, still waters
in the Monet painting the Kennedys had given to the White House
in memory of the President. Again, I was moved. Truly, this was the
end of an era.

I was seated on the President's left at table twelve, beneath the
painting of Abraham Lincoln, with the President's big easy chair
directly under the portrait, facing the room. My friend, Bessima
Al-Ghoussein, wife of the Kuwaiti Ambassador, the highest-ranking
female guest, was on his right. I realized the honor that had been
paid me, and for the third time, I had a catch in my throat. At our
table were Governor-elect Preston Smith of Texas; a Mrs. Harper
from Philadelphia, wife of an aluminum manufacturer; Mrs. William S. Paley from New York; the foreign minister of Kuwait; and

a young black athlete, a Job Corps graduate named George Foreman, who had just won an Olympic Gold Medal in boxing.

The President talked of Luci and Lynda, and their soldier-husbands—how Luci had spent five days with Pat on "R & R" in Hawaii, how Lynda was now with Chuck on "R & R" in Thailand. He talked about Richard Nixon, with no animosity whatsoever. "The new President needs all the help we can give him," he said, pointing out that transition teams were already working with the coming administration. There was a quality of equanimity about him tonight, almost of relief, it seemed. Later, in the East Room, as the New Christy Minstrels sang, "Glory, glory, I'm going to lay my burdens down," Birch whispered, "How appropriate."

There was no sadness about Lyndon Johnson. He reached over to take a match folder with "The President's House" printed on it, signed it LBJ, and handed it to me, saying, "Take this to your son." Then he took my place card and wrote, "To Marvella with love, Lyndon Johnson."

◦◦

We had been buoyed by the national reception of the "Bayh for Vice President" movement. If national office was to be his goal, a well-laid groundwork for 1972 must be begun now. "I'll need your help," Birch told me. "I couldn't have won without you."

I had knocked myself out on the 1968 campaign. I felt now, even more than in 1962, "a co-executive" with Birch, and that the staff was mine to share. After all, weren't we full partners again? The staff thought otherwise. And to my surprise, after the election, Birch sided with them. On matters where I felt that I could make a contribution—I'd studied the issues, too—I found myself ignored or snubbed. Some of those people who'd hitched their wagons to my husband's star had no room for my opinion; I was considered an outsider. Their attitude was that the people of Indiana had elected a senator—and his name wasn't Marvella.

I was furious. Had some of these same people not come to my house when Lyndon Johnson had offered me a plum of a job, and told me how badly I was "needed"? I was needed, all right—like a Barbie-doll who makes speeches; send me out on a campaign for a year, then fold me up and file me in a drawer until the next campaign! "Our campaign ran more efficiently in 1962, out of a garage with a borrowed typewriter, than with all these so-called brains you've hired," I cried to Birch. And he was furious. For me to criticize his staff was to criticize his judgment. He had chosen people for their skills, skills that he needed, he said. They tell you what they think you want to hear, I said. "And you didn't follow the President's advice—choose the best brains you can find," I said.

I was shocked that we were $150,000 in debt. For the first time, we had ended a campaign owing money. Some of it was a personal debt, for advertising, for office space, for hotel rooms—for expenses the staff had piled up. With my father's losses haunting me, and with my lifelong fear of getting into debt—a fear grounded in the stories of our Okie neighbors who lost their land—I became nearly irrational over the thought of that debt in our names.

To add salt to my wounds, Jill Ruckelshaus, who'd campaigned in Indiana for her husband and lost, now had a good, paying job in the Nixon White House. And I had none.

But what really rankled was that I felt Birch didn't take my part when there was a conflict between me and the staff. I'd be in tears, after a heated argument with a staff member, and Birch would say, "Are you sure it wasn't your fault," or "I'll talk to her"—and a week later the same thing would happen again. I felt so ill-used and hurt that I could hardly bring myself to call the office. But then somebody from Indiana would call me with a problem they didn't want to trust to office people, and I'd find myself making another demand.

It was in the midst of this feeling of tension and hurt that Birch and his staff began to work on his presidential campaign.

Chapter 10

*I*t was more than wifely pride that made me think Birch would make a good President someday. I had watched his political skills grow, his intellect sharpen, his good mind expand and grasp the complex issues of the nation and the world. He was not so rigid that he couldn't change his position, nor was he afraid to say when he had been wrong. He had a genuine feeling for people, which was reciprocated. Call it charisma, call it charm—I could see him move a crowd. He had a kind of bedrock strength that people sensed. He was equal to anybody we had met in Washington, I felt. Despite his staff, I was ready to work for Birch Bayh for President, but I wasn't sure that this was the time.

In early 1969, with the beginning of the Nixon Administration, we felt that Teddy Kennedy would be the Democratic nominee in 1972. And we would support him. Ted had qualities that were all of the above—and he had more: a mantle of leadership inherited from his two murdered brothers, a vast number of Kennedy supporters throughout the country who could be summoned at the drop of a hat-into-the-ring for a superb campaign organization, and a sizable family income from which to draw. All of the Kennedys, Ted included, were blessed with the ability to assemble an incredibly competent staff. If Ted were to be the Democratic nominee, then we would hope for a chance at the vice presidency.

However, there was doubt as to whether Ted should expose himself to the risk of running. There were sixteen children—his three, Jack's two, Bobby's eleven—to whom he felt responsible, as the only surviving Kennedy brother. As strongly as he felt a duty

193

to his country, or to the tasks his brothers had begun, we knew that he took very seriously the responsibilities to his family, to share greater amounts of his time and energy with a host of fatherless children. Not the least of their concerns were the passions and violence still running rampant in America, to which two Kennedys already had fallen victim. I had seen Ted, making a speech at a Democratic fundraiser in New York, turn white when a chunk of plaster fell, with a sharp crack, just in front of the stage. Joan confided her worries to me.

My private worry was diagnosed by Dr. Hawken, my gynecologist. I had to have a hysterectomy, and soon. I was out of commission for four weeks—but after that, I realized that the surgery probably should have been done years earlier. The difference in my energy level was amazing—as if I had been swimming with a heavy stone around my neck, and suddenly the stone was gone. Estrogen had been artificially running a naturally defective machine all those years. Now, at thirty-six, a new burst of physical well-being gave me the impetus to really get on with my life. To get on with Birch's life, that is.

He had asked me to help by inviting to dinner a small group of three senators once a week. I really enjoyed time spent with interesting people and friends; for me, it was a chance to get to know his colleagues and their wives better. We began with three senatorial couples. After a month of this, we noted that our guests seemed to enjoy an informal respite in our home from the mob scenes to which we all were overexposed. Just before the fifth dinner, Mark Hatfield came down with strep throat; we called our old friends Marge and Mel Elfin, Washington bureau chief for *Newsweek*, to fill in. The conversation was so sprightly, with ideas popping back and forth across the table, that I decided to include an "outsider," usually somebody from the press, at all our subsequent "Senate dinners."

On May 14, President Nixon made his first televised speech on Vietnam, proposing a gradual and mutual withdrawal of all foreign troops, including ours, and those of North Vietnam. Peace talks in Paris had been ridiculously stalled over the shape of the conference table. I felt despair; we had been at war five years, longer than World War II. But at least my husband and I now agreed that the war must stop.

The plans that Birch and his backers were setting in motion all assumed Ted Kennedy would be the presidential nominee in 1972. In mid-July, however, tragedy touched Ted once again. At Chappaquiddick, just off Martha's Vineyard, he was in an automobile accident. Miraculously, he was alive; his passenger, a member of his brother Bob's campaign staff, was not.

Birch was in Alaska. I was home, getting ready for a long-planned family trip to Russia. When we heard the news, I wanted to reach out as a friend, to respond in some way. I could imagine Ted's anguish. I had seen his pain at the loss of life before—at the two deaths in our plane crash, at the funerals of his two brothers. But my heart went out to Joan, that warm, buoyant, loving young woman, concerned about her husband's health, protective of her own family, masking a touching vulnerability with her own spunky ventures into politics. I remembered how hopeful she had been, during our campaign in Indiana, that she would become pregnant again. Now she was expecting another child. How could she stand all of this? I wrote her a letter, hoping that my feelings for her might be of some small meaning. One feels so helpless in times of grief, gestures seem so meaningless in the face of another's suffering. And yet, I would discover in my own life what a source of comfort it is just to know that people are caring.

The next day, of course, our astronauts landed on the moon, completing President Kennedy's promise to the nation. Thankfully, I felt this momentous event dimmed the public spotlights on the two suffering families of Chappaquiddick.

At midweek, on the Capitol steps, Ted told reporters he would remain in the Senate as Majority Whip, would seek a second full term next year, and, if reelected, serve out his entire six-year term. He took himself irrevocably out of the running for President in '72, stating flatly that nothing could change his mind. It was a decision that affected the Muskies, the Humphreys, the Harold Hugheses, the McGoverns, the Harrises—and ourselves.

Our tour of Russia, from August 18 to September 8, was a study trip as well as our family vacation with Evan. At Eastertime, after the Interparliamentary Union Conference in Vienna, I had visited Czechoslovakia, Yugoslavia, and Hungary, noting living and working conditions in those Communist countries. In Prague, I felt very much in a police state, with an overwhelming Russian presence. It was an intense educational experience to see that presence at its source, in the USSR. "Our children are our privileged class," we were told over and over. After a visit to a sparkling nursery school filled with the laughing, well-behaved children of working mothers, where learning was an integral part of the experience, I could comprehend what the positive effects of a voluntary, fully operating, adequately staffed Head Start program might be able to produce. "A teacher receives the same salary as a doctor," our guide told me, and I had to admit to myself that American teachers are woefully underpaid, in relation to the service they render.

It was a strenuous trip, one that expanded our knowledge but was hard on our marriage. It started out badly, with Birch nearly missing the plane while Evan and I sat nervously strapped in our seats. Birch was cross much of the time in Russia, and then more than cross, snapping at me in public and in front of Evan, until I'd shrivel inside. We got on each other's nerves, it seemed, and we tried to clear the air one night in a hot Odessa hotel room. But the next day it was thicker than ever, even on our "rest stop" in Portugal, on the way home.

Always on vacation, I thought. All those bottled-up complaints most people deal with and work through on a day-to-day basis suddenly surface. For us, there had been no day-to-day basis in the six years we had been in Washington, except for vacations. Then the bottle came uncorked. It was not a very good note on which to begin the tasks ahead.

On the day we left for Russia, President Nixon appointed Clement T. Haynsworth, a South Carolina judge on the U.S. Court of Appeals, to the Supreme Court. Birch, as a member of the Judiciary Committee, was disturbed about Judge Haynsworth's record, for labor and civil rights organizations denounced him as anti-labor and racist. The hearings began just after we returned from Russia, with Birch leading the charge to oppose Haynsworth.

On September 18, just after the hearings began, Birch's direct popular election proposal, abolishing the electoral college, passed the House of Representatives by an overwhelming majority. We were elated. Between this direct-election victory, with President Nixon now adding his support, and the Haynsworth hearings, our phone was ringing off the wall. Our scheduled entertaining picked up, and Birch's schedule of speaking picked up; he flew into Washington for the hearings, and back out again in the evenings.

For the first time we felt under siege. So pervasive were the tactics of the Nixon Administration that Birch began making private telephone calls from a public telephone, succumbing to the rumors that Attorney General John Mitchell had tapped the phones of "enemies." (As it turned out, this was not paranoia, but a justified precaution.) The hate calls came, too, as Birch turned up evidence that Haynsworth had made judicial rulings in favor of businesses in which he held stock. Our focus was narrowed, in those days, to the Haynsworth hearings, and, on my part, to a serious investigation into needs and possibilities for private-sector involvement in the field of child care.

On November 21, 1969, while I was in Indiana working on a child care center proposal, the Senate voted 55 to 45 to reject the Haynsworth nomination. It was the first time I had not been in the gallery to watch a Birch Bayh issue voted on, and I was sick to miss it. For him, it was a major political victory, as well as one of conscience. And on the NBC news, there were three minutes on the Senator from Shirkieville who might be President someday.

We went on a three-week study trip for the Interparliamentary Union that fall, to Russia, India, Nepal, Pakistan, Thailand, Korea, and Japan. Seeing life in those countries only reinforced my desire to become involved in my own. When I returned, I embarked on an even more intense search for a place for myself in the area of day care and child development. By this time, my reasons for studying child care projects had grown, for I keenly wanted to be able to help with my family's support. Birch and I were both supplementing our income with speechmaking. Our farm income and senator's salary put together were severely stretched to make ends meet, what with Evan's tuition and the soaring cost of living in Washington. I needed a paying job.

My worries about money were compounded by my father's woes. He had stopped drinking, he wrote me, but he thought he'd have to sell one of his farms to pay off his debts that year. And rains had come at harvest, beating the ripened wheat into the ground. (Aunty wrote that he hadn't stopped drinking at all.) Furthermore, we were staging fundraiser after fundraiser in an effort to pay off our old campaign debt—and thinking about the incredible amount needed to begin a presidential campaign. However, some of Birch's advisors began to worry that my going to work, even for a private corporation, might hurt his chances for the presidency.

By now Birch was gaining a great deal of national exposure on "Meet the Press" and "Issues and Answers," and was being mentioned in an occasional political column as a "possible presidential contender." President and Mrs. Johnson came up from Texas for a wedding; we met the former President in their hotel room, to ask for advice. Lyndon Johnson was heavier, more "western" than ever, it seemed to me. He ordered a roast beef sandwich ("Medium—and I want it *hot* this time"), and Sanka, taking huge bites as he gave us his comments.

"The field is wide open," he said, encouraging Birch to run. He thought Humphrey would be satisfied with the Senate; Muskie "hasn't quite struck a chord"; Scoop Jackson "might be good"; Harris "has no chance at all, as he's lost his grip in his home base [Oklahoma]"; and as for McGovern, "if we get out of Vietnam without an honorable peace, the peace movement, his major support, will boomerang." These would be the major contenders, for there were no governors "on the make," he said.

He advised Birch to plan twenty-five major speeches in the next twelve months. "Half a dozen or so in the Senate, others strategically around the country, well thought out, well-advanced." Show maturity, he counseled; always think before answering questions, and always precede the word "peace" with "honorable." "Good men to advise you politically are Clark Clifford, Cliff Carter, Jim Rowe, and Marvin Watson," he said, adding with a grin, "Those on my staff who talk the most [about the Johnson presidency] actually knew the least."

He cautioned Birch against letting anyone know about this meeting: "It would be bad for both you and me. Would look like I was trying to get back into politics—remember how ex-President Truman had come out unsuccessfully for Harriman—and it would look like you were 'LBJ's boy.'"

Then he turned to me. "If you had taken that job I offered you two and a half years ago, those contacts would have helped now."

I couldn't look at Birch. "I wanted it so badly," I said. "I still can't think of it without crying."

Nineteen seventy began with planning sessions in earnest on Birch's presidential effort. It was decided that I was needed in the campaign to accompany Birch. Our first trip, in January, was to Ohio, North Carolina, California, and Oklahoma. I flew in to Oklahoma ahead of him, hoping to wish my father a happy birthday.

Arriving, alone, in Oklahoma City on January 14, I looked over the visiting crowd for Daddy, who had promised to meet me. He wasn't there.

By this time, I had tried to condition myself to expect anything, but it still hurt. He had been gloomy about his financial situation. "Like a mule standing with his back to the storm, I will graze when the sun comes out—if ever," he had written. But I had at least held to the hope that he'd been sober. My cousin's wife, from Oklahoma City, found me at the airport, reporting that Daddy wasn't coming because his wife had run off with the car. I caught a small plane to Stillwater, then to Enid. Aunty and Uncle Oren met me. We went to the cemetery, then drove down West Oklahoma Street, past 2024. No car in the driveway; mail still in the box; evening paper lying on the sidewalk. We arrived at Aunty's house. There was no answer when I tried to phone Daddy. Nor on the following day.

Birch was to meet me in Oklahoma City the next day, when he would speak at Oklahoma City University. I had scheduled television interviews there. Just before leaving Enid, I tried one more phone call. His wife answered. In the background I could hear him staggering to the phone. When he spoke he did not sound like himself. "It's very sad," I said. "I've been here in Enid two days and you haven't even seen me."

He struggled to answer. In a voice so thick-tongued I could barely understand him, he said, "I know it, little darlin'. But I just couldn't help it."

Daddy's words and the subsequent letters from Oklahoma pounded a bitter counterpoint into the background of our lives during the next months. Two days after we returned to Washington, President Nixon's nomination of Judge G. Harrold Carswell of Florida for the Supreme Court was sent to the Senate and referred to the Judiciary Committee. The day Carswell's nomination was announced, we had held a campaign planning session in our rec room, outlining the national issues, the strategies, the organizational needs, the costs. Nat Kalikow, pointing out that Nixon spent $700,-000 a year, said that we would need at least $400,000 a year. Mike Sperling disagreed—we'd need a total of $8 to $10 million, he suggested. Mindful of how fast the staff had piled up expenses, and of how slowly our Indiana campaign debt was dwindling, I piped up: "We'll need someone to watch the money." The meeting put reality into our presidential dreams; we had the first pledges of seed money.

In this light, revelations about Carswell's segregationist past were especially troubling to Birch. If he opposed Carswell, it might harm him politically in the South.

The fight against Haynsworth had hurt him politically in Indiana, and he knew it. Birch did not like being in the position of appearing to tear down a person. It was one thing to oppose a piece of legislation, another thing to oppose a man. But this Carswell appointment gave the impression that Nixon was thumbing his nose at the Senate: "All right, you defeated Haynsworth; I'll send you somebody worse this time and you'll take whoever I send." There had been incredible pressure from the White House the first time; this time there would be more. Birch thought somebody else on the committee would lead the fight. But nobody else would. "There is not a chance at all that this can be won, but somebody has to oppose it," he told me. He spent sleepless nights, and then he said, "I can't help what votes I might lose because of this. I must do what my conscience dictates."

About this time, a letter came from Uncle Otis, my father's older brother: "Your daddy should have been declared incompetent. May be too late now. . . . He should be committed to be dried out from alcohol. I request you and Birch do something to save him." I had to write back that we had tried in so many ways; as long as he was married, I had no legal way to have him committed.

Every night I dreamed about Daddy not meeting me in Oklahoma. The week of my thirty-seventh birthday, Daddy had to sell off all his beloved machinery and his land, except one heavily mortgaged farm in which I had joint ownership: that farm where he and Mama started out as newlyweds. It was wrenching for him, the ultimate proof of failure. He had loved that land, which even included the farm his mother and father had carved out of the Oklahoma sod. I remember seeing him scoop up a fistful of that dirt with his hands just to look at it and smell it. It made me sad, but I didn't cry in Oklahoma when Daddy refused to see me; I didn't cry when he sold Grandma Hern's farm. I held the pain inside like a tight knot, until finally, literally hurting from too-dry eyes and my stinging contact lenses, I went to an eye doctor who, after two examinations, asked, "Is there something the matter emotionally?" and I burst into floods of tears.

But most days, either at home or out around the country speaking on the role of American women in the seventies, I had to wear my public face. Now Uncle Otis wrote about my father's marital troubles. "He is hurting badly to be on terms with you as in previous years. He loves you but is in a mess and doesn't know how to get out. . . . It is hard to do, but let him go his way, and after he has lost everything he will come to you for help and then will be your time to forgive him and be happy. . . ."

After a fundraising weekend in New York, and after a Washington dinner at which publisher Walter Ridder asked influential newsmen to give us their private views of Birch's chances, Birch cornered me for a rare dinner out together at the Sheraton-Park Hotel, near our house, to talk about our running for the presidency. For the first time, he said he'd stopped feeling he might not be "able enough" yet. "Just look at the others," he said, and we laughed. "He's really going for it," I wrote in my diary. "I only wish Mother knew."

On February 16, the Judiciary Committee had voted to send the Carswell nomination to the full Senate.

Mar. 16, 1970

We're entertaining 68 members of the press tonight. So tired. Birch opened the case against Carswell today. Slim chance of winning.

The hate calls began in earnest then. On weekends Birch was speaking in St. Louis, Detroit, Chicago, Albuquerque, New Orleans . . . and back to the hearings. A letter arrived from Uncle Otis: Daddy's wife had filed for divorce. "I am planning on leaving Oklahoma and until I am honorably reestablished," he had written Uncle Otis, "I don't wish to write anyone, not even Birch and Marvella."

✌

Birch asked me to help him decide whether to use the filibuster in leading the charge against Carswell. So many times, Birch had tried to have the filibuster abolished. "You should fight Carswell very hard," I said, "but *not* use the filibuster. And be sure the press knows why: that you won't stoop to use a method you believe is undemocratic."

The parliamentary tactic chosen would be a vote to "recommit" the nomination, a procedure that Senator Ed Brooke of Massachusetts assured Birch would cause the nomination "never to see the light of day again." After a March 25 meeting in the majority leader's office, with Brooke, Tydings, and Hart, it was decided to schedule the vote on April 6, to give the anti-Carswell forces time to organize their efforts.

I was pleased to hear about the two-week delay. The vote would be after the Easter recess—and we could take our planned trip to Monaco, to the Interparliamentary Union Conference. It would be work for Birch, but a change of scene was definitely needed. We had been charging nonstop since Thanksgiving—I needed a rest. Because of the Carswell situation, we didn't know until the evening before we left whether we would be able to go. But I packed hurriedly.

On Easter Sunday morning, we woke up in the Hermitage Hotel in Monaco, on a hillside overlooking a Mediterranean harbor. On the spur of the moment, Birch bought me an orchid hydrangea that evening, and we slipped away from the delegation to a quaint little restaurant beside the sea. We talked over candlelight, about, of all things, why I hadn't given him back his fraternity pin when I went to Indiana to do so. The evening was magic, the kind of personal talk we both had missed. We felt an old rush of love for each other.

But as we talked about the future, about the presidency, I worried about Birch. At the pace he was going, would his health hold? I worried about my father. Would he be an embarrassment?

"These special trips are what make the separations worthwhile," I wrote. "The most important thing in the world to me, next to family, is travel. I want to see as much of the world as possible, as I only pass through this way once."

The next day, April 1, Birch was called back to Washington for the Carswell hearings. I could have cried. This trip had brought a fine, special closeness. I decided to remain with the delegation. That afternoon, at a tea given by the British wives, Senator Sparkman, dear Alabama Senator Sparkman, Jan Shepard's father and our close friend, had me called out of the room. He and Mrs. Sparkman stood there, tears in their eyes. "Marvella, get your coat and come," he said, taking my arm.

"Oh, God!" I prayed, fearing a plane crash. "Has something

happened to Birch . . . or Evan?" I asked frantically. Senator Sparkman put his arms around me.

"Your father shot your mother and then shot himself," he said. "They are both dead."

I began to tremble.

"She's not my mother," I said weakly.

Birch was in midair; there was no way to reach him, no plane that night for me to go home. The Sparkmans were tender, sympathetic, listening as I poured out my heart. "Remember the wonderful Daddy you had as a child," the kindly old gentleman advised me. "Forget the recent one."

But it was this recent one who had been so driven, so deranged, that he would murder. The anguish, the torment he must have gone through. "Never kill a living thing, Marvella," he had told me.

I had to know the details, awful as they would be. Senator Sparkman placed the call to Oklahoma. Aunty was in the hospital, ill. The tenant who lived in Grandma Hern's little house out back had come by to pay the rent. There had been no answer at the door, but the lights were on. He had looked through the window, and had seen Pat, lying on the dining-room floor, and Daddy, in a chair in the living room.

The other members of the Congressional delegation and staff were very kind, supporting me that night. Senator Percy offered to fly home with me; I thought I could make it alone.

A heavy sleeping pill, Noladar. Waking, drugged, for the flight to Paris, the three-hour wait at the airport where Senator Sparkman had arranged for someone to meet me. The ten-hour ordeal getting to Washington. Headache. Six years ago this month Mother died. Now I am alone. The last time I heard his voice, in January. . . . "I know it, little darlin'. But I just can't help it." My face numb. On the plane home, I drank coffee to wake up, so dazed I forgot my allergy to coffee. I drank one cocktail, and then some champagne, to quiet me.

I looked up at the stewardess. "Are you all right now?" she asked.

"Yes, what do you mean?" I saw the concern in her face.

"You fainted. Collapsed in the bathroom. We had to use a special key to open it." There had been almost no pulse, she said. They had given me oxygen, helped me back to my seat. I had no memory of any of it. I barely remember coming to.

On the ground in Boston an hour and a half. They brought newspapers aboard. Big article in the Boston paper, with a photograph of my daddy. Delbert Hern, 60, father-in-law of Senator. . . .

Larry Cummings and Gail, my companions from former campaign days, met me at the Dulles Airport. The Senator was at the Capitol, making his major speech on the Carswell nomination.

❧

Birch went with me to Oklahoma, but I worried that he would have to leave me there to go through all the possessions, that dreadful lonely task for an only daughter, with memories from six years ago this month, when Mother died. By the time we arrived, however, I had a high fever. We went to the house, with the Krazy Kat sign still painted on the sidewalk outside. Somebody had tried to wash the blood off the carpet, but it was there. My daddy's and that of the woman he had married, a dark red blot that is forever stained in my mind. I see the size of it, the shape, even now. The body in the funeral home looked waxen, but this, this was my father's blood.

Her family was there, whose loss had been caused by my loss. It was to be a double funeral, two coffins in the front of the church. I worried, wondered how they would treat me. Mercifully, they were kind. They did not allow her to be buried underneath that garish marble stone, but took her to a town near Tulsa instead.

The minister did not know either of them. But I had a letter waiting for me, among the many that came to Enid, from Calvin Bergdall:

> Dear Marvella,
>
> When my first son was born, I was unemployed and had no hospital insurance. Delbert Hern loaned me money to take my wife and child out of the hospital. When I returned from World War II, Delbert Hern gave me employment for three summers, paid me a bonus for good work. When I was newly wed, Delbert Hern took time to attend my wedding; when I was seeking employment, Delbert Hern wrote impressive letters of recommendation for me. This is the Delbert Hern I shall remember.
>
> It must have been torment to the real Delbert Hern, the compassionate, intelligent, understanding person we know to *be* the real Delbert Hern, to contend with this strange individual he became, who usurped his earlier real identity.

I knew I owed it to my father to share the memory of that earlier Delbert Hern, and I told the minister so. "Are you sure you can get through it?" he asked. "I am not sure," I said. But when he came to that part of the service, he looked at me, and I nodded yes. I spoke at my father's funeral that cold April day, when the heavens poured rain into the red Oklahoma earth. I told of the Daddy I had known, my pal, often the only father at the school plays, the man who built the little seat beside his on the tractor, who wrote letters to Oklahoma A & M, some funny and some thought-provoking, who cared for his invalid mother, who gave people a chance, who lay on his back and looked at the sky and told his grandson about nature. I read them parts of Calvin Bergdall's letter.

And when I finished, I was too drained to stay in Enid and do what had to be done. After a day at my father's house, going over the necessary possessions and papers with Uncle Otis, I had to go home. Evan and I flew back to Washington with Birch.

The next day, April 6, I went to the Senate for the vote on recommittal of the Carswell nomination back to the Judiciary Committee. Birch lost that one, 44–52, and was very discouraged. He flew to Texas, to speak in Houston. While he was there, *his* father was taken to the hospital, with his second serious heart attack. Birch flew all night from Houston, arrived in Washington at 6 A.M., and slept two hours in his office; then a police car rushed him to the hospital to see Daddy Bayh. Then he rushed back to the Senate, where the vote on Carswell's nomination would take place at noon.

The White House had been working overtime to persuade each senator who was "undecided." On the day of the vote, success or failure would depend on three Republican senators—Marlow Cook, Winston Prouty, and Margaret Chase Smith. They voted against the nomination, standing up against pressure from their President, in a stunning 51–45 victory for my husband.

I sat in the gallery, which was first thick with suspense and then loud with sudden, unrestrained cheering, unable to take in this second milestone in my Birch's career, and that night, when Evan and I were at home watching the news, Eric Sevareid made a glowing statement about Birch in which he said, among other things, that Birch might very well be a midwestern John F. Kennedy. The phone rang and Evan answered it. A man's voice said, "You tell your father that if he is going to be a midwestern John F. Kennedy,

I am going to be another Lee Harvey Oswald," and hung up. Evan and I both began to cry, just as Birch walked in. After that he agreed we could have an unlisted phone number. No family should have to go through that.

I felt too weighted down to rejoice for Birch's victory. For Birch, the momentum was too great, now, to pause for personal reasons. Though Daddy Bayh was very ill, Birch had to fly to New Mexico and New York. There were fundraisers with movie stars and comedians, speeches, network television interviews—he was riding high on his new political stardom. I tried to submerge my grief, to accompany him.

May 5, 1970, was a key day in my life: Birch began hearings on a constitutional amendment for equal rights for women, a theme I had urged for five years. It was also the day they auctioned off my farm in Oklahoma. I couldn't go back. The lawyer, Earl Mitchell, took care of it for me. Aunty and Uncle Oren carried out the details of going through the house on West Oklahoma, disposing of things. To get rid of the farm—what was left of it with a very heavy mortgage—was one of those hasty decisions that I have come to regret. Although it was the poorest land of any of the farms Daddy had his name on, the value of farmland has shot up since then. Financially, it was a mistake to sell it, but I was so drained, so exhausted, so crushed, so hurt by the whole thing, I had to put it all behind me. And I couldn't so long as I had to make decisions about the farm.

On April 30, Nixon had announced he was sending troops to Cambodia, a statement that set off a new wave of student uprisings all over the country, leaving four dead at Kent State University four days later. On May 8 and 9, nearly 100,000 students, many from the 200 colleges on strike since Kent State, massed in Washington to protest the war. Birch, I am proud to say, went out to speak to them. And I impulsively wrote a check for $200 when two University of Maryland students came to the door, asking for help in renting a plane to fly over the demonstrations with a banner: "Let's buy peace in 1972."

Evan forgot about Mother's Day that year (as fourteen-year-olds will do), which caused a surprising hurt, perhaps because I was trying to focus my emotions too tightly on my own family. Birch flew into Washington that Sunday afternoon as those other mothers' children were camped around the Lincoln Memorial, with a love letter to me on American Airlines stationery. When he saw my tears, he wept, too, saying, "I am so busy, I am not with you enough."

He spent the afternoon with his secretary, working in our living room to try to repair a Democratic party split in Indiana, and then flew out again the next evening after dinner. Seated that night between Ben Bradlee, editor of the *Washington Post*, and Dick Helms, director of the CIA, I heard the peace march analyzed, dissected, put back together again. I felt, deep within me, that Birch could reach those young people, listen to them, give them the alternative to tearing down the system.

I had watched him on college campuses, where his rapport with students was extraordinary. Since his early days in the Indiana legislature, he had been a champion of the right to vote, for anyone of draft age. Now Birch was trying to engineer in the Senate a constitutional amendment to lower the voting age to eighteen.

But his time was ever more fragmented, with increased travel back and forth to Indiana to deal with that Democratic party split eating into what little time he might have for thoughtful planning as to how he might reach those young people—or his family. In the midst of this, he had to find a nursing home for his father, a wrenching move for both of them. And then he had to leave again. "Birch mustn't let politics push out everything else in his life," his father said plaintively.

I, too, was shaky, needing love, attention, security. My father's death was a far greater blow than I could possibly tell anyone. If only there had been time to be held a bit, to be comforted, to adjust, to be calm.

But there wasn't.

At our dinner party on May 19, in honor of John Brademas, the Tom Bradens and the Mel Elfins discussed Birch's chances for the presidency. Editorials were beginning to appear, in the *Christian Science Monitor*, in the *New York Times*, mentioning him as presidential material. With Haynsworth and Carswell, and now again with electoral college reform, the spotlight was on him, the momentum going. The volume of hate mail, too, increased. I worried even more each time he traveled; I was concerned especially about the next day's trip to Mississippi, to investigate the deaths of two black Jackson State College students killed in a confrontation with police. For Birch, these trips were a matter of conviction. With death so close, I began to feel an unnatural (or, in retrospect, a natural) panic about his safety.

I wrote in my diary that Braden and Elfin seemed to think, that evening, that Birch was the only candidate who could find the path to the nation's conscience.

The Senator returned safely from Mississippi, two days later, forty-five minutes before our next dinner party. The George Mc-Governs, the Ramsey Clarks, the James Restons, the Joe Califanos, Randy and Jim Fellers from Oklahoma, Jan Shepard, and Walter Cronkite gathered around our table, talking: Vietnam. Vietnam. Vietnam. McGovern graciously proposed a toast to Birch, saying that winning on Haynsworth, and especially Carswell, did more than anything to convince the kids that the system would respond.

The issues for '72 were lining up, and instinctively I seized the thread that would bring focus to my thinking. I was alarmed about the vast difference in child care and development between our country and others I had visited. Child development centers, providing far more than custodial care, should be available for mothers who need them in this country, I thought. It was a natural theme on which to hang my efforts for Birch's presidential campaign. But somehow those efforts got all mixed up. In the background were feelings of insecurity—and fear. I woke up screaming the night of June 1. I'd dreamed that Birch had committed suicide.

The implications of what a presidential race would mean hit me with a thud during the Indainapolis "500," in May, 1970. Birch rode around the track in an open convertible; there were cheers down in the bleachers, from the low-priced seats. From the high-priced seats with the good views, for the first time since he'd been senator, there were boos. Nationally, Birch was taking positions that were unpopular in Indiana. If he failed in '72, it would be tough for his Senate race in '74. "So we very well may face four years of campaigning," I thought. It seemed there had been almost no campaign letup since 1967.

In the next month I would speak in California, Oklahoma, Oregon, Kansas, Indiana, and New York State—and I worried about Evan's reaction and my tiredness. When Birch spoke to Evan on June 2 about his running for the presidency, Evan cried, "Daddy, you're never home now. And if you get to be President, we'll never ever be normal again."

At school's closing, Evan had been singled out as a class leader.

We were so proud of him. I felt that we ought to take time to bask in his glory more, as my parents had done for me. But mainly, for me, it was the wrong time to embark on a campaign. I wanted to draw inward, to gather my family about me and cherish them. The blow of Daddy's death left an emotional wound that needed to be healed, a void that needed to be filled, and try as I might, I couldn't seem to fill it, even with my very real concerns about care centers for small children.

That's why I got off on such bad footing with some of the staff. I felt that they were scheduling Birch so tightly that he would not have a moment, ever again, to be with us. Evan, especially, entering adolescence with the usual sensitivities, wanted to have a "normal" life, whatever that is.

There is a natural tug-of-war for the politician's time, between his staff, who, after all, have hung their careers upon his, and his wife, who may yearn for a normal family relationship. But in those days I did not know that this was a common occurrence; it was not something political wives discussed with one another. It was not until I read Abigail McCarthy's thoughtful *Private Faces/Public Places* in 1972 that I discovered other wives suffered from rivalry with the staff. In 1970, I thought only I was having trouble.

The built-in conflict between staff and home was heightened during the presidential campaign—but the stakes now were bigger for those who had hitched their wagons to his star. They wanted Birch out on the stump constantly, and when there was a break, they wanted him back in Indiana, or wherever else he could get the most political mileage. All too often they told him what they thought he wanted to hear, for those same reasons. I soon realized how very important our heavy schedule of entertaining at home was —not just to establish contacts, but also to expose Birch to ideas and opinions from strong people outside his staff.

That it was the same staff who had brought us out of the 1968 campaign into debt still bothered me, too. I saw the same petty jealousies at work among them, the same inattention to details, the same "clods and kings" mentality that had divided the office then. When I'd cry, at dinner, because some secretary had been rude to me, he'd say, "Haven't you been too demanding?" I never could understand why he let them treat me that way.

I *was* demanding—less so with others than with myself, but nevertheless, I was insistent on performance. I now realize that if they made me feel an outsider, I must have been anathema to them. My career was so intertwined with his that I suffered from endless frustration when things weren't done exactly the way I'd have them done, or as I'd seen them done with split-second precision during the 1964 LBJ campaign.

On June 25, 1970, I wrote: "I really hope Birch never runs for the Senate again. Life is too short to live like this. As far as what happens in 1972, for President or Vice President, I will roll with the punches. But Birch has served long enough in public life not to seek another term. We never see him. When he is in town, it's only because there are night sessions in the Senate, and he gets home at midnight. I married for companionship, not this, and I told him so."

It was no way to begin a strenuous national campaign, and I knew it. Jane Sinnenberg may have saved my life that summer—at least until the campaign began in the fall. We took our sons, her Steven and my Evan, and spent two weeks driving through the British Isles. (Birch couldn't join us; he was wrestling to get his electoral college reform bill, which had passed the House, up before the Senate, the first step for a constitutional amendment on direct election of the President.) Ours was a liberating trip, two women and two teenage boys sightseeing in London, and then renting a car to travel on "the wrong side of the road" through the countryside.

But Jane let me talk on and on about my father, talk that had been bottled up in my system since April Fool's Day, talk for which there was no time at home. From Edinburgh to Killarney, she listened, until some of the pain was drained out.

Flowers, hedges, stone fences, lakes, castles, and the greenest grass I'd ever seen; easy companionship, funny fourteen-year-olds, not reading about Vietnam in the newspapers; it was a soothing trip, a shaking-down of values. I yearned to share these quiet experiences with Birch.

On July 31, outside Newmarket-on-Fergus, Ireland, I awoke in Dromoland Castle at 7:50 A.M. and took a long walk, past the biggest roses I'd ever seen. Down a narrow path, there was a huge tree, like an umbrella, with branches that touched the ground. I stopped there, just to feel its presence. "Be still, and know that I am God," I suddenly thought, the verse from the Bible filling my mind with peace.

I wish that I had taken that message as a sign, a lesson for my life.

Birch was waiting at the airport when we arrived home, looking at me with those sky-colored eyes like a young boy in love. I had missed him, but not as painfully as when he left *me* at home for two weeks; I didn't stop to wonder why. There wasn't time.

"Would you like to be First Lady?" Birch asked me.

"It would be a job," I answered.

While I was gone he had written a song for me; on our eighteenth anniversary he played his guitar and sang the song.

"Nixon really can be beaten," Birch said. "We can get away to Camp David together."

"That's really dreaming," I laughed. "I'd rather go to the Greenbrier."

"I'd like to get him away together without having to beat Nixon," I thought, as we left for New York and his latest appearance on the "Today" show, another for the both of us on the David Frost show.

By mid-October we were rushing about the country on the pre-campaign trail and I was back to square one.

Tranquilizers to sleep again, and a basketful of tension all day long. Night after night, dreaming about Daddy, I would wake up sobbing. Perhaps if grief had not been at the base of my physical problems, I could have thrown myself into the campaign as heartily as I had in 1962.

"I want to die of old age, and with my boots on," I told Dr. Fulcher late that year, when I went to him about a racing heart. "Not from this."

The price of a presidential race, I now saw, was more pressure —more than I honestly thought I was able to endure. The other part of me was organized, neatly put together, writing speeches and delivering them, always smiling in public, always giving the appropriate response for a proud wife. One reporter called me "saccharine" —and no wonder. What natural sweetness I might have felt was tempered by the misery inside me.

When you are caught up in this plethora of campaign plans, the opponent somehow never seems as formidable as he actually is. In early 1971, Richard Nixon's "six great goals, to change the framework of government itself," spelled out in his State of the Union message, were met with less than excitement, giving each of the Democratic hopefuls the idea he might be able to heal the rifts in the Democratic party and, by 1972, to build up a groundswell to defeat the President.

George McGovern announced right away, pledging his campaign directly to the Vietnam issue, on an early and definite date for U.S. withdrawal. The others of us, including Ed Muskie (who, considered the frontrunner, already reportedly had a campaign budget of $1.25 million), quietly opened our Washington campaign offices, and set about looking for enough money to keep them open.

The California convention, which was scrutinized by the national press, filled Birch with optimism, for his speech there was enthusiastically received. ("In First Heat of Demo Run for '72, Muskie Leads, Bayh Edges McGovern," announced a headline in the *Miami Herald*.) To add fuel to his optimism and exposure as well, there was an important two-part story by Richard Harris in *The New Yorker* about the Carswell fight, and the announcement that actor Hal Holbrook had studied Birch as the prototype for his popular "Senator" role on television's "The Bold Ones."

For me, there was a "typical" Washington dinner party at my house, covered by the *Ladies' Home Journal*, a full-page article in *Women's Wear Daily*, speeches in Washington, Philadelphia, and Detroit, and a trip to Israel with Birch, where he studied politics and I studied their methods and expenditures for child care.

As I had dumped on him all my statistics and outrage about the treatment of women in this country, which led to his sponsorship of the Equal Rights Amendment (then still in Judiciary Committee), I also was honored by his taking seriously all my study, comparisons, findings on child care. In December, he had announced a proposal to provide national child care for fourteen million children of American working mothers.

It should have been a glorious time. But weighing upon my already low emotional state was the continuing problem of maintaining a new home that seemed to be falling apart faster than it could be fixed. We were in for a siege of floods, through the window wells below and from the humidifier through the ceiling; the dishwasher simply gave up, the new furnace quit. And I had no household help. Our lovely Lachina Morrison had married, and now was working in a bank in Virginia. Dorothy Coutain, who tided us over the rough spots last year, had gone back to Trinidad. Macel, bless her, came up from West Virginia for emergencies, but could not stay. There had been a series of helpers who moved in and out, bewildered perhaps by our unpredictable hours, our pressured existence. (One simply stole away in the middle of the night.) If I were to enter into a strenuous campaign, especially one that Evan opposed, I would need a calm, firm hand managing the house. Precious, frustrating time was being spent trying to find her.

I would need new clothes for a campaign. By now, fashion had become something of an adventure, rather than the fearsome challenge of my first days in Washington. I had a small wardrobe, but it rotated rapidly. (Dorothy Stead had taught me well.) In February, in New York for a birthday celebration with the Rogerses and Jan Shepard, I shopped for American designer clothes, remembering how awed I was when those names appeared at my first Washington fashion show.

It was there in New York, on my thirty-eighth birthday, that my right breast began to hurt.

The x-ray was okay, the physical exam showed no lump. I was vastly relieved. Birch was away, speaking in Texas; I was home, feeling dizzy and a little disoriented. I drove out to the nursing home to see Birch's father, and was distressed by how much he had deteriorated. I wanted to cling to him that bleak February day, to stop time. He was the only parent we had.

I was feeling awful. Back to the doctor: low blood pressure. B-12 shots. Speeches were ahead, traveling all spring and summer. Birch would announce in the fall.

The B-12 shots did not pull up my spirits, however. And even now, when I think of 1970 and '71, I shudder. They were the worst years of my life, especially 1971, as we built up to the announcement. I remember running into George McGovern, early in March. He was alone, at a dinner party; "Eleanor is in Spain for three weeks taking a rest." I'm sure I turned a bright green, wishing I could move to Spain and come back after the election.

From my point of view, the campaign was in a mess. There was dissension between the campaign staff and the office staff, and in the office there was in-fighting and jealousy, some workers not speaking to others, secretaries yelling at administrative assistants . . . and at Birch.

Birch was trying to be conscientious about his job as a senator, and at the same time he was flying around the country, back and forth, writing his own speeches on the plane because they couldn't afford to hire a top-notch speechwriter, appearing jovial and alert at all these speeches; he was sometimes delicately, sometimes blatantly asking for money. To me, he looked exhausted. And when he walked in the front door after all this, he began to growl.

At a fundraiser in New York, a woman walked up to me and said, "Why do you want your husband to be President? You'd never see him."

I felt like answering, "I don't see him now."

Nixon's announcement relaxing the trade embargo with China was a coup. But it did not cut much ice with the young, for two days later, he again refused to set a date for withdrawal of our troops from Vietnam—and the May Day anti-war demonstrations in Washington erupted, with more than 10,000 arrests. We still have a number of touching thank-you letters from those students and professors who slept in our campaign office during this time.

By June, money had become so scarce for the campaign that they had trouble keeping the phones going. Creditors started bringing the bills to the house or phoning: "Mrs. Bayh, we are embarrassed to do this, but we have sent four bills to the presidential campaign committee and haven't had any response." Credit cards were being canceled, phones being taken out. I felt the old panic about the debt being placed on my own back.

On vacation that summer, trying to show Evan the West, Yosemite, the Grand Canyon, Birch and I argued until we were spent. By this time, I was sick of politics, and what it was doing to our lives.

"I wish he would make sure we get enough [money] to get out of debt," I wrote in my diary, "and then forget the whole crazy business. I think 1972 will be a bad year anyway. Nixon will have toned down the war, gone to China, and pumped in the dollars he should be spending now on the economy, but isn't. Money the Congress has already appropriated."

Birch was angry, curt with me. I was shrill, almost frantic about the money problems. By now he had campaign organizations in eight states, and the groundswell was something he could feel. I became the rain on his parade, and he shut me out. Evan saw us fighting too much; I had begged for some time with Birch. No, he had to fly out to be best man in Alan Rachels' wedding. "Alan is my friend," he said. "I am your friend, too," I cried. He walked out the door and flew to Indiana.

Sally Quinn of the *Washington Post* came to interview us. I pasted on a smile, tried to act the part of the energetic candidate's wife. "I live, totally, through my husband," I told her. The piece appeared on June 20, showing a surface relationship between typical candidate and wife, guardedly trying to say the Right Thing. She could not know what lay seething below the surface.

Less than a month after that, I arrived home to find that Birch had called a staff meeting in the basement of our home, to talk about the debt. "I don't want us fighting about the debt in front of the staff," he said. That was the lowest point.

"May I just read Jim's memo?" I asked.

"No, I don't want you to read it. You'll just agree with everything he says."

Shut out. I had made his career my career, had dragged myself all over the country all summer giving speeches, like a puppet on a string, mouthing a false enthusiasm, feeling like a hypocrite, and now I was excluded in my own home. While the meeting went on, my spirits dropped to rock bottom. Emotionally, my bitterness was beyond description. I felt our marriage was deeply in trouble, that I could no longer reach Birch. For the first time, I considered leaving him. And I believe he felt the same way.

Birch's father died on August 26, two days after our nineteenth wedding anniversary, and we went to Terre Haute for the funeral. Birch was devastated. Birch Evans Bayh, Sr., was a wonderful man, whose legacy to Birch was a good name—a fine, clean name with an unblemished reputation—a strong moral code, and a passion for physical fitness. He was always gentle, supportive to me, and I felt the loss acutely. But Birch submerged his grief in the campaign. I knew how much his father had meant to him; I could see the sadness in his eyes, but for Birch, there was no time to talk it out, to share his grief. Again, there was no time to mourn. The campaign meetings went on in our basement, the staff running in and out. I wondered if there were no personal sacrifice too great for the campaign to demand. I saw this presidential campaign as a monster, eating up everything in its path. The candidate feels constant, unrelenting pressure, not the least of which is responsibility for so many people, some who have quit their jobs to work for him. He must not let these people down. Moreover, the candidate is only one individual, but he is wanted, needed, in thousands of places at once, or so it seems. The candidate must present himself to millions of people, and millions of dollars must be raised, for transportation, television, staff, to make this presentation; the campaign fires must be stoked to keep the momentum building. The campaign had eaten up our marriage; in my bitterness, I saw it swallowing Birch himself.

After the funeral services, our dear friend Auntie Katherine, close as family, who had mothered Birch and Mary Alice after her friend Leah died, talked to me at her house. "What is wrong with Bud?" she asked. "He is not himself at all." He was preoccupied, snappish, constantly being called to the phone by the campaign organization.

"It's the campaign," I answered. "It has taken over his life. Nothing else matters."

She was disturbed. "Is it worth all this?"

But in JFK's 1958 words, "the ball may come across the plate only once"—and Birch was ready to take his swing. He was building up to an announcement in November.

"When you're in the Senate," I tried to explain to her, "you have bills, goals, tangible things you're trying to accomplish. And when you have been there for awhile, and adjusted to the effort it takes, you do see that there is more power in the White House, to accomplish those goals."

"Our system of choosing a President is absolutely barbaric," I continued. "The average person has no idea of the demands on a presidential candidate and his family. How anybody comes out of this with his health intact is beyond me." I shudder to think of our country, every four years, in the hands of the marathon winner, who is so drained and exhausted from the campaign he can hardly think. He is facing immediate decisions—choosing a cabinet, for one—that will affect the entire nation. He should be prepared, rested, thoughtful, to take on the most weighty job in the world. Instead, he has emerged from this meatgrinder, the campaign, as its victim, its captive.

It had to be a test of the strength of our marriage that we survived it.

Two days after Daddy Bayh's funeral, there was an especially important Interparliamentary Union trip to Paris because Birch had scheduled a meeting with the North Vietnamese delegation to the peace talks, in which he made sure I was also included. While he met with the parliamentary delegates, I toured day care centers, each one more impressive than the last. Back at the hotel Birch and I argued, about the staff, about the debt. The campaign now owed $200,000—$60,000 of it was ours personally. I delivered an ultimatum: I would refuse to campaign at all until the debt was paid. "I wish so much that you'd be satisfied with being a great senator," I told him.

But Paris softened us. We sat at a sidewalk cafe our last evening there; we held hands, we loved. I relented. Yes, I would go to Wisconsin, to Oregon, to speak for him. He was off and running—to California, to Wisconsin, to New Hampshire. He planned to announce his candidacy in November, with a morning news conference in Washington, then a dash by jet to Tallahassee, Milwaukee, Lincoln (Nebraska), and Los Angeles, all in the same day, for "simultaneous" announcements. There would be a primary in each state.

It was September 23, and I was just back from speaking for Birch to a group of Democratic women in New Jersey. Birch had taken off for Florida that day; he would return to Pennsylvania, not Washington. I also checked in with Dr. Hawken on September 23, for a mammogram. My right breast, the same one that had bothered me in February, felt swollen again. Now, there was an occasional zip of pain, like a small electric shock.

A week later, I went back to Dr. Hawken to find out the results. As in February, the x-rays were okay, he told me. There was no lump he could feel, either. But he wanted a biopsy, because the skin around my nipple seemed "a little unusual." He couldn't get an operating room for eight days.

Birch had called that morning from New York, with jubilant news. He had pledges of money in his pocket to erase our entire campaign debt. We could now officially announce his candidacy "in the black."

Now, that afternoon, he was in Ohio. When he called, I told him my frightening news. He flew to Washington that night to be with me, and flew back out again the next morning.

There was an 80 to 85 percent chance I would be all right, the doctor told me. But still. The night before I entered the hospital, as I performed in a show for the Women's National Democratic

Club, I wondered: would I ever be able to wear a dress like this again? It was a flapper dress, low-cut, with spaghetti straps, worn with no bra.

Birch watched me dance in the show; then he flew to Florida afterward. Bob Blaemire, Birch's aide, drove me to the hospital the next day. That evening Birch flew back from Florida to have dinner with me in the hospital room. He brought in steaks, I remember, that were just about the best steaks I'd ever eaten. We talked about the campaign, about how things were looking up. "If I get out of here all right," I promised, "I'll help you in the campaign—in any way that I can."

We laughed and joked a little, but I was worried about tomorrow's biopsy. I had insisted on a biopsy only—because I couldn't stand not knowing if they were going to remove my breast. Besides, I felt more comfortable with the pathologist having longer to study the report.

An intern came by to examine me. "I can't understand what you're in here for," he said cheerfully. "If it were up to me, I'd send you on home."

But I worried. Birch could see it.

"Everything's going to be all right," he said. "I just know it."

"You said that just before the plane crash," I said.

But I wrote in my diary: "Scared. Pray, pray breast condition not cancerous."

It was.

Chapter 11

I could not believe it. With only a 10 percent chance of it being so, with no palpable lump, no indications from the x-rays, I had breast cancer. I was that cold statistic: One out of every thirteen American women.

When I awoke in the recovery room, groggy from the anesthesia, Dr. Hawken was standing over me, Birch kneeling by my side. I could see the distress in their eyes.

"I'm afraid I have bad news," the doctor said. "It's malignant. We'll have to remove the breast."

I went into shock, my chin trembling out of my control.

"Bad news. Bad news," I cried out, over and over again. "I'm only thirty-eight years old. I don't want to die." And then, with wrenching fear, I thought about Evan, mischievous, challenging, fifteen-year-old Evan. "But I have the most wonderful boy. . . ." I cried to Dr. Hawken.

It didn't occur to me then to worry about losing a breast. I was afraid of cancer. The word itself revolted me.

I called Aunty and Macel, to pray for me. Dr. Hawken, too, said he had prayed, "but this time prayer didn't help."

On October 8, at eight in the morning, I went in for surgery. It took two hours, a modified radical mastectomy, in which Dr. Hawken and Dr. Scully removed my right breast, a portion of the chest muscle, and the lymph glands in the armpit. If none of the lymph nodes are malignant, the cancer is said to be in "stage one," or localized. If nodes, these little defenders of the body against infection, are involved, the cancer has spread, and is in "stage two." Birch and

Dr. Hawken told me that there were only two nodes involved, which I took to be a good sign.

"Everything's fine," Dr. Hawken told me in the recovery room. "I think we surrounded it."

It slowly began to occur to me that he may have saved my life, this doctor who had felt something was wrong even though the mammogram had detected nothing, because he noticed a slight skin change below my right nipple, and a certain "lack of mobility" in that particular area. He took the chance, insisting on a biopsy when others might have said "wait."

Immediately after the biopsy, Birch had called Paul Rogers, our dear friend who, as chairman of the House Subcommittee on Public Health and the Environment, had become very knowledgeable in the health field. Paul helped give both of us reassurance, as he and Birch called top cancer experts around the country, who concurred with the diagnosis and the prescribed treatment. Dr. Hawken put me in touch with a cancer specialist, an oncologist. I would have twenty-five radiation treatments on my chest where my right breast had been, five times a week, then eighteen months of weekly chemotherapy, a drug injected into my veins.

It all seemed a nightmare, some horror movie I was watching. I couldn't take in that it was happening to me. . . .

Four days after surgery, it hit. Even with shots, sedatives, and sleeping pills, I stayed awake all night, wrestling with the fear of mutilation, and death. Why had it happened to me? I rolled over, facing the wall, crying. All I could think of was that I wanted my mother.

The next evening, Jane Sinnenberg beside me, I lay there in Columbia Hospital for Women, watching the television set high above my head. There was my husband, on the evening news, speaking at a packed press conference from a room in the Senate building.

"During the last several months, I have seriously considered becoming a candidate for the presidency," he said. "I have made this effort because of my concern for the problems that confront our country and each of us as individuals. . . ."

He talked about Vietnam, where Americans were still dying, and about this country, where millions of Americans can't find work. He spoke of how he had been encouraged—"how *we* had been encouraged," he said—by citizens all over the country declaring their support, and how he had planned to announce within the next few weeks his intention to seek the Democratic presidential nomination.

Then he paused. I could feel those clear blue eyes looking straight at me. "Whenever I have had an important decision to make during the seventeen years I have had the good fortune to serve in public life, my wife, Marvella, has always been there." Another pause. "But Marvella is not here today. She is not here because she underwent critical surgery for a malignancy.

"We have every reason to believe the operation was a success," he went on in a choked voice. "However, her complete recovery may require a lengthy period of recuperation. During this time, I want to be at her side—not in Miami, Milwaukee, or Los Angeles. . . .

"Therefore I am not a candidate for the presidency."

I lay there, tears streaming down my face, feeling more pain for my husband than in the wound in my chest where my right breast had been. He had worked so hard—and had been so hopeful. The 1972 elections were hardly a year away, and Birch's bandwagon now appeared to be rolling along. More than anyone, I realized how much it had meant to him.

I turned to Jane. "I feel like Wallis Simpson," I said.

"Oh, no, this is better!" Jane replied. "Her man was only in the first blush of romance when he gave up the throne to be by her side. You've been married for nineteen years, and Birch knows all your faults. Now that's *really* something!"

It was something, as it turned out. Because, as my scars were healing and the chemotherapy took its effect, the wounds in our marriage began to heal, as well. Birch and I had allowed the great disease of political life—time and energy and priorities for everything except ourselves—to eat its way through our home as the disease was eating its way through my body. Beneath the facade of the "perfect political partnership" that we tried to portray, there had been too much tension and anger, frustration, and pain—mostly *my* anger and frustration, I now realize, because I had tried to live out my life through his life's work.

That was too big a burden for either Birch or me to carry. It took a look at death itself—at the possibility of losing, not Birch, but my own life—to make me take stock of my values, my priorities. And now Birch made this choice. I had asked him as he was leaving for that press conference, "Are you sure, sure you are doing the right thing?" He held me. "I've never been so sure of anything in my life." From him came my greatest support, my will to fight. "We're going to lick this thing," he kept repeating to me, that strong Bayh chin jutting out as if he were still the old Golden Gloves contender—until those words just burned into my brain. When fear of dying sank me into a pit of despair, Birch held my hand, and forced me to think only of living.

That first hard question, "Why me?"—why did I have cancer —spun through my head as I searched back. I gathered up possible reasons, to share with the doctors:

Did DDT cause my cancer? When I was a little girl, I had stood by the fence and watched a tiny airplane spray a white cloud of poison over my father's wheat field to kill the destructive "green bugs." The wind blew the cloud over me. Now cancer was linked with DDT in recent reports.

Or could it have been radiation? When I was eleven, recovering from pneumonia, I had had weeks of x-ray treatments on my bronchial tubes—a treatment that has long been discontinued because of the link to cancer. Was it the x-rays (which would be minor compared to the radiation I was to receive now)?

Another thought: For years I had dieted, knowing that my metabolism would rather put on fat than give me energy. I had depended on years and years of artificial sweeteners, diet colas. There had been reports linking additives and dyes to cancer. I also worried about having eaten so much red meat.

Only recently had the reports on hormones come in. Women were being warned against overuse of estrogen. For years I had relied on estrogen to regulate my cycles. Had that caused my cancer?

It seemed that just about everything I had read about as being carcinogenic, or even suspected of causing cancer, I had used, eaten, or been subjected to, except tobacco. (I had never smoked, thank Heaven.) In addition, I read that many cancer victims are people who have undergone periods of severe physical or emotional stress. I couldn't help but wonder if the stress under which I had been living had caused my malignancy—in particular the years of worry about my father. Nor had I fully coped with the strain of my father's death, the ensuing insomnia and anxiety. I had tried to bury it under the pressure of the campaign. Moreover, I had not been able to deal with the strain of the campaign upon my marriage.

I brought my concern to Dr. Hawken, hopeful that he could isolate the reason.

"What has caused this?"

He was quiet, just looking out the window.

"Oh, if we only knew the answer to that question," he finally said.

There was less pain and discomfort after the surgery than I expected. That would come later, with the radiation treatments. Under the bandages, I only felt rather . . . lopsided. And my arm didn't work very well. Though for some reason I'd always paid more attention to my hair than to my bosom, still the thought of mutilation of that part was hard, as any woman who has had the experience knows.

I had cried out to Birch, "How am I going to go through the rest of my life with only one breast?"

And he had answered, causing me to laugh until tears came, "Well, I've made it all right through forty-three years without even one!"

But then he said, "Do you think I married you for your breasts? I married you for *you*."

He will never be able to comprehend how much that statement meant to me, at that time. I had been worrying, as all women do, what would I see in the mirror? I felt embarrassed by all the publicity. Because of Birch's announcement, I thought that everybody now knew I'd lost a breast. Would they stare? And Birch? I had wondered if he would find me repulsive. Now that I knew the answer to that, the other questions meant nothing. I was more worried about survival than appearance.

As I was feeling down, stringy-haired, and unattractive after a week in the hospital, into my room walked a woman looking like a million dollars, in a jersey blouse, slit midi skirt, and stunning hairdo. I was tempted to pull the covers over my head. "I'm Virginia Newman, from Reach to Recovery," she said. "And I want to talk to you." As a volunteer from the American Cancer Society, her job was to show me how to wear a prosthesis (artificial breast), to exercise my right arm with a ball and rope, which she brought along in her kit—and most important, to make me feel a whole woman again.

Virginia Newman, with her sleek figure, looked me in the

eye and said, "A few years ago, I had a breast removed, just like you. You must remember that you are the same person today that you were before surgery—in every way." She talked with me for more than an hour, while I looked her up and down, deciding that I'd better get on with it and look as smart as this woman did. She gave me advice that meant more from her than it would have from any doctor—unless the doctor were a woman who had also had a mastectomy. "Act as you always did with your family and friends. They will feel more at ease, and so will you. Go back to your normal way of life as soon as possible, whether it is home or career. You'll feel better for it." (I wondered if I could explain the madness that was my "normal" way of life. Or, now, if I could ever go back to it.) "Do you enjoy sports?"

"No," I answered, "but I do take exercises."

"Then resume them. And drive your car just as soon as your doctor gives the green light. But be sure not to overdo. Getting tired will only retard your recovery."

She cautioned me about having blood pressure taken or injections given on my right arm, on the side where the surgery had been done, and then she grinned.

"Don't neglect your appearance. And don't allow yourself to become discouraged."

She left her phone number in case I had further questions, and she left me, in addition to her kit, a precious gift—hope.

I had been listless. Now, I decided to get all dressed up. There were to be some special tests on spleen and liver over at George Washington University Hospital, for which I determined not to appear in a hospital robe. The nurse had to help me pin the padding in my bra—and then take out padding again and again to reduce it to balance with my small, natural left side. (We were both giggling, during that exercise.)

I called Birch at his office. "Come quickly, I need to see you. It's an emergency." I was in the parking lot getting ready to go when he came, late as usual, rushing across the lot. He saw me, realized what was up, and threw his arms around me. It was a very happy time, because I looked normal, dressed, and with this temporary prosthesis, just as I had when I entered the hospital. Dr. Hawken took interest—and delight—in this, as well.

Another unexpected gift was the rush of encouraging mail from all over the country. From my initial embarrassment over Birch's public announcement, I was first astonished, then grateful, at the letters from friends and strangers, many of whom were writing to say that they, too, were "mastectomees," and life was just fine, thank you. A senator's wife whom I had always considered attractive greeted me with a grin: "You know, I had both my breasts removed." (I hadn't known.) My hospital room was overflowing with flowers, the phone rang off the hook, telegrams and get-well cards filled up the mailbasket, giving me a clue about the basic goodness of the human condition and causing me to wish, strongly, to remain a part of it. Three weeks after leaving the hospital, I went to a dinner party at the Sulgrave Club wearing the lowest-cut dress I owned, just to prove I could do it.

The operation and my initial terror were survivable, I was helped to discover. But the radiation treatments almost did me in. They burned my chest until it was raw, and I felt my spirits sag with each treatment. Not everybody reacts the same way. But for me, it was the low point of the experience—worse than the surgery, worse than the one-drug chemotherapy that followed,* which did not have devastating side effects.

Not only did the radiation sap my strength, but the physical surroundings in which radiation was administered were very depressing. I have toured hospitals since then, and found that many have made a successful effort to keep the radiation department from being a dungeon. In my low state, the absence of any cheerful touches in the large Washington hospital to which I had been assigned wore on my spirits. Five days a week, I drove down to the hospital, took the elevator to the basement, took a number, and settled myself in the bleak room for perhaps a two-hour wait. Some of the patients were obviously in the last stages of cancer, dying, while others of us were having our first encounter with the disease. To see those very seriously ill patients, fear in their eyes, lying on stretchers or hospital carts, waiting for their numbers to be called, was very depressing, as I knew I had the same disease. We waited together, silently.

When my number was called, I would go into a little cubicle, strip, and put on a clean, shapeless, mud-colored robe. Then I would be taken to the x-ray room, with its heavy concrete walls, and told to climb up on a table. The technicians placed the machine at

* More effective combination-drug chemotherapies have been put into practice since that time.

measured distances from me, then left the room. I lay there, alone, wondering about the effect of x-rays on the rest of my body. A red light flashed on, followed by an eerie grating noise, like the whine of a train coming to a halt.

I was bleeding from the treatments, my chest like raw meat, my back burned light brown. I had difficulty swallowing, and my arm ached. My energy was sapped, depleted. Some mornings it took all the effort I could muster just to get to the bathroom and brush my teeth. But if this is what it took to save my life, it was worth it. At home I kept a chart. Each day I would mark off one more day, knowing that on a certain day the treatment would end. Birch was more than wonderful. His loving notes, his precious time kept me from buckling under.

One day after my radiation treatment I found a note, scrawled on a page of school notebook paper, tucked underneath my wind-shield wiper: "I see your car parked here very day, Mrs. Bayh. I just wanted you to know others are thinking of you and wishing you a complete recovery. Hang in there." It was unsigned, but it must have been from a university student, going to classes nearby. (That writer will never know what a lift it gave me. It struck me how each one of us can do so much to help others by taking a tiny moment of time.)

Mike Sperling died in November, of a heart attack. This loss of our benefactor, who was like a father to both of us, added heart-ache to the pain I was bearing. As I had felt once before, after the double blow of losing my mother and the plane crash, the spectre of death seemed just beyond the edge of my vision, although one part of me was fighting for my life.

I was talking about this life with Stewart Alsop just after Thanksgiving, at Tom and Joan Braden's dinner party for Kirk and Anne Douglas. Stewart, grappling with leukemia, and I, with my lopsided chest, quietly compared notes about cancer. I confessed to loving life almost too much—even the silly feeling of thinking, "me, Marvella Hern, sitting here with a movie star." And Stewart said to me, in almost the same words that so many other cancer patients had written to me, "It wasn't until I knew I might lose my life that I really began to live it." On the way home, that thought stayed with me—and the next day, and the next . . . "Until I knew I might lose my life. . . ."

The old question of my identity, which had been shelved year after year while I was out making political speeches for Birch, came back to haunt me. Who *is* this person who might lose her life? There had never been time to spread my own wings all alone, to be *me*.

That one great regret grew, filling me first with rancor—toward Birch's political advisors who had persuaded me to turn down President Johnson's job offer, and then treated me like excess baggage after the campaign; then with rage at myself—at having spent my life like a robot, always doing what others expected of me, using my God-given talents and my youth to do whatever my parents, or my husband, or that larger enemy, society ("serve on this committee, that committee"; "don't speak your own opinion, speak his"; "go to this luncheon, that reception, they expect you to be there") had dictated. And all this time I had never struck out, earned a regular paycheck, stood on my own two feet alone, and said, "I did this."

While I had all this time to think, I promised myself that if I were given another opportunity at life, I was going to correct that gaping hole in my life's experience. Cancer made me realize for the first time that life is going to be over before we know it, and that if there is something important for you to do, *do* it. To a certain degree, what John Kennedy said about the presidency is true for each of us. When the ball comes across the plate, you had better take your swing, because you might not get another chance. I had passed by many chances. I wanted my own career and didn't pursue it. Now here I was facing up to the fact that it might all be over. "If I get out of this alive," I vowed, "if I get another crack at life, when my chemotherapy is finished, I am going to pursue my career, whatever it might be, and make my own contribution in my own way."

This, aside from my wedding vow, was the most important promise I had ever made. It was like getting a new lease on life. It fueled my will, and with Birch in the background repeating, "we're going to lick this thing," I focused so hard on getting well I was sure my will was entering my bloodstream along with the chemotherapy, to seek out and kill any rapidly dividing cells that might have escaped. I was determined to be one of that 85 percent of all mastectomees who live to celebrate the five-year anniversary of surgery.

With that vow behind me, my life changed dramatically. Soon after the radiation treatments ended, my energy began to return. And true to his word, Birch was by my side. We cranked the ice-cream freezer; I served up fried chicken, green beans, angel-food cake, as on the farm. We three actually spent evenings together as a family.

Birch and I laughed together—in truth, we rediscovered the kind of day-to-day marriage we hadn't had since those young days amid the pigs and flies in Shirkieville, or in law school. I found such pleasure in his company, my blue-eyed Birch of the strong, loving arms, who made up songs to me and played them on his guitar. We went out with our friends, and kicked up our heels, and I felt wonderfully free of the old niggling fear that they'd think we were seeking their support. And as a tough parental team, we ganged up on Evan, who was having a "normal" life and beginning to feel his own teenage oats. We set rules and limits, and weathered the explosions—and sat in the bleachers for his ball games, held our breath while he drove us around flexing his new driver's license, complimented his taste when he brought home his first girl friend. We celebrated a lot—the end of radiation on December 10; the paying off of Birch's presidential campaign debt just after Christmas; our trip to New York for the sixth year in a row with the Shepards and Rogerses; Birch's Equal Rights Amendment being voted out of committee on March 1, and approved by the Senate on March 22, 1972.

Birch had held to a strong schedule in the Senate, holding hearings on juvenile delinquency and drug abuse, shepherding his amendment on equal rights for women. Except for the latter, in which I took vicarious pleasure, I felt my involvement in politics receding. It was a good feeling.

I could sit next to Henry Kissinger at a dinner party and be as thoroughly charmed as anybody else, without worrying that my husband was pitted against his boss. I could listen, in a detached way, to Muskie and Humphrey vie for Birch's endorsement (in essence, for the organization he had built), and, when asked, give my opinion, not tumbling all over myself to impose it on him. (I could also call his office, now, without a knot in my stomach.)

I could look at Nixon's trip to China, and watch this historic event crumble Muskie's lead in the polls with a sure sense that Nixon would probably be unbeatable this year. I read a lot, a luxury that I had denied myself for so long, and felt rather removed from the political scene, except for watching the debate on the Equal Rights Amendment.

Perhaps if we had known of the "dirty tricks" the Committee to Reelect the President was already employing to sabotage Democratic candidates, we would all have been so outraged it would have overcome the "Nixon is unbeatable" frame of mind. But we, like the rest of the country, just assumed that politics this year was no different from usual—just tough. Joan Mondale confided to me at a dinner party that she couldn't get excited about the campaign this year, not as she had been about Stevenson or Kennedy, and wondered if we were all "just getting old." George McGovern, a truly gentle man, was out methodically organizing a new group of voters who had not participated in politics before, but who by no stretch of the imagination constituted a majority. Nixon was flexing his diplomatic feats, first in China, then in Russia; George Wallace was out fanning the fires of backlash with "send them a message."

Birch and I were relaxing at the Greenbrier, a lovely, private Mother's Day celebration, when we heard about the assassination attempt on George Wallace. We clung together, my husband and I, grateful to be out of the madness of presidential politics. Aware of the unpredictability of life itself. Appreciative of the gift of life, and of each other, as individuals in our own right.

Until now I had not stopped to think that my parents had lived totally through me, and that was a grave mistake for them and a burden for me. I realized I had made the same mistake. By living through Birch, I had not only thwarted my own development, but placed a heavy burden on him, as well. I have always struggled hard to be in control. Imagine the frustration that built up when I saw a campaign in which I was only vicariously running, careening out of my control. Imagine Birch's frustration at my frustration. How he tolerated my trying to run everything, I will never know. Now, as I withdrew, retreating into my own strengths, I realized that I did not have to be inextricably bound up in Birch's life. So I would have run a tighter ship than he ran. So what? It was his ship, not mine. What freedom, for both of us, to release my career from his. Had being "Mrs. Birch Bayh" erased Marvella Hern, as it had erased her name? Of course it hadn't, for Mrs. Birch Bayh had truly enjoyed a great portion of that roller-coaster ride. But in that assessment of life that comes when one is fearing death, it came to me that the accomplishments of which I was most proud, the ones I could count as my own, were those from way back in high school. And here I was, almost forty.

Had I pursued it on my own, politics might have been fulfilling for me, an occupation combining my abilities and my ambition. But having lived it second-hand, I knew that politics was not the right direction for me. It was Birch's life, *his* star to follow.

In June, one of those fortuitous events in life's journey occurred. A writer named Lester David had asked to interview me for an article on breast cancer that he was writing for *Today's Health* magazine. I had known so little about the disease when I was so suddenly confronted with it that I felt I could help to inform other women about what to expect—especially the important role that the Reach to Recovery volunteer had played in helping me to accept myself—and I would be happy to cooperate.

When the article appeared, carefully researched and full of information, carrying my experience to "humanize" it a bit, the impact was stronger than I had ever dreamed. Mostly, letters came from doctors, thanking me for speaking out, urging me to continue to do so, saying that I could help women face this disease. I had not thought much about the public's lack of knowledge, thinking that my own ignorance was due to my not having read up on the subject. The truth was that very little had been written for women about mastectomy back then. Now, I realized that breast cancer had been a fearful, shameful subject to many women—and editors. The approximately 72,000 American women in 1972 * who would discover they had it were faced with a situation that was still "in the closet," so to speak. So when the Indiana chapter of the American Cancer Society asked Birch and me to be honorary co-chairmen of its annual Crusade, both of us readily accepted.

I was in Indiana for my annual teaching stint at Girls' State when the CREEP burglars broke into Democratic headquarters at the Watergate. I didn't even notice the news item. Later I was pleased to sit quietly at the Democratic Convention in Miami, feeling no envy whatsoever for George and Eleanor McGovern. Shortly after the convention, Birch was elected to a spot on the Senate Appropriations Committee, to which he had aspired for a long time. He was excited—and so was I. Being a distinguished senator was a valuable career, I thought. And when I was strong enough, I could pursue my own career without being dragged around in a presidential race.

He and I had been off to Africa together, six months after the surgery, for the spring meeting of the Interparliamentary Union in the Cameroons, taking time this trip to enjoy each other, learning new manners for greeting African tribal potentates, visiting

* Since then the number has increased markedly each year. In 1979, there would be 107,000 new cases.

missionary schools and those untiring Peace Corps workers in the jungle. At home, we took long walks, watching the squirrels play, seeing the beauty of the clouds and the colors of the sunset more clearly. This was a time for realizing the value of quiet in our lives—time spent observing, reflecting, enjoying—not just achieving. This feeling of well-being, of coming into focus, was not limited to me, I discovered. Stewart Alsop told me, "I feel more tolerant than I was before."

We took off to spend our twentieth wedding anniversary at the Greenbrier, with Evan. A woman there asked Birch and me if we were honeymooners. We laughed. "Your mother is prettier today than she was when I married her," Birch told Evan. "I mean that."

It was that kind of summer, crowned by a visit to a hideaway near Front Royal, Virginia, owned by our friend Bea Keller. We walked through the woods, discovering bear prints, listening to birds, watching a fox and a deer. "I feel like I've been to Heaven," I wrote. Birch and I both felt a need for the country, for the rhythms of nature. "When I get my job," I told him, "I'm going to buy us a country place."

In November, on election night, my strongest feeling was heartbreak for Eleanor McGovern. There followed deep sadness for good friends lost—Hale Boggs, in a plane crash in Alaska in October ("You and Birch kiss each other for me," Lindy, his wife, told us); Eve Symington, on Christmas Eve; President Truman, on December 26; and, on Birch's forty-fifth birthday, January 22, 1973, Lyndon Baines Johnson.

My grief could bear no description. On the way to the graveside service, I looked out the bus window at the Texas hill country that he loved so much, at the scrub oak trees and the little towns with filling stations, just like Oklahoma. No wonder he never felt comfortable with the Harvard or Georgetown crowds. At the family cemetery, with beautiful live-oak trees spreading their arms to the sky, they buried President Johnson. My heart went out to Lady Bird and their daughters—and to all of us. He was a mountain of a man. Having learned from those earlier losses, when I was so hard on myself, holding in grief, this time I cried it out. And I learned, finally, to take time to mourn.

We spent my fortieth birthday in New York, with the Shepards and Rogerses. I had only four more chemotherapy injections to go. But I was already exercising my new lease on life.

There was an article in the *Medical Tribune* telling my story, pointing out that "Reach to Recovery volunteers cannot visit a cancer patient unless called in by the patient's doctor," which brought a spate of letters from doctors. One wrote: "As a physician who has specialized in the treatment of cancer patients with radiation therapy for the past fifteen years, I am fully aware of the tremendous trauma, both physical and psychological, to patients undergoing mastectomies. . . . the Reach to Recovery program has not reached its full potential because of the large number of physicians who do not know about it. Your article will do much to correct this deficiency."

And another letter, which I cherish, came from Terese Lasser, who founded Reach to Recovery in 1952 and who has done so much to help others: ". . . May I thank you for being as forthright and encouraging as you are. I have the feeling that many lives will be saved by what you have written. . . . May you and your husband walk in God's sunshine always. . . ."

And for an entirely different audience, there was an article in the *National Enquirer*: "Operation for Breast Cancer Has Brought My Family Closer Together." There were television programs in which I was questioned about the cancer, and then speaking for the American Cancer Society's Indiana Cancer Drive, in March and April.

It was not a hard-hitting impassioned speech on the issues, as I was accustomed to giving, but just the plain simple story of my own cancer surgery. After seeing and hearing their reactions, I realized that open and frank discussion of breast cancer was a great step forward. I truly wanted to rush up to every woman on the street and say "Have you had your checkup lately? Have you had your Pap smear this year? Have you examined your own breasts this month for a possible lump?" If I could warn even one more person, I would be, as my mother urged, "putting back in" something that I had taken out of life.

Had I lost all interest in the business of Washington? Of course not. But my focus began to narrow to those things I could actually do something about.

Politically, I was thankful that there had been a ceasefire in Vietnam—but sad that President Johnson did not live to see it. With my new involvement in life itself, the Watergate investigation just was not on the front of my "scope" in 1973, as it certainly would have been in another year. But as the revelations showed more and more scurrilous activity in the White House, I almost didn't appear there for the Senate Ladies' luncheon on May 8. However, in the end Myrtle McIntyre and I went, as did Eleanor McGovern and Joan Kennedy. I felt sorry for Pat Nixon, though. There she was, having to greet those of us who were outraged at what had gone on, when none of it was her doing. She stood alone in the receiving line, and shook each Senate wife's hand, while the Air Force Strolling Strings played, of all things, selections from *Camelot*.

Two days later, at a dinner party at our house, Eric Sevareid made an interesting remark: "Because of Richard Nixon's makeup, his disposition, he probably won't be able to get himself out of this Watergate mess. Birch's Twenty-fifth Amendment might come into play." Eric said that even on his China trip back in February, Nixon was stooped and haggard, brightening only when there were photographers around. When it was revealed that Birch was at the top of a Nixon "Enemies List," I was proud to be in such good company.

We had given a dinner party for twenty friends, at home, an evening rich in fun and laughter. The next morning, there was a note under my door:

> You were great last night
> You are wonderful this morning
> and
> I'm madly in love with you
> and
> Will be for the rest of my life
> and
> A little bit longer than that, too.

"I'm so lucky," I wrote. "I must keep my health so I can go with him to the White House someday if he ever goes."

A few weeks later, an article appeared in the *Washington Star*, under the headline "Marriages under Pressure," in which it described the strains on Washington marriages. There were photographs of Ted Kennedy, Eugene McCarthy, Lyndon Johnson, and Birch, captioned "Quartet of Casanovas."

I have never seen Birch more disgusted. He stomped around the house, fuming and fussing, and the madder he got, the funnier I thought it was. Finally, I came up behind him and gave him a squeeze. "Do you think that if I ever for one moment doubted that you were faithful to me, I would have been out there all those years breaking my neck to campaign for you?"

For weeks, our friends teased him with "Casanova," until he soon laughed at it, too. Birch is a handsome man, attractive fodder for the gossip mill. But if there were one thing in which I believed, it was his singular devotion to me, as mine to him. "He has a mistress," I once joked to a friend, "but it's not another woman, it's politics."

But politics certainly did not intrude on my happiness that second summer and autumn of my new lease on life.

And then I took on a mission. The American Cancer Society had asked me, along with actor Peter Graves, to serve as national co-chairman for the 1974 Crusade. We were two of two million volunteers. From the outset I was impressed with the Cancer Society officials, doctors and laymen alike. Their dedication to the eradication of this disease that had become my personal enemy, and to be of service to its victims, spurred me to volunteer as much time as I could to their nationwide effort. As the late Dr. George Papanicolaou, renowned cancer researcher, wrote, "It is a great satisfaction to make a discovery in the laboratory, but we do not save lives in the laboratory. Lives are saved where people are."

The Society's main objective is to disseminate information about cancer, to make the public aware of the disease, and alert to ways of guarding against it. In addition, its funds support research toward prevention, treatment, and cure of cancer. As I write this, I shudder with rage at the knowledge that 55 million Americans living today will get cancer. Major cancer will strike one in every four of us sometime during our lives, as it struck me.

But my volunteer work was propelled by the knowledge that one-third of all cancer patients are being cured while many of the others . . . although not cured . . . are able, with treatment, to live reasonably normal, active lives. When cancer struck twelve-year-old Teddy Kennedy, Jr., in November, 1973, I was heartbroken for Ted and Joan—but I gave her the encouraging statistic that there are two million cured cancer patients out there. I hope that number gave them as much hope as it had given me.

The 1974 Cancer Crusade began in Atlanta, with a tea for 300 at Betty Talmadge's "Gone with the Wind" home, Lovejoy. The next morning, at the National Crusade Kickoff meeting, they showed a film, *The Marvella Bayh Story*. Then I spoke, telling of my own experience, the role that cancer society volunteers had played in my life, and of the progress that was being made in treatment of cancer. There was a standing ovation, which touched me immeasurably because I realized that I had made a connection with people. The momentum built, with Peter Graves as a terrific master of ceremonies at that evening's banquet, and I felt that 1974 was off to a hopeful, purposeful start.

From that January kickoff in Atlanta, I literally flew about the country, accompanied by *The Marvella Bayh Story* film, speaking to volunteers, urging that people memorize the seven warning signals for cancer* and act upon them. Peter Graves flew to different cities, on his own schedule. As in a political foray, the speeches were well "advanced," adding local radio and television and newspaper interviews to the number of people I could reach. In many ways, the technique is similar to a campaign, though we call it a crusade. But it is also different, in a way, because you are not asking something for yourself.

From Atlanta to Los Angeles, Salt Lake City, Louisville, Chicago, Boston, Buffalo, Oklahoma City (with a side trip to Enid to see Aunty, a fringe benefit)—my act on the road was a tryout, I joked to Jane Sinnenberg, who traveled with me. New York, on March 25–27, was the "big time." There were television, newspaper, and magazine interviews, and then the Cancer Society luncheon for New York businessmen, who gave me a standing ovation. The proof that I was effective was the number of letters I was beginning to receive from women who had been watching, and decided to practice breast self-examination, and had discovered a lump. "I'm so glad I can be of some help," I wrote.

---

* 1. Unusual bleeding or discharge;
  2. A lump or thickening in the breast or elsewhere;
  3. A sore that does not heal;
  4. Change in the bowel or bladder habits;
  5. Hoarseness or cough;
  6. Indigestion or difficulty in swallowing;
  7. Change in size or color of a wart or mole.

Chapter 12

In a hard year, 1974, Birch was up for reelection to the Senate. He had given up his main chance, his crack at the Democratic presidential nomination, because I had needed him. I would help him now, because he had asked me. Now that I was feeling better, my career would again be put on the back burner—until this campaign was over. I wanted to help my husband, but I dreaded the coming weeks when we would be apart, aimed in different directions by another strenuous campaign schedule. My marriage was happier than it had been in years, but my heart wasn't in this campaign.

I know that Birch valued my contribution to his career in those early days in Indiana, when I helped write speeches, helped him rehearse them, studied with him over how to address the issues, and made my own speeches in his behalf; and in the early days in Washington, when I learned how to be his hostess. And I also know that many on his 49-person staff had been wonderful to me, and very helpful, but I still had no real position there. Perhaps if there had been a role for me in his Senate office, those early satisfactions in making a tangible contribution might have grown, alongside his own satisfactions in his soaring career. I will never know. I only know that my early substantive role had been supplanted by staff, that some of them preferred me in mothballs, or exile, between campaigns. Birch's career was now an unquestioned success, his reputation as an outstanding legislator firmly established. How much was I actually needed in the campaign, at this stage, even though I "owed him one"? How could I tell if my campaigning really made any difference in the outcome of the election? Did I, as a campaigning wife, think I made more of a contribution than I in fact did?

I thought about all those things on April 24, 1974, as I was, ironically, scrubbing my kitchen carpet. At Lindy Boggs' dinner party that evening, I sat next to Congressman Gillespie (Sonny) Montgomery of Mississippi, a bachelor. "He didn't need a wife to get reelected," I thought, and teased him about his making it tough for us wives. It *was* tough for wives that spring.

The annual Senate Ladies' luncheon for the First Lady came the day after Richard Nixon announced on television that he was releasing the "relevant portions" of the taped conversations of "what I knew about Watergate or the cover-up and what I did about it . . . the President has nothing to hide in this matter." The publication of even those "expurgated versions" exposed Nixon to the public in a way that could not help but mortify any wife. But Mrs. Nixon kept her composure at the luncheon, "a political wife" to the end.

Two weeks later, on May 13, I went to the First Lady's luncheon for the Senate wives, at the White House. Neither Joan Kennedy nor Eleanor McGovern attended this year. As we walked through the receiving line, Mrs. Nixon welcomed us, the women reporters beside her scribbling notes on her every word. The revelations on the White House tapes had been devastating, the presidency seemed denuded and dirty. It was later revealed that Mrs. Nixon had advised her husband to burn the tapes before they were subpoenaed, but he had gone against her advice, wanting to use them to ensure his place in history. (Now, they were certainly being used for just that purpose.) She looked us in the eye as if the awful mess did not exist, and had something pleasant to say to each of us. She had just returned, with the President, from Vance Air Force Base near Enid. "You've just come from my home town," I said to her. "Oh, they were wonderful," she replied. "There were thousands of people who had driven far to see us—and not one boo."

After lunch, as we were walking into the Blue Room for coffee, Donna Metcalf suddenly stepped back and I took a nose-dive over her foot, hitting the table on my way down. I was badly enough cut and bruised to have to be taken to the doctor's office on the ground floor. I was still there when Mrs. Nixon came down to see about me. "My pride was hurt more than anything," I said. Pat Nixon could not have been more gracious, warm, or concerned. She put her arm through mine and walked me to the door herself, making sure I was able to drive myself home. Walking through the Diplomatic Reception Room where once my purple tranquilizers had rolled into the fireplace, we were two in the sorority of political wives.

Quick as a flash, it seemed, Evan was graduating from high school. Evan would work in the campaign this summer, and then enter the University of Indiana in the fall. I now had to gear up for Birch's reelection campaign.

Announcement day was June 10. Then there was the state convention at Indianapolis' new convention center, where Birch was unopposed for the nomination, followed by my stint at Girls' State. Jane Sinnenberg traveled with me, bless her soul, and kept me sane as I dragged around the state of Indiana to speak. Tom Koutsoumpas drove us, a gentle young man who had been on Birch's staff since 1969. Only a few years older than Evan, Tom had become a second son to me. Sometimes he'd spend the night at our house while we were away, because Evan was too old for a sitter but not for the company (and restraining presence) of an "older brother." It was Tom who drove me to my chemotherapy treatments, whose sensitivity and compassion endeared him to me forever. With Tom and Jane, I survived the 1974 campaign.

There was history in the making, of course, during those final days of July and early August, when, before a mesmerized country, the House Judiciary Committee voted three articles of impeachment against President Nixon: one for obstruction of justice in the Watergate cover-up; the second, for abuse of power; a third, for refusing to obey the committee's subpoenas. The full House would begin debate in about two weeks. Behind the scenes, the Senate leadership was preparing for an impeachment trial that was made unnecessary when President Richard M. Nixon resigned from office at noon on August 9.

Because of Birch and the presidential succession amendment, Gerald Ford had been named to the vice presidency when Spiro Agnew resigned under a cloud of scandal in 1973. Now, Gerald Ford ascended to the presidency smoothly, constitutionally—and, again because of Birch's 25th Amendment, could appoint Nelson Rockefeller as his Vice President. We were proud. Birch's time "writing history" had eased the country through this wrenching period.

I was impressed with President Ford's speech of acceptance—

and felt sorry for Betty Ford. She hadn't wanted this. He had promised her that he was going to retire from politics. But most of all, I felt sorry for Mrs. Nixon and her daughters. This disgrace would follow them for the rest of their lives. There is an old maxim of the press that I had come to detest: "You live in the public eye, you die in the public eye." I hated watching the agony in Pat Nixon's eyes.

In Indiana, both candidates for the Senate denounced Nixon. Both were attractive, articulate, and intelligent, and both were campaigning hard: the Republican, Richard Lugar, former Rhodes Scholar, mayor of Indianapolis; Birch Bayh, the Democrat, who, I stated in the "Last-Minute Appeal," is "the United States senator who has cast four thousand votes, and who . . . I have shared with you for the last twelve years."

Our friend Abigail Van Buren came out to help in what we called the "Dear Abby days"; she charmed Hoosiers up and down the state with her best advice: "Vote for Birch Bayh." With her wit and wisdom, she gained us valuable publicity, and, I'm sure, votes.

After the campaign, it would be farewell to politics for me. I hoped that it would be for Birch, too. I had enjoyed his company so much after the mastectomy when he had chosen to be "by my side." On Labor Day, we had slipped away for three glorious all-alone days at Bea Keller's country place in the Blue Ridge Mountains. We walked in the woods, listening to our footsteps, stopping to watch butterflies play, looking at raindrops cling to a spiderweb. If Birch were not in politics, if he had a job in what we call the "private sector," would we have more time for each other, like this? From Labor Day until Election Day, he would be home for only three nights.

On September 27, I saw Betty Ford at the groundbreaking ceremonies for the Lyndon Baines Johnson Memorial Park. I thought she looked tired and drawn. That evening she was in the hospital for a biopsy. On Saturday, she had a radical mastectomy. I wrote her, as I write to each person who reaches out to me.

Sept. 29, 1974

Dear Mrs. Ford,

I am so sorry that you have joined the large sorority of women who have had this surgery. It was three years ago next week that I had the same experience.

I just wanted you to know that today I feel great, and I'm happier and busier than I've ever been.

While I was in the hospital a friend sent me this book. [*Always a Woman*, by Sylvia S. Seaman.*] I read it the night before I went home, and it helped me a great deal. I hope it is useful to you.

I'm leaving for Indiana tomorrow, but will return on the sixth. Please know that I'm hoping I can be of service to you in answering some of the "girlie" questions that the doctors can't cover. When the time comes for you to shop for a prosthesis, perhaps I can help. They come in every size and are terrific. Mrs. Cherry at the downtown Garfinckels is the best person in Washington to do fitting. She has a great deal of experience and is *so* nice.

Please know that your world will return to normal soon. I was in Africa with Birch six months after my surgery.

You are a terrific woman, and I know this experience will not get you down. *Please* call me if I can help in *any* way.

> With admiration,
> Marvella Bayh

Suddenly, with the First Lady's mastectomy in front-page headlines, and because of my volunteer work for the American Cancer Society, I was called for a spate of interviews about breast cancer: AP, UPI, NBC, CBS, *Newsweek*, the *Chicago Tribune*, *Chicago Daily News*, and *People* magazine. I tried to stress two points: (1) The need for more cancer research money (the appropriations bill was in conference committee at that moment)—half of the approved research programs were not funded last year; and (2) the need for more education for women to practice breast self-examinations monthly. On the "Today" show and on "Not For Women Only" with Barbara Walters, I made the same points. I had been able to speak to a cancer conference in Denver a few weeks earlier, telling doctors what a mastectomy is like for the patient; and from that, there was a teaching film produced and distributed in which I told the same story for medical students.

Less than a month after Betty Ford, Happy Rockefeller also had a mastectomy, then another. I wrote to Happy Rockefeller also, explaining again how life can actually be enriched after this experience—because you learn to value it.

* Argonaut, 1965.

A funny thing happened to me on the way to Birch's reelection. In September I had an appointment at television station WRC, Washington's NBC affiliate, for a job interview. By now, I had been on television hundreds of times, and should have been at ease. They were considering me for an eight-minute spot on Sunday mornings. You would have thought I was up for president of the network. I trembled. My heart raced. I forgot my script (and had to run back for it). Just as I handed it to the producer, Jim Silman, my right earring dropped down the front of my dress, and I had to stand up and shake until the thing fell on the floor. They hired me, nervousness notwithstanding. I cannot describe my excitement at that first salaried job of my entire life. Here I was, in my forties, and Jim Silman couldn't believe that I'd never even paid into Social Security before.

I was to be the "Bicentennial Reporter"—every Sunday morning until July 4, 1976. I'd be interviewing government officials and historians on various aspects of the celebration and its history. I would be Marvella Bayh, not "Mrs. Birch," a point that had become increasingly important as I fought to establish my own identity.

That same fall, I had lunch with Lane Adams, the executive vice president of the American Cancer Society, whose efficiency and compassion I had come to admire during my work as a volunteer. I was telling him of my excitement about being a working woman when he said, "We really need you. You have done all this as a volunteer for years. Now would you consider going to work for the Society? We'd like to hire you as a consultant and special representative."

I almost jumped out of my chair. A job doing work that I loved, for an organization that had helped so many millions of people—one that had helped me—I couldn't believe it. By the time election day came around, I had one job and another waiting for me.

Inflation and high taxes were Birch's campaign issues, along with President Ford's pardon of Richard Nixon. Birch was having as much trouble with the "gun nuts" about his "Saturday night special" stand as if he had voted for gun control—which, to my sorrow, he hadn't. The anti-abortion people, collecting signatures for a petition to overthrow the hard-won 1973 Supreme Court decision granting a woman the legal right to terminate an unwanted pregnancy, challenged Birch's brave stand, in which he said, "We are talking about whether a woman has the right to make that personal decision, or whether the federal government is going to have to make it for her—or prohibit her from making it. Although I am not prepared to make it, as a man, I am not prepared to make it for a woman."

The matter of life concerns me, and greatly. War. Murder. Suicide. Cancer. All of those have touched my life, and have left me with the strongest conviction that all of life is precious. I could not have an abortion. (And, thank God, I'd never had to face that agonizing personal decision for myself.) However, I feel just as strongly that I, or the federal government, do not have the right to make that decision for another woman. It was so unfair to Birch, who has championed the right to life and freedom in so many ways, to be the object of the frenzied screams of the anti-abortion lobby. But when I complained to Dear Abby about the intensity and unfairness of the anti-abortionists' attacks against Birch, she reminded me, "If you want a place in the sun, you have to be prepared for a few blisters."

"That's true," I said. "But then each of us has a different opinion as to what is our place in the sun."

This time around, the entire Democratic state ticket was elected. Our first day home together (Birch's third since Labor Day), I wrote:

> I want to walk through the leaves with Birch.
> I want him to play his guitar and sing love songs to me.
> I want him to have the time and energy to feel deeply and write moving poems. I want to love.

And thus began the liberation of Marvella Belle Hern. One of the greatest thrills of my life came a few weeks later, entering England for a NATO Conference. On the entry card was a line, Occupation: _____. Always before, I, with my unused college degree, grimaced and wrote down "housewife."

Now, on November 7, 1974, I was nearly trembling with pleasure to write in "American Cancer Society special representative and television reporter."

Birch was scheduled to debate at Cambridge. "Resolved: That one should still have faith in the American government." But for that same evening, there came an invitation on a card with the gold-

embossed royal crest, E-R II. Birch couldn't change his debate, but
I decided to go.

Nov. 14, 1974

Worried about wearing black gloves, most everyone else wore
white. Left them on the seat of the car, anyway. Went running
back after them, in the mist.

The Palace was brilliant. The Queen was warmer, prettier than
her photographs, with a feminine, crinkly-eyed smile. Prince
Charles stood next to her, celebrating his 26th birthday at the
occasion. Queen Elizabeth mingled with us for two hours, taking
time to talk to us, to really visit. Gracious, I thought, befitting a
queen.

When we returned home we found that Evan, our freshman,
had been accepted on the Indiana University debating team. Both
of us were exceedingly proud.

Two weeks after our return, on a December Sunday morning,
Evan took Birch to Dulles airport to catch a flight to Indiana for
the swearing-in of state officials. Then we heard there was a plane
crash in Virginia, and all aboard were killed. That was the plane
Birch was waiting to board on its return flight. He stayed at the
airport the rest of the day and tried to comfort people waiting to
greet loved ones.

Our lives were changing—and for the better. Not only were we
constantly conscious of the preciousness of life itself, we were in
awe of how close death had come to touching us.

The television job was great fun. I took my eight minutes a
week very seriously, interviewing a whole range of people, government officials, historians, investigative reporter Jack Anderson, and
others, on various aspects of the bicentennial celebration, from
Thomas Jefferson's recipes to the origins of lynching, from the
Colonial Dames to the Peoples' Bicentennial, from the British Ambassador to American Indians, and, of course, much on the role of
women in the Revolution.

I found myself researching, writing, studying museums and
galleries, interviewing fascinating people. It was a refreshing ab-
sorption in history, an old passion of mine that had bowed to politics.
It would come to an end on July 4, 1976, and I found myself wish-

ing the work on our Declaration of Independence had stretched on to 1777, at least.

But the career of a lifetime was my work with the American Cancer Society, which began in December, 1974. There could be no more fulfilling work for me. It was the culmination of all my training and experience. It also brought a deeper gratification: helping others to face this awful disease with hope; warning others of its danger signals, and being rewarded with a letter: "Mrs. Bayh, I saw you on television, thank you for saving my life."

I began, of course, fired by a personal vengeance. Cancer is a thief. Cancer is a foul, foul villain that can rob you of your time and energy, that can cause you great pain. Cancer is a murderer. I hate this disease with a venom, a passionate hatred that I had no idea I possessed.

I tried to make the statistics meaningful to my audience: "Cancer takes 395,000 lives a *year* in the United States. From World War II through Vietnam, thirty-four years, this country lost only 372,000 of its men in battle. One in four Americans who will have cancer is just a frightening number—until that one is a member of your family—or you."

In my new job, I spoke out on the subject of safeguards. I urged people to stop smoking, or never to start. I talked about the importance of early detection—of the need for everybody to have regular physical examinations: for those over forty, a proctoscopic examination every year; for all women, breast self-examination, once a month, after one's period; for every woman over twenty, a Pap test at least once a year; for everyone, a careful mouth examination by a dentist or doctor; and, since many skin cancers are caused by overexposure to direct sunlight, reasonable protection from the sun. And, for the most elementary safeguards of all, memorize the seven warning signals for cancer (page 235).

Part of my job has been reporting on the progress that has been made in treatment for cancer. Since my mastectomy, advances have been made in combined therapy: surgery, radiation therapy, chemotherapy. There are results in treatment by ultrasound and immunotherapy, and many exciting reports are coming out of laboratories.

I speak to cancer patients and their families about hope—and how it is possible to lead a useful, productive, reasonably normal life, with treatment. I speak to groups of doctors and nurses and hospital administrators about the need for them to give hope, about how their words affect the attitude of cancer patients.

From the responses of my audiences, from the letters I have received, I know that my work has been worthwhile. Cancer is the great equalizer, no respecter of race, sex, wealth, or position. Once, driving from LaGuardia Airport, a burly New York taxi driver recognized me. "My wife is dying of cancer," he said, big tears coursing down his face. "Please write to her." There have been letters from strangers, thanking me for showing how to live with cancer, and from doctors, thanking me for educating them on how to deal with cancer patients. And learning, learning, learning from the courage of the cancer patients I meet.

Cancer makes you get your priorities in order. Looking at the calendar and thinking that "the rest of your life" might not be all of infinity gives you great impetus to say, "Am I going to be doing what I want to be doing for what is left of my life?" The rewards from my work were so great, I knew that was what I wanted to do with my life. In 1976, I did not want to be the wife of a presidential candidate.

In the spring of 1975, I pleaded with Birch, begged him not to enter the presidential race. I had a real fear of an assassination attempt, or a maiming. Our unlisted phone number did not hide us from threats on Birch's life. I also feared the toll on our family life from another campaign. We had not had time to recover from the 1974 Senate race. It was so soon, too soon to be gearing up again, building an organization, looking for money, living under constant strain.

Living from campaign to campaign, from paycheck to paycheck, was taking its toll on me. I had never had the feeling of financial security; I had seen firsthand what it's like to reach retirement age without it. What a difference it makes in one's old age, I told him. Moreover, if he ran, or ever were elected President of the United States, I worried that I'd have to give up my work.

"I'm not ashamed to ask this of you," I wrote to Birch. "I've waited to do my own thing until I was forty. I've had three close calls with death. It's my time, now. I can wait no longer. . . .

"Please don't run," I wrote. "You've done this constant campaigning for eighteen years. It's *not* the only way to leave your mark and help people. . . ."

I had not yet grown enough to realize that I was asking him to limit his dreams for my sake, the way I had limited mine for his.

Chapter 13

*B*irch knew I didn't want him to run. So did the press, some of his potential backers, and, rather particularly, Evan. By the beginning of 1975, three other Democratic candidates had already announced: Morris Udall, Fred Harris, and Fritz Mondale. The former governor of Georgia, Jimmy Carter, who had officially announced in November of 1974, had been carrying on a campaign for two years, but few in Washington were paying much attention to his candidacy. Mondale dropped out (saying it wasn't worth it), but Henry Jackson, Lloyd Bentsen, and Terry Sanford came in, although at midsummer nobody's campaign seemed to be picking up steam. Ted Kennedy had taken himself out of the running; in September, Sargent Shriver announced. Everybody knew Birch was interested, and Evan particularly wanted him to run. But as yet, he'd made no official move.

Being First Lady had no appeal, at this stage of my life. My job was as important to me as Birch's concept of the presidency was to him. My fear was that my employment would be threatened by his being "political." I worried that the Cancer Society would think Birch's national political campaign, as a Democrat, would jeopardize my effectiveness. The television job, my precious eight minutes on Sunday morning, would also be in danger because of "equal time" provisions in the law.

Perhaps if I had not been so propelled to use what time I had left on the earth to make my own contribution, I might have been enthusiastic and supportive. There was no question in my mind that Birch would have made an excellent President. But there was a sword dangling over my neck, held up by a thread of hope from cancer check to cancer check. I didn't want to make any more sacrifices to politics, even though I agreed with Evan that Birch Bayh had every qualification for leading this country.

I did not want it for Birch, either. "How can he risk his life?" I thought. "And once you get it, what have you got—the incredible burden of the job itself."

Birch put off his decision to run, based on my objections.

That summer, with my own salary, I made a down payment on a vacation cabin, high on a hill near Front Royal, Virginia, overlooking the Shenandoah River. For several years I had longed for such a place, searched for it, envied other Senate couples, such as the Churches and Longs, who could escape the pressure-cooker on weekends. Now it was ours, a tiny A-frame cabin surrounded by virgin timber, looking out at the most spectacular view I have ever seen, with birds and deer, squirrels, chipmunks, and gophers as our neighbors, a blanket of quiet to surround us, a picture-book farm across the river to remind us of our roots.

We worked together to make the house livable, the kind of physical work we hadn't done in ages, which brought a surprising happiness in itself. Birch split logs for firewood, and laid seventy-two steps all the way down to the river. I painted woodwork and furniture, and Birch had a sign made to be placed by the road: "God's Little Acre." I thought of this place of respite, quiet, pleasure in nature and each other, as a gift from God. Living there was like discovering two old selves who were just waiting to share each other in a new way, a new setting.

It was in the country, with peace of mind for thinking, that I realized I was about to make a mistake—the same mistake Birch had made in January, 1967. In so strongly opposing his candidacy for the presidency, I was laying the same kind of burden on him that he had imposed on me in rejecting President Johnson's job offer. It was *his* life, his career, his decision. I had no more right to put my wishes or needs ahead of that decision than he had in placing his ahead of mine. I knew, now, that I could never forgive myself if I stood in his way.

But I would not campaign for him. Birch understood. His pride in my independence was considerable. And if his candidacy would affect my job, he assured me that he would not run. From our cabin, he called Lane Adams, executive director of ACS, receiving assurance that if I did not campaign, the nonpartisan Cancer Society would allow me to keep my job. Birch and I made a pact. I would no longer oppose his presidential bid; but if he did not win, it would be his last political campaign.

On October 21, 1975, after a year of speculation in the press (including a prediction from a syndicated-columnist psychic that Birch would get the Democratic nomination), and Evans and Novak calling him the "liberal with the best chance of winning," he announced his candidacy. Before doing so, Birch had flown that month from Washington to Michigan, to Iowa, to Kansas City, to Boston, to New Hampshire, to Virginia. Then out again to San Francisco, back to Boston, to New Jersey, New York, Philadelphia, Boston, and to California. That same month I had campaigned against cancer in Kansas City and in Orlando, Florida, and had spoken on women's rights in behalf of International Women's Year in Toledo, Ohio, and at St. Mary's College in Indiana. Birch had spent ten days in New Hampshire, had flown from there to New York, to Iowa, and on to Ohio.

We met in a Terre Haute motel on October 21, and drove to our farm, past the familiar gob piles, which sported a homemade sign: "The Capitol Hill of Shirkieville supports Birch Bayh for President." There were about a thousand people standing there on Granddad Hollingsworth's place, listening to this forty-seven-year-old Hoosier who hoped to be President. Later we drove to the State House, where he'd served as Speaker, for his official announcement at the podium of the Indiana House of Representatives—and then to Bloomington to a rally at Indiana University, where Evan announced that he was dropping out of school in January to help Birch campaign in New Hampshire. Like an old firehorse at the smell of smoke, I must admit I was tempted to join them, but I stuck to my guns.

And I went my way, speaking to radiologists, to the Committee on Prevention of Heart Disease, Cancer, and Stroke, and to audiences in New York City, Annapolis, Maryland, San Francisco, Kansas City, Boston. Sometimes Birch and I passed in midair. Sometimes he would take time to send one of his funny little telegrams to me where I was speaking.

The Secret Service entered our lives. I welcomed the protection for him; but I'm afraid I resented terribly the intrusion on what little privacy we had. Three cars with flashing lights arriving with Birch on our quiet country road. Tires and gravel waking me every hour on the hour as they changed guard at night. Our mail being scrutinized by machines for letter-bombs before it got to us. I went through the ceiling when those mail inspections delayed my TV scripts. I felt I couldn't hug my husband with their eyes watching me. At the cabin, we had asked them to stay up on the road, and not down by the house or the woods. That was the one place we could go to unwind, to be alone. The day Evan joined us for Thanksgiving vacation, a beautiful, cold, clear day, the three of us walked down the hill to the river. There was a fallen tree. It was a private, family time, all alone there in my precious wilderness, love in the air. We hugged and kissed, and giggled, and frolicked over that fallen tree, laughing like loons. I turned around and there one of them stood, following some distance behind us, a total stranger watching our most private moments. I burst into tears. (But I often thought that if Birch were elected President, we would have the Secret Service around for all of our lives, even after leaving public office.)

Birch had opened his New Hampshire headquarters, and Joseph Kraft called him the Democrats' "candidate of the month." On December 7, he just missed getting the required 60 percent vote for endorsement by the New Democratic Coalition in New York. Later that month, the *New York Times* called him "electable," and *Newsweek* teased him with "For an Indiana farm boy, Birch Bayh comes straight out of 'Oklahoma'—a don't-sigh-and-gaze-at-me liberal with deep blue eyes, apple cheeks, and an unshakable conviction that the Democratic nomination will be his come harvest time." (They should have known what a good laugh that gave me. All those early years I'd tried to get him to move to Oklahoma!)

Birch and Evan were in frozen New Hampshire that January of 1976, talking to paper-mill workers, college professors and students, electronics workers, shipyard workers, environmentalists, trying to cement a coalition of all their divergent interests, to project Birch Bayh as the one Democratic candidate to represent them in that state's February primary. Because of his late start, he was frustrated because he couldn't also spend enough time in Iowa. He'd hoped that being a midwesterner, familiar to neighboring Iowans, would give him an edge there, and he sent Evan out to campaign. Other wives had been in Iowa campaigning for their husbands: Eunice Shriver, LaDonna Harris, Rosalynn Carter. "Maybe I should be there, too," I thought. But then I steadied my new self.

The results of the Iowa caucuses on January 19 were: Carter first, with 28 percent; Birch second, with 13 percent; Harris, 10 percent; Udall, 5 percent; Shriver, 3 percent; Jackson, 1 percent—and the highest number, 37 percent, were uncommitted. Birch was very disappointed, Evan almost disconsolate.

There was so little money for Massachusetts that Birch could only take one TV spot. The experts had decided that Birch's big strength was his fourteen years of experience, so they devised an ad in which Birch came on camera and said, "Hello. I am Birch Bayh. I am a politician. And it takes a politician with experience to get the job done." When I saw it, I pleaded with Birch not to use it. As a typical American looking on, I realized that the average person was going to be turned off. The ad proved to be a big mistake —even the press mentioned it as such.

Birch seemed as interested in where I'd been speaking or whom I'd interviewed on television as he was in reporting on the campaign. Once he brought home a button—"Susan B. Anthony Would Vote for Birch Bayh"—that charmed me. I picked up a paper and read an article about candidates' wives, which quoted Ella Udall as saying, "I could be sitting at home, like Marvella Bayh, and not out here on the rubber-chicken circuit."

"Dear Ella," I thought. "Marvella has paid her dues."

My only trip to New Hampshire was for election day, February 24. There was no Bayh victory celebration. Birch ran third, behind Carter and Udall. Despite my initial opposition, my heart was torn to see him so disappointed. After all these years, it was his first political defeat. There would be six days before the Massachusetts primary. I agonized over whether to offer to help, even though I would have to give up my wonderful job.

It was too late, Birch felt. He told me he was glad for my sake that I didn't come up there, because he was so exhausted.

Boston, March 2, 1976

Evan was so hopeful when he met me. It was sad to see him so upbeat when all indications pointed otherwise. The three of us ordered dinner in the hotel room. About twelve photographers came in. Evan had hardly finished eating when he left to hear returns. He came back shortly, really down, saying that in his worst nightmare, he didn't think it would be that bad. The big Irishman who was in charge of his campaign in Massachusetts just

cried like a baby. It was pointed out that the candidates finished
in the same position as the amount of money they spent on
television. Birch had no money to spend on television spots,
except for that one. We are one hundred thousand dollars in debt.
The assessment was that Birch should have entered the race
earlier, should have had his whole campaign strategy planned, the
image to be created outlined, the timing worked out.

Evan feels that if I had been for the campaign, Birch would
have stepped into it earlier. Perhaps so, but I will not feel guilty.
We cannot rewrite history any more than we can predict the
future. I had to be true to what I am.

Birch and I talked until two in the morning, and on March 4,
1976, he formally withdrew after four and a half months of an
honest swing at bat. "It's the country's loss, and my gain," I told
the press, and meant it.

Birch, strong as his Indiana roots, set about his future with
good humor and equanimity, endorsing the candidacy of Jimmy
Carter in May. But our Evan, who had worked so hard, was deeply
wounded. Returning to Bloomington, he wrote a college paper based
on his experience. In it, he touched upon the roles played by families
of the candidates—and he came down, hard, upon me:

> One cannot underestimate the impact that the family situation
> had on the candidacy of Birch Bayh. . . .
>
> The political repercussion of all this was the substantial delay
> of Bayh's entry into the race. . . . Birch Bayh became a candidate
> on October 21, 1975, barely three months before the crucial Iowa
> caucus. One cannot complete the intricate strategy, organization,
> media, and financial preparation necessary to be President of
> the United States in three months. Nor can one develop a
> competent and efficient staff in such time or compete with men
> who have prepared for years.
>
> Yet with precision and expediency these handicaps might have
> been overcome if Marvella Bayh had reconciled herself to the
> contest; she did not. . . .

It was Evan's first campaign—and his role in it was similar
to the one I had played for so many years. I felt that it was a tribute
to our relationship that he felt free to voice his criticism openly, and
that I could respond openly, explaining to my now adult son the
reasons for my opposition. I wrote him about my own current
priorities, reasons I described earlier in this chapter. And I explained

the impact of cancer, not only on my physical life, but on my emotional and psychological outlook as well.

Evan did, in time, understand—and it was the exchange of our views in writing that led to the beginning of a mature friendship between my son and me, with the mutual respect and honesty that such friendship requires.

The pressure was off. The marriage was on, our relationship growing steadily deeper and stronger than if we had just begun. We took time together, planning in advance our busy travel schedules so that we could enjoy the cabin, the woods, and each other. Birch planted a garden, and we waited for the little sprouts as eagerly as for election returns.

Just as our idyll was beginning, however, we had a shock. In May, Birch came down with a bronchitis he couldn't shake. He went for an x-ray, and then he had to tell me. For two years, he had had a spot on his lung. Surgery had not been indicated, but nevertheless it had to be watched. Now, it was growing. There had to be a biopsy.

My heart almost stopped. For two weeks, waiting for his bronchitis to clear, I worried and prayed. It would be major surgery, cutting through layers of muscle, through the ribs, to the back, and removing one lobe of his lung. Fear tore through me, fear of my sworn enemy, cancer.

June 2, 1976

> This was one of the longest days of my life. They came to take Birch to the operating room. Evan and I walked beside his cart, to the door of the operating room. I looked up, and at the end of the hall were sitting P. A. Mack, Tom Koutsoumpas—and Jane—What a friend!
>
> We all waited in Birch's room, the longest hour I have ever spent, hardly able to speak to each other. Only now did I really know what Birch had gone through, waiting to hear Dr. Hawken report on my breast.
>
> Finally Dr. Peabody came into the room with the best news in the world! It was not malignant. They hadn't had to remove **any** of the lung.

There is no describing my excitement at that news. Evan and I held each other, wondering what quirk of fate had given us a lucky break this time.

While Birch was recuperating, I filled in for him at a graduation speech at Front Royal High School, the town nearest our cabin. Mostly, though, I said "no" to invitations that would tax our time and energy. Our time together was just too rich, too important.

My television job as Bicentennial reporter ended with the Fourth of July. Evan, Birch, and I spent that Bicentennial Day in Enid, Oklahoma, where I spoke on the Bicentennial—and read Grandma Hern's account of her life on the prairie—to my high school reunion. Birch and I rode in the rumble seat of an antique car in the Enid parade, with a poster on the side that said, "Senator Birch Bayh, Marvella Bayh," underneath which my friends had written, "This is Marvella country." It was like the Cherokee Strip parades of my youth, and very stirring.

We drove around my old haunts, and I showed Evan where I came from. And then we ate homemade ice cream in Norma Jean Hoover's front yard, and watched the fireworks on Meadowlake Farm. It couldn't have been a better celebration.

At the Democratic Convention in New York, I responded to Barbara Jordan's stunning oratory, the nomination of Jimmy Carter, and later there was dinner at the top of the World Trade Center, looking over the whole of New York City, lights twinkling, with the Statue of Liberty in the distance. Just being alive, being able to appreciate our heritage and the beauty of our country that Bicentennial summer, was a gift to treasure.

That summer we visited Iran, and I had a private meeting with the Empress. On returning, we were invited to a dinner at the Iranian Embassy by her ambassador, Ardeshir Zahedi, who had also become our friend. It was October 12, the fifth anniversary of my mastectomy—and my recent cancer check had been "all clear." During dinner, Birch sent me a note by way of a waiter. "Five years! Going on a wonderful 25!"—signed with a heart. After dinner, we danced and danced, celebrating our good fortune.

Another celebration, three weeks later, was the election of Jimmy Carter.

November 4, 1976

This was a dream of an evening. We went to the Israeli Embassy as guests of Ambassador and Mrs. Dinitz for a small dinner party to honor Elizabeth Taylor and John Warner, who will be married

soon. Elizabeth Taylor is so nice and friendly, full of laughter.
She wore a beautiful heavy gold chain and a brown and gold caftan.
I told her I've thought she is the most beautiful woman in the
world, ever since *National Velvet*. I noticed that she declined the
yummy dessert. She offered a lovely toast to John.

I was seated next to Henry Kissinger. He never takes anything
alcoholic to drink. Before dinner, he received a call from Vice
President Rockefeller.

The next afternoon Henry Kissinger gave us a briefing at the
State Department on the People's Republic of China. We would
leave the next day for three of the most interesting weeks of my
life, to visit a culture 3,500 years old, unified by a totalitarian government less than thirty years old.

China. Loudspeakers blaring martial music, laborers toiling
in the fields underneath a red flag, people outside at 6:30 in the
morning doing calisthenics—children playing in a schoolyard, throwing hardballs at a poster of the Gang of Four. Out the train window, however, there was neat, clean countryside, no litter anywhere
—nor in Nanking, a city dressed in greenery, nor in the wide
Boulevard of Eternal Tranquility in Peking.

I thought the country was beautiful, each city with its own
character; the wondrous Great Wall, 2,000 years old, that would
stretch from New York to Denver; Kweilin, with its steep, exotic
hills, caverns, underground channels, a quiet river rambling through
sugar cane fields and villages, people traveling, on junks.

Their health care was interesting, with its "barefoot doctor"
concept—training a local youth for a year or two, like a paramedic,
to return to his or her own village to deliver basic medical care—
vaccinations, preliminary examinations. I witnessed surgery under
acupuncture anesthesia, performed by a nineteen-year-old woman.
As we entered a new phase of our life in Washington—the Carter
Administration—I kept thinking of a poster in China, a Mao saying: "Women Hold Up Half the Sky."

❧

I look at young women today with pride, as they state their
choices clearly—whether to focus their lives in the home or outside, pursuing their own dreams, walking down the road that was
opened for them by the women's movement. But it is the mature
women I really admire, those who take stock of their lives, find

them wanting, and then proceed to take charge of their destiny.

One such woman, of whom I am especially proud, is Birch's sister Mary Alice, who, after leaving her career as an actress, survived some emotionally turbulent years, made a happy marriage, and now, in her late forties, has just graduated from nursing school. She confesses that it is hard work keeping up with those energetic twenty-year-olds. But she says that she has never been happier or more at peace, and is convinced that it is not too late to make her contribution.

If the women's movement had not reached me when it did, I do not know what would have become of me, or of our marriage. It was of great comfort to realize that I was not alone in my frustrations, and of great encouragement to me in my determination to stand on my own feet at last—to be in control of my own life.

We live our lives in phases. At any time during those years I could have picked up my career, or furthered my education, or done almost anything under the sun I wanted to do (except when Evan was little; then I truly believe a mother should stay home, if she can afford to)—I was one of the lucky ones with choices—but I did not realize that I had the right to choose. I did not know.

I know other political wives who never once took to the stumps on behalf of their husbands, who are content either with separate careers (many in real estate, some as writers, decorators, artists, lecture-bureau directors—interests as varied as their backgrounds are) or with maintaining a household and family as a full-time occupation. There are still others who are out there campaigning as vigorously as I did (I know of at least one who even directed her husband's campaigns), who are secure in their identities as political partners. I have not heard one wife, however, admit to enjoying the separations that the life-style Ellen Proxmire describes—one foot in Washington, the other always back home—entails.

There is no such thing as a "typical" political wife. We in this sorority are as different from each other as are the political precepts in which we believe, as are the divergent regions of this country in which we grew up, as are our own talents and interests. We are individuals in our own right, and many are beginning to speak out candidly about the psychological pressures of being submerged in a husband's career.

How difficult it is to emerge from a political marriage intact is voiced by Susan Goldwater, who left Washington and her husband, Barry, Jr., to embark on a television career in Columbus, Ohio: "I always worked hard for *his* goals. If the transition was hard, it wasn't leaving Washington or going to Columbus, but in being goal-oriented toward my own goals. It's easy to go out and knock on doors for your husband, and sell him. To go and work for yourself, that's harder."

Except for that one time, the nadir of our marriage in the summer of 1971, I never considered leaving Birch, in order to find my goals or for any other reason.

For Birch and me, our twenty-fifth year together saw a marriage between equals—between two people who are mature and happy, each secure in our life-style, each making a contribution—a marriage definitely better than when I was trying to ride along on his coattails. It is amazing that we came through the hurricane, but we did.

His support, enthusiasm, and pride in my work has been one of the greatest joys of my life. He has given me the courage to make an effort to influence public policy in health care, as well as public perceptions about this disease we fight. From the day we met over that lunch table in Chicago, we were both mesmerized by the notion that we could work together to effect change in the lives of human beings. Throughout all our difficulties, that idea has been at the base of our relationship, the strongest bond between us. It was the challenge of the political process, of trying to make government move to help our people, that propelled us from the beginning. Now that I had left the stressful world of elective politics, I once again found that our goals were the same: We really believed that we had the opportunity in our society to affect our destiny and the destiny of other generations.

In my work, I found that people out in the country somehow responded to me as an individual—they came to me with their personal problems, which I could take back to Washington. Through questioning and prodding, I could try to make the system work for them. A poor seventy-year-old widow in Denver told me that she could not get a breast prosthesis under Medicare—she was humiliated by having to stuff socks into her bra; another cancer victim had worked for a company for fifteen years, but was fired, even though he might have ten good years to work, because their insurance rates might go up. Another man, also jobless because of the cruel cancer news "six months to live," discovered that Social Security takes five months to establish disability. My anger really flared when I found out from a woman who had heard me speak that you could get a hair transplant on Medicare—but not a Pap smear.

It was those people reaching out to me for help who sent me back down the halls of government to see what I could do to change regulations, laws, policy, to help the cancer victims I met or who wrote to me after my speaking/teaching trips. As Birch's wife, I had the opportunity to use his resources to effect these changes.

And then, of course, I found myself engaged in the huge battle for prevention—the war against tobacco, to be specific—that must take place in the arena of public policy, because private industry continues to pump cancer-causing agents into our environment. Working with Health, Education and Welfare Secretary Joe Califano on a serious anti-smoking campaign is one skirmish I entered with a great deal of zeal.

My work had grown, and so had the enormous satisfactions from it, which Birch shares with me. Not the least of my satisfactions has been knowing the dedicated, outstanding people with whom I work: My boss, Lane Adams, is a prince of a man. Working with a humanitarian like Mary Lasker has enlarged my appreciation for the dimensions of generosity and commitment. Ellie Montgomery of Georgia, Carolyn Amory from New York, Deeda Blair from Washington, Helene Brown of California, workers among the thousands of women in the front lines of the fight. Dr. Arthur Holleb, senior vice president for medical affairs, and Dr. LaSalle Leffall, the national president of the American Cancer Society, whose compassion and intellect are equal to none, and the two million organized volunteers who join them—these are my colleagues who are consumer advocates for all 55 million of us. But mainly, my work is meaningful to me because it has drawn me closer to people.

In May, 1977, there was recognition from the medical profession as to the value of my work. The American Society of Surgical Oncologists presented me with the James Ewing Memorial Award, honoring one of the pioneer doctors in experimenting with chemotherapy and radiation treatments, which is given annually to a layman in the cancer field. I felt very humble, I who had survived cancer because of Dr. Ewing's work. The real affirmation of the award's worth, however, came from a young woman after a speech I had given in Atlanta. She came up to me with tears in her eyes. "I can't believe I'm meeting you," she said. At the age of thirty-one, just three years ago, she had breast cancer, she told me. "Mrs. Bayh, you were my shining example." Statements like those were the real rewards, the heart of the fulfillment from my work.

In October, 1977, I felt I was sitting on top of the world. My health and energy had never been better. I felt great—the old neck pain had not bothered me for two years. I had flown to Florida for a speech on cancer in Tampa. There was a television interview. I flew to Denver, changed planes, and arrived in Salt Lake City, in another time zone, where I addressed 3,500 women on equal rights for women. Then I went straight to the airport to fly to Des Moines, Iowa, in still another time zone, for a speech on cancer. I arrived in Des Moines in pouring rain, and addressed the statewide convention of the American Cancer Society. What wiped out the fatigue was the satisfaction, the fulfillment, the gratitude that I feel for my work. I woke up in a hotel room in Des Moines, at 5 A.M., and I couldn't go back to sleep. I rolled over and wrote on a little notepad beside my bed, "I can't stand it. I am exploding. I am so happy."

You've seen children who seem to be just bursting with energy. I was bursting, like that, with excitement. Anything that is deferred—that you have waited for and dreamed about, for a long, long time—you treasure so much more, once you get it, than if you always had it.

I called Birch later that morning in Indiana. "I am about to explode," I said.

"Why?" he asked.

"I am so happy."

Birch got that little catch in his throat.

"I am so happy that you are happy," he said.

Chapter 14

Just five months after I wrote on that little notepad in Iowa, "I am exploding with happiness," I had an appointment for my three-times-a-year cancer check. I was not too worried. After all, it had been six years and three months, with "all clear" blood tests. We had celebrated the five-year mark; my life during those years had been one of fulfillment, of usefulness, of hope.

That afternoon, January 25, 1978, when I went in to my cancer doctor, hoping for the expected "all clear," I didn't get it.

This, then, is a chapter that I didn't intend to write. But through my experience over this year of my recurrence, the forty-fifth year of my life, I have gained something far more valuable that I hope to share. So many times, as I fought the sleepless battles within my own mind, I have said, "Oh, to have Aunty's faith." No matter how heavy her pain and tribulations, she has been able to deposit her troubles with God. Her simple, abiding faith has given her a serenity that I envied, and I often turned to her, in my own despair, for help. "Pray for me, Aunty," I said. "I need it."

I did not know that same faith was mine for the asking.

༄

The cancer doctor found a lump that afternoon, one I hadn't noticed, on the left side of my neck, near my collarbone. It was flat, hard, about the size of my little fingernail, a swollen lymph node. Perhaps it would be only an ear infection.

Dr. Hawken, my surgeon and gynecologist, examined me next.

259

"It's not on my schedule to go to the hospital just now," I told him. "I know," he said, quietly. "I know."

He took me over to an ear specialist, Dr. Webb, who was not as hopeful about an ear infection, because none of the lymph nodes around the ear were involved. Nevertheless, they gave me penicillin for a few days, just in case there was a hidden infection somewhere in my body that would cause a swollen lymph node.

We drove up to the country, creeping along because of the ice, marveling at the patterns of ice and snow drawn like diamonds on the trees. On the picnic table was a birthday cake for Birch, a perfectly round snow form about six inches from the edge. He had just turned fifty the Sunday before, an event we would mark, along with my approaching forty-fifth, with two dinner parties the first week in February.

Birch built a big log fire in the fireplace, we looked out the window at our world. In the tall woods down the path to the river, a woodpecker, with the brightest red head I had ever seen, pecked a sharp tattoo in a treetop.

And I developed a slight earache. It was a wonderful pain.

But on Monday, I had an appointment with Dr. Gutierrez, the surgeon who would remove the lymph node for examination. He had all my previous records, and he was not hopeful about an ear infection. Moreover, he explained to me some things about my previous breast cancer that had been withheld from me.

All these years, I had thought my "spread" was minimal—that only two lymph nodes were involved. Dr. Gutierrez now told me there had been five, all in the first level. And two, not one, types of cancer had been found in that right breast, one highly invasive, that had spread throughout the tissue of the breast, and even into the skin.

"How long had it been growing before I had my mastectomy?" I asked.

"Probably not long," he estimated. "Maybe a year or two."

A year or two. 1970, 1971—those horrible years of my father, that presidential campaign, with all the tension, tears, debts. If stress could cause cancer, I thought bitterly, that could have caused mine. (Later, I learned other doctors think cancer develops much more slowly.)

Surgery was scheduled for February 1, and I worried, of all things, about the scar. The scar on my chest is hidden by prosthesis and by my clothes, the one on my leg from that tumble in 1966 by makeup and stockings. Now there would be a scar on my neck for people to stare at. Jane Sinnenberg made me laugh: "Just have Birch buy you a diamond necklace to cover it up."

"I'm afraid it would be something like a little Vera scarf, instead," I said. Then: "Oh, Jane, I'm not ready for this."

"I'm not, either," she said quietly.

I knew what I would be in for, if it were malignant. And it was the loss of my time and energy that I would resent. The body scans, all the blood tests, probably radiation and chemotherapy, all those hours in doctors' offices, the endless waiting for results—those procedures rob you of time and energy, and add stress as surely as do the pressures of outside life. I resented the thought of days, hours, minutes, being taken from my life, for cancer tests, cancer therapy.

Ironically, I'd received a letter from Dear Abby that day, saying that she and Mort, her husband, had never seen us looking so well and happy. "Whatever you are doing, keep it up," she said.

Also, ironically, the day before surgery, I had a call from another cancer victim who used to telephone when she got depressed during the months of radiation treatment, for she said I cheered her up. I did my best. I couldn't tell her about me.

I had felt proud, useful, of service, to be held as an "example" to cancer victims these last few years. Now, if I had recurrence, would it shatter their hopes?

I took a sleeping pill and went to bed, worried about many things. One was the operating room—I dreaded looking up into those masked faces, those gruesome instruments, before they put me to sleep.

Birch spent the night of my surgery in the hospital, in an empty room across the hall. Mercifully, Dr. Gutierrez allowed the anesthesiologist to put me to sleep in my hospital room. But the masks, the tiny scar—those were such minor worries. The node was malignant, the same type of cancer that had invaded my breast.

The next three days were back-and-forth for scans—the liver scans, x-ray of the lung, the bone scans. The results were not yet in when we gave the first of the two dinner parties for fifty, to celebrate our birthdays. It was a merciful diversion.

The next morning I was back in the hospital for scans, Jane Sinnenberg beside me through the exhausting procedure. "Should you tell someone if they probably aren't going to live?" a young man asked Jane. His wife, the mother of three young children, was having a brain scan. After the scans I came home and laid out my evening clothes. We were going out for dinner with Ann and Lloyd Hand, friends from the Johnson White House days. I lay down to rest, but I could not sleep.

At six o'clock, I was standing in the kitchen when the phone rang. It was the man who had been my cancer doctor for more than six years. "I am afraid I have bad news," he said. "The cancer has spread to your bones."

"What does that mean?" I asked, clutching the phone as if it was a lifeline being pulled away.

"The bone scan was positive in several areas—the mid-back, the neck area, the pelvic region." I began to take notes. I felt as if my mind were separating from me.

It is inoperable, I wrote. I'll be on therapy for the rest of my life. It will be terminal in the future. Then I asked him a question no doctor should ever answer: "How long do I have to live?"

"A year for sure," he said. "A good year. And perhaps five or six more, with treatment."

My fingers, writing down this information, didn't want to work. I felt so totally alone, and helpless, a death sentence coming through the telephone.

But during the call, Birch ran in the front door.

"Birch, Birch, pick up the phone," I screamed. "It's in my bones."

"I know, I know," he said. The doctor had called him at his office; he had rushed home, but not in time. (On his way off the Senate floor, he'd run into Senator Cranston. "You look so bad, Birch," he had said. "You shouldn't let being head of the Intelligence Committee get you down.") We talked to the doctor a bit more, about chemotherapy, about consultations. And then the conversation ended.

We held each other, and we cried.

It could not be real. I felt so well, I looked so well—how could it be in me? The chemotherapy was supposed to stop this. Perhaps if they had had the combination drugs six years that they have today, we could have licked it. All the cancer speeches I had made, the facts and figures, research and progress, whirled around, jumbled in my head. The unfunded projects—the research at the National Cancer Institute that has been approved, but Congress has not funded. Could the cure to my cancer be lying in one of those projects?

I thought of Evan, pride of my life, graduating from college this year. How could we tell Evan? I thought of my doctor's call. No more bad news over the telephone. No, I must tell Evan myself. We canceled our dinner with the Hands. Finally, we had to eat something. Birch drove down to Roy Rogers and brought back some fried chicken. As he walked in, the smell of fried chicken suddenly seemed like life to me, a pleasure to savor, to hold on to. Rain was pattering on the roof; I wanted to hold on to the sound. To hold on.

With that one phone call, all the trivial things that had always concerned me shrank into nothingness. This life, that I have loved so much, that I have tasted and savored with an appetite that would not be filled . . . why is it to be over?

"Please, Birch, let's promise never to have another fight, never another cross word," I said.

I called Jane Sinnenberg, closer than a sister. We wept together. "What can I do, Jane?" I asked. "Where can I go?"

And from the past, from Grandma Hern's little country church in Lahoma, came the melody of an old hymn, "Where could I go, but to the Lord?"

I wanted to pray. I tried, once, twice, but I felt inadequate. I believed in God, of course. But did I have any right to ask for a miracle, I, who had drifted away from the church? Did I have any right to pray?

I called Jane Suydam, who lives next door. This Jane, who had worked in the Kennedy campaigns, had learned to cope with sadness in her own life through prayer. She is a born-again Christian. There were frequent prayer meetings at her house, a "Jesus is Lord" bumpersticker on her car. "Please come over and help me," I asked. She walked over, bringing her Bible, praying for words that would reach me.

"Where is God's love?" I cried. "Tell me about God's love. I want to live! Surely I'm being taught a lesson. What can I do? How can I have stronger faith? How can I believe in miracles?"

"There are miracles," she said softly. "They do happen." She talked to me about God's love—how His love would never leave me. She said His love was mine, for the asking, quoting those words from the book of Matthew: "*Ask, and ye shall receive; seek, and ye* shall find; knock, and the door shall be opened." God's healing love was there, all around me, like the strongest current of electricity. All I had to do was to plug into it. To believe.

She read the Twenty-third Psalm to Birch and me. And as she read, each old familiar word suddenly came to me in a new way as a gift, to treasure: "*I shall not want . . .*" "*He restores my soul . . .*" "*Yea, though I walk through the valley of the shadow of death, I fear no evil . . .*" "*And I shall dwell in the House of the Lord forever . . .*" I began to pray, silently. I asked for the faith to believe, to conquer doubt, simply to have stronger faith.

There was no flash of lightning, no roll of drums. But I felt, slowly, a relaxation in my mind, and in my taut body, a strange and welcome feeling of calm. It was as though a path were being opened for me, a way toward help with this incredible burden that had fallen on my shoulders. I took my first steps along that path that night, by saying, "I want to believe." The help was there, and still is there, as I embarked on the difficult journey of searching for medical help for my cancer, and for God's miraculous healing power to touch me, as I believe it has touched so many others.

God brought me to my knees, humbled me, and then, as I learned to pray and to trust, gave me the strength to ask that my remaining years be used, in whatever way He can use me, to further His work, through my work.

The next evening, the second of what was to have been our double celebration dinner party, was bearable only because of the strength of those prayers. I decided to go through with it. It made me receptive to the love around me, the gifts of caring friends. We did not tell anybody, of course. It was hard to make light conversation. But when Birch lifted his glass in a toast, he paused, turning to me. There was emotion in his voice. "I want to toast someone who has always been by my side . . . my best friend and advisor, my wife." Our guests could see on his face that something was wrong. I stood up, trying to lighten the mood a bit, saying that my father used to say that the most amazing thing was that Birch and I could live together without an atomic explosion. "But, Daddy, we do have atomic explosions," I had told him. Nevertheless, I asked our friends to indulge me in a personal, private toast to the most wonderful husband and friend in the world. And then Birch and I drank to our friends, and reached out with all our hearts to the love in that room.

Dr. George Blumenschein, of M. D. Anderson Hospital in Houston, Texas, flew up to consult with the Washington cancer doctor, Birch, and me. I took with me a card that Yaqub-Khan, the Pakistani ambassador, had handed me at our party the night before: "Life is full of tragedies which never occur."

I also had a list of questions to ask the doctor: What are the dos and don'ts? What about my heart racing? About not sleeping? Will diet help? Will I end up in a wheelchair? What about exercises? What about treatments? Side effects? Nausea? Hair loss? What about the pain? What is the best hope? What is the worst? What about the quality of life? How long do I have?

I liked Dr. Blumenschein immediately. He began to answer my questions straightforwardly, but kindly. I now have stage four cancer, the last stage (stage one is when it is localized to the breast; stage two is when it involves the lymph nodes; stage three is when it appears in larger volume and is possibly operable; stage four is when it has spread, metastasized to a degree where it is inoperable). But I had options for treatment, they told me: If my tumor was estrogen-receptive, and if we take away estrogen, there would be a 50 percent chance that the tumor would recede for a while. I thought ironically of all those years when doctors were pumping estrogen *into* my body. Now other doctors wanted to take it out.

They recommended a new drug—one that wasn't available six years ago—to block any estrogen my body would be producing. There would be no side effects from this pill. They would check my blood every two weeks, scan me every four weeks. "There are more therapies coming," Dr. Blumenschein said. "We have to buy valuable time."

Pills, not the hated injections. "Aha, you won't get to shoot my veins," I teased my cancer doctor. "Wait a minute," he said. "At some point chemotherapy must be started."

Then they told me about a hard drug, new since my mastectomy, tough, more effective than any previous drugs. But the side effects would take a heavy toll. Nausea. Hair loss. Possible heart damage. They threw the names of other drugs at me until my head was spinning.

They told me statistics, and defined "remission," when the cancer goes below the clinical line. Yes, the "hard drug" treatments would sap my energy. But, they said, without treatment, at some point the tumor would rear *its* head and sap my energy. It slowly sank in: Not only were they telling me my days were numbered, but they were telling me my productive, quality days with energy are numbered, *whether or not* I take the drugs.

And then they talked about "buying time" with these drugs, until new drugs appear. "Live one day at a time," Dr. Blumenschein said.

In one breath, doctors talked about positive thinking and removing stress from one's life; in the next, they describe a situation that is fraught with more stress than even the most tension-packed professional life: the interruptions of your living, to go back and forth to doctors, to hospitals; the endless waits in impersonal offices; the painful injections; the waits for results; the harmful side effects. When they speak of eliminating stress in your life, I suppose they mean that you must cut out everything else so you will be able to bear the stress imposed by the torturous procedures of fighting cancer. I prayed for the strength to fight this disease.

That night, at a dinner party at Deeda and Bill Blair's, who are great supporters of the fight against cancer, I sat next to the young cancer specialist who heads the Georgetown University Cancer Wing, one of the nineteen comprehensive cancer centers in the nation. He had no idea I had had a recurrence, as I pumped him with questions. And I learned—maybe too much for my own good. But then, after telling me all the damage the new hard drug can do (they don't know yet about the long-term results, as they have been using it only for two or three years), he said, "If I had a patient with cancer in the bones, I would definitely use it. We have to buy as many years as we can, and not worry about the possibility of it damaging the heart." That night I turned again to prayer. I would need guidance in determining my therapy, and guidance in telling my son.

I'm bursting with pride in Evan. And he doesn't need me as he did six years ago, I thought. I could leave him now. I thanked God for having spared me those years, not only to achieve my own personal fulfillment but to guide Evan through his adolescence, through those turbulent years when the man he is now was being shaped. Yes, I could leave him—but oh, I don't want to. I want desperately to see him graduate from law school, to meet the girl he will marry, and someday, maybe even hear his children call me "Gran."

But how to tell him? Should we wait for his spring break,

when he comes home? Should I fly out to Indiana? I prayed for guidance, and the next morning it came to me, with certainty: Bring him home for a weekend, tell him here, with Birch and me to put our arms around him. We called him, explaining that his trip home would be my birthday present from Birch.

My prayers were already being answered, each in its own way, I felt. Friends, as they heard about it, began to pray as well, encircling me in love. It was a joy to discover the Scriptures, as a "baby" Christian, and to soak myself in the comforting words. Out in the country, the beauty of nature was my own special birthday gift. The problems of Washington—Panama Canal treaty, Korean scandal, wiretap investigation—were far behind. We watched the parade of cardinals, bluejays, woodpeckers, and we walked in the snow, laughing. "How long will I be able to do this?" I wondered, as I ran ahead of Birch in the snow. We watched television and laughed at Archie Bunker, later calling actor Carroll O'Connor, our good friend, to thank him for having made us laugh. I read the booklets Jane Suydam had given me, stories of miraculous healings, lessons on how to pray, how to receive God's blessing. I felt myself growing spiritually, more than I had grown in the last twenty-five years.

We came back to the White House once again, for my birthday. President Carter had called Birch over to talk about the Intelligence Committee, and had told Birch he was praying for me. Now, we were invited there to a reception for the Finance Committee of the Democratic party, and to a movie afterward with the Carter family. Seeing President Johnson's portrait in the foyer filled me with memories, as I stood on the spot where, on Lynda's wedding day, I could see her and her father walking down the stairway. We went downstairs to the theater, where we had watched a movie with the Kennedys when we were so young and excited about Washington. Once, I had wondered if I would live in this house; now, I only hoped to live.

The Carters were warm and friendly—they'd changed from their party clothes to comfortable slacks (not jeans). Amy came down with a little suitcase of toys, which she spread out on the floor in front of us, in case she got bored. Behind us sat a few members of the staff, Zbigniew Brzezinski (whom we remembered as another "outstanding young man" of 1964), Jody Powell, Mary Hoyt, and

Gretchen Poston, an old friend of mine, now Mrs. Carter's social secretary. I thanked the President for his prayers—and told him I would like to meet his sister, Ruth.

The next days were filled with investigating alternative medical therapies—and a healing service at St. Margaret's Episcopal Church. And all the while I was reading, praying, reading, praying. I had been tempted to cancel my scheduled ERA debate with Phyllis Schlafly, on February 25 in Lynchburg, Virginia, but I am glad that I did not. Birch had promised to fill in for me if I didn't feel up to it, but I felt strongly that this was something I wanted to do myself.

I believe many wives and mothers—and widows—who would benefit economically from the enactment of the Equal Rights Amendment have been confused by the STOP-ERA people. Hubert Humphrey once said, "The poorest people in the world are not those who lack money, but those who have no options." Millions of women have had very few choices in our society. If you are married, with little children, and you have no way of supporting yourself, and your husband comes home and beats you, you have no choice. If he comes home drunk and you do not have job skills of your own to fall back on, and have a couple of children who need to be fed, you have no choices. You are trapped.

I have been one of the lucky ones. There are so many women who are vulnerable to economic disaster. Over sixteen million of America's mothers of young children are working mothers; 44 percent of mothers who are heads of households have incomes below the poverty line. For one reason or another, many housewives find themselves facing financial insecurity—or disaster—at midlife. Facing old age without Social Security or comprehensive insurance is a frightening prospect for a dependent, widowed woman. But it is a reality in which millions of women, including those whose husbands were in government service, find themselves.

It is these women, even more than the militant young marchers, who would benefit from the Equal Rights Amendment. Indeed, many women who already have benefited from the women's movement do not identify with the movement because of the strident voices of those leaders who broke ground for us. It is time, I feel, that more women speak out—wives and mothers who are comfortable in their femininity, yet who insist on equal opportunities for women to pursue and advance in a career if that is their choice. Though I was nervous about that debate, I made my points and felt that the debate went well.

There was important work to be done in Washington. ACS had asked me to open the Washington office of its newly formed Public Issues Committee, in which I could direct our educational programs about cancer. It would be a small office, but a beginning, to help combat the $5,000,000 a year the tobacco lobby was funneling into its Washington office, and to seek government support for cancer research (though not for the ACS, which is a volunteer organization) and other cancer-associated legislation. There would be the inevitable conflict-of-interest charges leveled against such a job for the wife of a public official. But Birch had been a strong supporter of cancer legislation all his years in the Senate. He had lost his mother to cancer, and had suffered through my ordeal. Nobody needed to lobby him.

The office furniture was all donated. Jane Sinnenberg took over as decorator, while I worked with Lane Adams to set it up administratively. There were speeches to be made around the country, on cancer. "I just don't have the time for this disease," I prayed, as my schedule loaded up. "Surely I am doing Your work."

"*Be still. And know that I am God,*" was my answer.

I had read Dr. O. Carl Simonton's book, *Getting Well Again,* in which he suggests that the psyche not only can help produce cancer, but also can help cure it. In other words, if stress hinders the body's immune system, could not *absence* of stress allow our natural immune system to do its work? Could "positive pressure" from the psyche work with radiation and chemotherapy to help evoke a cure? Now I was also reading Agnes Sanford's books about emotional and mental healing. And still praying for guidance in making a decision about the "hard" chemotherapy.

The cancer doctor said to me, firmly, as he took my next blood test: "You *will* go on the hard drug at some point, Mrs. Bayh."

"He ought to know better than to dictate to me," I wrote that night.

A friend had sent me an article about the drug that very day, pointing out that it had caused deafness in some patients. It is a powerful poison, capable of killing cancer cells. I was reminded of that statement from Vietnam: "We had to destroy the village to save it." But I knew many people had been helped by this drug.

I called Dr. Blumenschein in Texas. "We don't promise you the moon—a cure—or huge advantages in taking it," he said. But he said he had known no instance of deafness in the cases he has handled since 1973—and that the heart, if damaged, could lose half of its functionability and still, with its reserve capacity, function rather normally. And then he said, "Mrs. Bayh, do you realize that you have 'stage four' cancer, which is the last stage? The prognosis is not bright. There is some evidence, with this drug, that it might be altered. And we can just keep our eye on new drugs. Three years from now, we'll know so much more."

The prognosis is not bright. Three years from now. . . .

I was ready for some good news—and it came. The results from my blood tests showed that the estrogen-block pills appeared to be working. I thanked God. It was a sign, I believed, that I could be healed.

Evan came home in March. That month's worth of prayer had given me the courage to tell him. Birch and I brought him into our blue sitting room, where we talked about my recurrence. There were tears, from all of us. But I remember most that he was so understanding, so sympathetic, so mature. I told him how much prayer had helped me. "It's been helping me, too," he said. "I've been attending a prayer group at school."

We drove to the country that next weekend, a harmonious, close-knit family, and spent quiet time in prayer together. I felt that my cup was "running over," as in the Bible. Later that week, back in Washington, we three went out to the Shoreham Hotel, where comedian Mark Russell pokes fun at the foibles of politicians. We laughed at his jokes. There was music, and Evan asked me to dance. As we danced, laughing about his old, hated dancing class, he looked down at me, my tall, strong son. "Mom, you've really got class," he said. "I so admire you for the way you are taking this."

Another gift: God had let me live long enough to hear my son give me his highest form of compliment—"class."

Birch was supportive in many ways. He learned to bake bread. He attempted a pecan pie from Colleen Nunn's old Georgia recipe, and even eggs benedict, and when I flew to New York for an ACS meeting, he sent one of his telegrams: "Have a great day in the Big Apple, but beware of those big city boys. Remember I love you." The next week, while I was in Roswell Park Hospital in Buffalo, New York, for consultation, he wired: "I have 12 pints of blood and a very strong heart just for you if you need it."

I had gone to Roswell Park at the suggestion of Rose Kushner, author of an important book, *Breast Cancer: A Personal History and an Investigative Report.** Dr. Thomas L. Dao, whom I consulted there, has been a pioneer in hormone therapy for breast cancer. A soft-spoken gentleman who was born in China, Dr. Dao was reassuring about the possibilities of controlling the disease at this time, without the "hard drug" that I feared. "But, Dr. Dao, if you have bugs in your house, the natural urge is to kill them all, and stamp them out," I said.

"That is fine, if you have a method of stamping them out, but we don't have such a method. And we don't burn down the house to get rid of the bug." He, like so many others, reiterated that we are just "buying time" for new drugs. There were more tests, more x-rays.

I had tried to reach my cancer doctor in Washington before leaving for Buffalo. Unfortunately, he had not been in, and he was surprised now to receive my call from Dr. Dao's hospital, asking that he share his information on my blood tests. The tone of his voice as he said, "Mrs. Bayh, you can go anywhere you want to go and see any doctor you want to see," made me uncomfortable. I remembered Dr. Frank Rauscher, the Cancer Society's vice president for research, who had told me not to be intimidated by doctors: "Anybody worth his salt welcomes someone else's input on a situation like this."

Meanwhile, we had been continuing to investigate new drugs, some showing positive results in controlled tests in this country, and some being tested abroad. Some sounded *so* promising. I went back to my cancer doctor in Washington, excited and hopeful. "Oh well, that may not appear to be anything—we just don't know about that yet." I had gone into his office, hopes high, and left in tears. I did not question his skill or his ability, it was just that he was so . . . blunt. And this was the same doctor who said that "attitude is just as important as what I put in your veins." A patient in a life-or-death struggle is a very difficult patient, I realize. We ask for straight answers, and then we are horrified to hear them. Nevertheless, if I could insert a required course in every medical school in the country, I would. I'd call it "Hope."

Doctors forget, I think, how we cling to every nuance, every

* Harcourt Brace Jovanovich, New York, 1975.

tone-of-voice change, for a shred of hope. There are ways, and there are ways of saying things. If he had only said, when I asked him how long I had to live, "None of us can answer that question. . . ." Or now, about that new drug being tested, something like, "we just don't know, it hasn't been tested yet, but we have hope. . . ." perhaps I might have reacted more calmly. I am no psychologist, but I realized that I was becoming more and more depressed after each visit with this doctor. It was a striking contrast when Dr. Blumenschein from M. D. Anderson Hospital in Texas called. Although he might not agree with what another doctor said, he was gentle in the way he said so, encouraging about the new drugs, and optimistic about some of the results. He realized I was clutching at straws, and while he offered no answers, he did not deny me hope.

Throughout that first ordeal of searching the country for the therapy I needed, I, who had always been a bundle of nerves, needed no tranquilizers, no sleeping pills. That was the first miracle faith had given me. My neighbor and good friend, Myrtle McIntyre, said to Jane, "Isn't it wonderful what they've given Marvella to make her relax after this terrible news?" I just smiled.

I believed that God works His miracles in many ways—through doctors, through scientists, through the unselfish love of friends and strangers, and through those unexplainable events we so often, gratefully, call "coincidence."

I had been reading a book, *The Power To Heal*,* by Father Francis MacNutt, a highly educated Catholic priest whose ministry has been in healing through prayer. That book had given me such a lift, such hope in the face of all my devastating news from doctors, that I hoped to meet him, to ask to be included in his prayers. Shortly after I returned from Roswell Park Hospital in Buffalo, Jane Suydam and I left for Staten Island, New York, for a weekend retreat at Mt. Augustine, conducted by Father MacNutt.

A giant of a man, handsome, Father MacNutt spoke in the softest, most gentle voice that I have ever heard. He prayed for healing—first in English, and then in what they call "Tongues," beautiful, unintelligible (to me) sounds that are, they say, inspired by God. Afterward, he pointed out that it was important to continue prayer, and to practice what he called "soaking" prayer, a lingering, continuing, quiet, but intense prayer every day, after we have ini-

* Ave Maria Press, Notre Dame, Ind., 1977.

tially asked God to heal. "It helps to think of soaking prayer as being like radiation or x-ray therapy," he has written, in an analogy that was easy for me to understand. "The longer the diseased area is held under the radiation of God's healing power, the more diseased cells are killed. . . ."

I felt his intensity, warmth, and sincerity, and was moved by it. I prayed that the soaking prayer would help the medicine I was taking to work upon the cancer in my body.

Prayer in place of medicine? Indeed not. As I had told Evan, God's healing power is worked through doctors, in scientific break-throughs, as well as in other, unexplained ways.

There were 170 of us at the retreat, a group seeking, in one voice, the power of God and a closer personal relationship with Jesus. We learned about ways of living with grace, and praying, being quiet, waiting for the Holy Spirit to perform.

"Enter into His rest. Rest from our work. Even God rested from His work," said Father MacNutt.

I thought of all the years of my life when I compulsively jumped out of bed to tackle that desk, race through that schedule, pushing a tired body and mind to do work that amounted to—what? No time to rest, no time to mourn, no time to receive God in my life. Had it taken this blow to stop me?

There were more comforting words: "Don't have false guilt. Don't think God will punish you for something for the rest of your life.

"Jesus doesn't want people to be sick. It is never His will to have anyone sick.

"You really can't communicate well with God if you harbor resentments or hate toward anyone.

"There has to be continuity: Prayer is not limited to time or place."

Although Jane and I are not Catholic, we were made to feel a part of this family, as surely as if we were nuns like Sister Jean or Sister Beth, who, with Father Bill Kerr, run Mt. Augustine. The healing sessions at Mt. Augustine, I discovered, are part of a grow-ing religious movement in this country known as "charismatic re-newal," which is both interdenominational and nondenominational. It reaches straight back to the Bible for its source, calling believers to come together and pray, believing that the Holy Spirit changes lives.

After we returned, I joined Jane Suydam in attending the New Life Series led by Father Everett Fullam, a Connecticut Episcopalian, at Washington's St. Luke's Methodist Church. Later, he told Jane that after his church service in Connecticut, a woman came up to him and said, "You know, the Lord has told me to pray for a Mrs. 'Bye.' Isn't that the funniest name? I don't know nor have I ever heard of anybody by that name."

Easter Sunday in the country was a quiet time for Birch and me, highlighted by a visit to the church, and listening to religious tapes. Birch came into the cabin with a load of firewood.

"The power to live is so strong that the tulip bulbs are sprouting right through the hard, icy crust," he said.

I felt it, too.

Birch appeared, unexpectedly, at Georgetown University Hospital on April 3, as I checked in for my new bone scans. My prayer was that they would reveal to me some sign, some tangible effect of the healing power I had felt at Father MacNutt's Mt. Augustine retreat. My new cancer doctor in Washington was reassuring, hopeful. "Is there any chance that I might live for ten years?" I asked him. "With luck, yes," he answered.

"There are new drugs being developed all the time," I said.

"That is true."

"Many prayers are going up for me. You also must reckon with the power of God," I told him.

"To be sure!" the young doctor answered.

I had changed doctors at this crucial point, not on a whim, but because I was convinced a key ingredient in any cancer therapy is hope. Once I would have stood by meekly and accepted a doctor's negative attitude. Now I am no longer the docile patient that I once was. I am fighting for my life.

This physician's credentials are impeccable; his knowledge of cancer is comprehensive. He has cared for many cancer patients whom I know. He had joined Birch and me at a dinner meeting with Dr. Dao, to discuss consultations and a working relationship between them. He was willing at the outset, he said, to help me search for the most effective therapy.

And from the results of that bone scan, it appeared that the prayers and the pills were working. All my praying friends (and there were many, individuals and prayer groups) and I rejoiced, and gave thanks.

The previous Sunday, Birch and I had watched a television program new to us, Rev. Robert Schuller's Hour of Power, from Garden Grove, California. I had been thinking of Hubert Humphrey that week, at an annual Cancer Society luncheon, where last year he had received an award for courage. Reverend Schuller had been of great comfort to him. Now, coincidentally, a friend called from California. Robert Schuller was coming to Washington; would I like to talk with him? Birch's cousin, Bill Bayh, and his wife Janie had also written to him of their prayers for me.

Reverend Schuller came to my house, to talk and pray together. I felt that he was a fine person. After we talked about my religious renewal, he asked me to speak about it on his television program. "I don't know if it is time for me to do that yet," I answered.

I hadn't minded that word was spreading around Washington about my recurrence, now that I had received this renewed faith. The sustenance of caring friends has always carried me through the deepest valleys. Now, when I needed it most, I was almost in-undated with the kind thoughts and offers of help from friends. How much that has meant to me, I can never describe. There were so many—Betty Vanik from Ohio, who called to tell about her answered prayers in her healing from cancer; Walter Ridder, the newspaper publisher, telling of progress in his valiant fight against illness; Joan Gardner, who touched my arm and said, simply, "It just isn't fair. . . ."; Joan Mondale, who asked to help in any way she could; Tom Koutsoumpas, from Birch's office, who drew happy faces on his notes, and wept when I wept, and his mother, Alice, and gentle, patient Susan Tigani. Jean-Paul, the hairdresser, and Ken, from the beauty shop, who brought plantain tea; Buffy Cafritz, with whom we spend quiet New Year's Eves, who brought a special pillow; Ardeshir Zahedi, who offered his Embassy of Iran in any way to help with my work; the two Janes, rocks of strength; friends from the Senate, like the Hatfields, and the Chiles, and the Nunns, many of the Senate wives, who wrote, called, dropped by, sent food —these are only a few. But I had not thought of my health and my life being used in a ministry to strangers. Except for these friends who sustained me, I felt that my recurrence of cancer would be a private matter. I was inclined not to accept Rev. Schuller's invitation.

Then two things happened. Vice President Mondale, an old friend as well as a fellow Christian, mentioned in Indiana that "both Bayhs have my prayers," setting off a flood of press inquiries. In

Indiana, my health is news. Birch sent out a simple confirmation: "Marvella has had a recurrence of her cancer. She is undergoing appropriate treatment." I guess it was news beyond Indiana, as the notice appeared in newspapers around the country. I began to receive such an outpouring of letters, from old friends, from people who had once heard me speak, from perfect strangers who had survived cancer and just wanted to reach out to me, letters about religious healing, letters that were an affirmation that my work had been worthwhile, and I was glad that Fritz Mondale had mentioned it. Should I also share my new-found comfort in my relationship with my Lord with these people who were comforting me?

Then Larry Ziemianski, a Catholic deacon active in the charismatic movement, talked to me as I was wrestling with the decision on Reverend Schuller's invitation, pointing out that Jesus had said, "Whosoever shall confess me before men . . . will I confess also before my Father who is in Heaven."

Still, I worried. I was so new at this, I was afraid I would say the wrong thing—something that might be counterproductive, causing nonbelievers to think I had become a "religious fanatic," doing more harm than good. I was also afraid that something I would say might be offensive to people of other religions, whose faith I also had come to respect. In addition, from the tone of the letters I was receiving, it was clear that people had gone to doctors because I had urged them to do so, sometimes writing that because of early detection of cancer, I had saved their lives. I would not want people to misinterpret my faith in God's miraculous power, or to think I was even considering abandoning medical science. That would be a disservice beyond all conscience.

Bill and Janie Bayh had told me of a place in their hometown where retreats were held, healing prayers offered. A spring visit to this place, the Martinsville Ministry Center, in Martinsville, Indiana, helped guide me toward a decision. It was an experience, in warmth and intensity, that paralleled the Mt. Augustine retreat with Father MacNutt. The Ministry Center is Protestant-sponsored. Its director, Jack Winter, prayed with me that weekend, and as he was praying he slipped into first person, which he said indicated that he was receiving the gift of prophecy.

"This is not a sickness unto death," he spoke, "but that you might come to know me. You will be a vessel to help many sick, needy, hurting people that they might know My love and mercy.

Even when men come against you you will continue to be an instrument of My love. There are many in distress, many needing comfort. You will be a vessel to bring comfort and love to many."

Those who joined in our prayers at the Center that day said that they were aware of the presence of the Holy Spirit, a vibrant assurance. I prayed. And decided to accept Rev. Schuller's invitation. I would pray for God to give me the right words, to be a witness in a way that would give comfort, and not confusion, to others.

And I prayed constantly for stronger faith. I prayed to have faith if pain should come, to ask for healing. I prayed for forgiveness —for my doubts and for hurt that I have caused others. I prayed for the faith that I would be forgiven.

It was a glorious spring. I was energetic, free from anxiety and pain, immersing myself in prayer and hope, attending a White House ceremony where President Carter presented the ACS Courage Award to Tom Harper from the Naval Academy. And my blood tests showed no further progression. On a trip to California with Birch, I was reading on the plane. He reached over, took my bookmark card from my hand, and wrote, "Thank you for loving me for more than a quarter of a century. P.S. I am looking forward to the next 25 years!!! At least." And signed it with his usual heart-and-arrow. In May, we watched Evan graduate from college, a milestone event in our lives. And also in May, my faith was tested.

Chapter 15

It was May 18, the morning of the Pap Stamp ceremony at the White House, and Mrs. Carter and I were to speak.
The U.S. Postal Service was publishing a commemorative stamp to
honor the work of Dr. George Nicholas Papanicolaou, who developed the "Pap smear" method of detecting uterine cancer that
has saved so many lives.

It was all I could do to get through that speech about cancer.
Just as I was leaving home, my new cancer doctor called with the
result of my latest C.E.A. blood test, the one that since February
had been encouraging—"in the average zone." Today he had bad
news: On the diagnostic scale, my previous test had read 3.5,
well below the "clinical level" of 5. Now, this one read 10—tumor
activity which he interpreted to mean the cancer was growing, or
spreading.

I stood there, Rosalynn Carter beside me in the East Room of
the White House, speaking words about cancer. I could not look
at Birch, or at Jane Sinnenberg, for fear the tears would come. The
fear began, all over again.

Perhaps it was a mistake. "Labs do make mistakes, sometimes,"
Jane said, to cheer me up. "Oh, that's probably something that my
son, the intern, would do. Can you imagine me unleashing him on
the world as a doctor?" Another test, to check against this one. A
whole week to wait for results. No, we wouldn't wait a week, the
oncologist said. We'd have another bone scan, tomorrow. I'd hoped
to consult with Dr. Dao, in Buffalo, too. My blood sample was
mailed to him, packed in ice, but it never arrived. Lost in the mail.

New blood-taking for this purpose, and my veins collapsed. Too many tests lately. Pressure. Birch was with me for the bone scan, where they jabbed and jabbed trying to hit a vein. They missed, injecting dye into the body tissues. It was too much. I went into the hospital bathroom to cry. As I stood before the big bone-scan machines, where they would chart the progress of the dye they had injected, I prayed.

It wasn't a mistake. The next test, duplicated by Dr. Dao in Buffalo, also showed increased cancer activity. And now there was another swollen node in my neck. The intensity of worry that week attacked my faith, both in God and in doctors. What to do next? Did this mean that the pills were not working, that they would want me to go on the "hard drug" immediately? I thought at one point that I was sitting on the edge of a volcano, which below me was rumbling and trembling, and I could not move. The two doctors did not agree on what course to take. In Washington, the oncologist said, "Irradiate [x-ray] the swollen lymph nodes"; Dr. Dao, in Buffalo, said, "Remove them, determine if they are estrogen-receptive." There was firm disagreement over the long-distance telephone, while Birch and I were sitting in the Washington doctor's office. Neither doctor would budge. It's my *life*, I wanted to scream. Radiation or surgery? The decision would be mine. Birch and I prayed. We flew to Buffalo to see Dr. Dao. After talking to Dr. Dao we decided on surgery. When we returned to Washington, however, the doctor here was very persuasive. We talked to *him* last—and gave in to his recommendations, and started the radiation. But then, after agonizing over the decision, after I had had three of the x-ray treatments, the Washington doctor changed his mind, and decided to operate. Someone he "respected" at the National Cancer Institute had agreed with Dao. I panicked, feeling that we had lost valuable time. And now, before surgery, I would have to wait ten days, without the pills I had felt were my lifeline.

I was discovering the attitudes, the words, the uncertainties of some doctors were almost as difficult to cope with as the disease itself. My confidence could not have been lower. Watching the Washington doctor disagree so vehemently with Dr. Dao, then as suddenly change his mind, put me through a nightmare.

Surgery brought more bad news. These new tumors, too, were malignant, and they were not estrogen-receptive. More x-rays, more graphic descriptions: "When you have pain in your right pelvic area we use radiation and, if needed, later put a pin in." Or "We can remove your pituitary gland, which is at the base of your brain, through your nose." Or "We can remove your adrenal gland—of course you will be on cortisone for the rest of your life."

"When I begin chemotherapy, how long will I be on it?"

"For the rest of your life."

By this time, I felt like Muhammad Ali's punching bag. The stuffing was beginning to come out.

Although I still had plenty of energy, the thieving of my time had begun.

June 3, 1978

So they tell you you have a lot less time to live than you thought or planned on. Your life is threatened. Then they proceed to rob you of what time you do have left by absolutely taking over your time. Either you are at the doctor's office or you are talking to doctors on the phone or you are trying to make doctor's decisions. You get up early in the morning and it is a beautiful day outside that God is giving you and you feel wonderful and you have no pain and you are really ready to enjoy the day, but then you talk to them and they say, "Now, how much weight have you lost? Do you have a good appetite?" I say, "Look, I am fighting gaining weight. I have a fantastic appetite." "Are you in pain?" "No, I am not in pain." "Most people who have your amount of spread are in great pain." And then they say, "You realize, of course, that we are just fighting a holding action. We have no magic bullet, there is no cure for this. We can use these drugs. Of course, they deplete the bone marrow and you lose all your hair and they cause nausea. The side effects are very grim but of course we are buying time." By the time you sit and listen to all this, and you go out and look at that beautiful day, you feel like some duck that's been held under water until it is just about dead, and then thrown out on the grass. And you have to just lie there until you get a little strength back.

My faith was so new, it was strained at that first test. As long as I was feeling well, as long as the laboratory offered good results, the faith was easy, like a tranquilizer, bringing me comfort from the fear of death. Now that the cancer was moving again, how should I pray?

In Father MacNutt's book, he had described a miraculous

healing. A little girl's leg was stunted from an accident, an infection, then osteomyelitis. The child's mother had given her away to a convent, thinking the nuns could take better care of her because she was crippled, one leg six inches shorter than the other. After an intense session of Father MacNutt's "soaking prayer," the child's leg grew two inches in two days; then growth stopped. Something was blocking the healing. Something negative had crept into the path of communication to God. They found, after questioning, that the child hated her mother, felt deserted because the mother had given her away. Once she learned to forgive her mother, realizing that the mother's intentions were to help her, the block was removed. The child's leg began to grow again.

Reading that story, I began to wonder what kind of block I had. Jane Suydam helped guide me. "Is there someone you have not forgiven?" Or: "Have you forgiven yourself?"

I had prayed for forgiveness. My trespasses have haunted me. I have ached from the aftermath of realizing I caused hurt to others. There have been times when I have lashed out at people in a quick flareup of anger that for me is therapeutic ("Marvella, you'll never get an ulcer," somebody once told me) and is over as quickly as it boils up. Then I worry that I've hurt the other person, and often I'll quickly apologize. I have prayed for control of my temper, prayed to be forgiven for the times that temper has hurt another of God's children. I had asked Birch to forgive me, also, for all the times I have hurt him. Any couple that has been married this long has some hurts and resentments that need to be dealt with. But asking his forgiveness was easier than my forgiving him.

Jane Suydam reminded me that the Lord's Prayer also requires that we forgive those who "trespass against us." For years, I had thought about President Johnson's job offer, back in 1967, and how I had been thwarted. But here in 1978, we were having dinner with Dan and Jean Rather in the Rive Gauche restaurant, and the conversation turned to the late Lyndon Johnson. I told them about turning down that job because of Birch's career, and to my surprise found myself crying. Despite all my progress, all my liberation, I had been hanging onto a knot of bitterness, blaming Birch. Truly, I thought I had worked it out, by saying in the long run it had been my decision, etc., etc., but I guess even that had not purged me of resentment. Only by forgiving Birch could I purge myself of the residue of bitter resentment.

"Do you need to forgive anybody else?" Jane probed. And if as by design, two people I hadn't seen in a long time, people I had studiously avoided and for whom I had harbored a resentment that bordered on hatred, crossed my path. Now, in one painful week, I realized that God had thrown me up against both of them for a purpose. I could not ask forgiveness for *me* as long as I held unforgiveness in my heart for those I felt had wronged me. "Forgive us our trespasses, as we forgive those who trespass against us." I had to pray hard, for the ability to forgive.

It wasn't easy, but with prayer forgiveness finally came, and a burden lifted. God directed me to call both of them, to tell them I held no more hard feelings for what they had done to me, and to ask their forgiveness for any wrong I had done them. I was warmly received, and the wounds healed. Life is too short to harbor hate or resentment toward anyone.

With each prayer, I offered thanks for God's peace, and I asked that He might guide my life, to use my remaining years in some way to further His work on earth. Perhaps He answered that prayer that summer. In an interview on the "Today" show, ostensibly to speak about Dr. Papanicolaou and his contributions, I had found myself answering Jane Pauley's questions about life, and living with the knowledge that I have cancer, and the comfort that I have found in religion. I spoke, in the context of Dr. "Pap," about the contributions of science, about the progress that has been made and that will be made in fighting this disease, and how I believe that God is working through our growing knowledge of science. The response, measured by letters I received after that one brief interview, was an outpouring from hundreds of strangers who *had* been touched, who took time to sit down and write me about it.

One wrote: ". . . You have something infinitely more powerful than any 'disease' and you are a winner . . . the love and strength I saw in your eyes compelled me to write this. I love you."

A chaplain wrote: "I was deeply moved by your witness on television as to your faith in Christ. . . . I do not wish to build up false hopes but on the other hand be ready if a miracle comes. I pray for you."

From an English teacher, "I chose a thank-you card to say thank you for everything you've done on behalf of women's rights. . . . Most of all, thank you for making your cancer public, because I know you may be saving lives by raising the public's consciousness about this disease. Even more important, the peace you radiate in spite of imminent death is truly remarkable and can only have a beneficial effect, not only on other cancer sufferers, but on anyone. . . ."

From a sixty-two-year-old woman: ". . . Three years ago I accidentally heard you on Channel 4, talking to Barbara Walters about your mastectomy. With similar symptoms to mine, your encouragement persuaded me to have a biopsy, which proved to be cancerous, and then a mastectomy. . . . With all adversity I've restrengthened my faith in God . . . Thank God for Marvella Bayh. . . ."

Answering those letters was a pleasure. Some wrote to ask for help, but most just wrote to say "Thank you." I took that response to be a sign from God that I was to continue His work, by speaking out not only to warn people against cancer, but also to share the knowledge of God's comforting presence with others who might be suffering.

I went to California to tape my testimony for Robert Schuller's service at the Garden Grove Community Church. Arvella Schuller, the minister's wife, became a radiant new friend in my life.

I prayed for words that would be used to further God's work, and the Schullers prayed with me. On the program, which would be televised in October and again the following February, I told of enduring the suffering and losses of my life without having turned to God, and of the difference, now that I was facing another crisis, that prayer has made. All those years of tragedy that I tried to battle by exercising that old Oklahoma will unfolded before me. Had I only known the comfort of God's peace, the feeling that He was walking beside me, what a difference that would have made during those times of suffering. It could have been mine at any time if only I had asked, and been ready to receive. I had thought I was a survivor, that I had handled each crisis, but my trembling hands and sleepless nights were clues that I hadn't handled them that well. The Lord had knocked at my door before, and I didn't answer. That automobile accident, which dealt trauma to my body and mind, the unexpected death of my mother, the emotional scars following the plane crash, the horrible murder-suicide that ended my father's life, my anguish during Birch's presidential campaign, the cancer in my breast—God was just waiting, all those years, as I had been trying to carry those burdens by myself. This time, He nearly knocked my door down. "Terminal" is the hardest word a person who loves life can face. But I know God is here to walk this road with me.

Abigail McCarthy, a devout Catholic whose own spiritual search has enriched all of us, helped me with a definition of the Holy Spirit, about which theologians have wrestled for centuries. "It is also known as the Holy Comforter," she told me. I pursued the Holy Comforter throughout the spring and summer, making contact with some special people who have made their lives a ministry. Canon Charles Martin, an Episcopal minister who had been Evan's headmaster at St. Albans, reached out often in friendship and prayer. Eight Martinsville Ministry Center people, in Washington on other business, came out to pray with me. I thought that I had forgiven Daddy long ago, but here, when I least expected it, was that old well of pain. We spent four hours, a beautiful, concentrated, consecrated session, in which I felt a cleansing, healing power. The next day in the country, Birch and I watched Rev. Schuller's "Hour of Power" on television. In the evening I also saw an hour-long special on the evangelist Oral Roberts' life.

Oral Roberts had gone to Phillips University in Enid, and his first ministry was in my home town; I had heard of him all my life—God's first healing miracle through him, of a woman's deformed hand, had occurred in Enid. Since then, he has devoted his life to the healing ministry, and he is building a new hospital, The City of Faith, to be connected with his university medical school in Tulsa, which will incorporate Christian faith and prayer as part of the medical healing process. As I watched that program, I realized that I was scheduled to speak in Enid the next month. I was being led to this man.

I placed a call to him.

I was feeling better and better. Before my trip to Oklahoma, we spent a glorious Fourth of July weekend in Ottawa as guests of our American ambassador Tom Enders and his wife, Gaetana. As soon as we returned, I had a call from Ruth Carter Stapleton, the President's sister. She could visit with me on July 10, a Sunday. It was a beautiful experience. She is a lovely, gentle woman, with a soft southern voice, and her manner is one of understanding. She has a calming presence. She prayed for healing, for *inner* healing. I think, through the studies of Dr. Simonton and others, we are learning that "inner," or emotional, healing and physical healing are intertwined. Ruth Carter Stapleton prays for God to remove the deep emotional scars, the tension, frustration, agony, that people have borne all their lives. Her approach is different from most. She goes way back into one's life, even to the moment before conception, and brings the understanding, forgiving love of Jesus into life's hurtful experiences. I found her spirit very powerful, her commitment persuasive. The next morning, as I flew to New York for American Cancer Society meetings, I felt fantastic, like my old self—sharp, with energy and drive, not whipping myself to move. I thanked the Lord for that burst of energy.

We had a party with the Shepards to celebrate Paul Rogers' birthday, and the important news that Paul was retiring from the House of Representatives. "He's got sense enough to retire at the top of his career, and still have time for a second career in law and more security for his family," I told Becky, not without envy. I did not look forward to Birch's being gone for his next campaign. It was a blessed relief to laugh and giggle with old friends, to be able to put aside the overpowering concern for my health that had simply taken over.

The ensuing four days in Oklahoma lifted me even higher. I watched Oral Roberts preach a sermon on the subject of being able to receive from God. Afterward, he talked with me about the faith to move mountains, as promised in the Bible. He prayed with me that my mountain be moved. ("Mountain, I have tried to go around you, over you, and through you. And so now, mountain, you have just got to move!") Then he asked me to pray for him. I met his wife, Evelyn, and planted new seeds of friendship, as well as faith.

In Enid, speaking at a meeting to raise money for a costly new piece of cancer-detection equipment for Bass Hospital (it was General Hospital, when I was born there), I felt the most positive connection to the past I had had for a long time. This time, the connection was my new experience with an old friend, the religion of my childhood. Thomas Jefferson Murphy had believed this way, and had so lived his life; Laura Hern and her Earnest believed this way, worshiping in that lilac-filled country church; Aunty Lillian Tharp, with whom I spent precious hours that weekend, believed this way, making Christ the center of her life. This "old time religion" now sweeping the country under the name of charismatic renewal was not exactly a foreign language to me, as for some other new believers. In Enid I realized that it was more like coming home.

The old home place, where Grandma Hern bore her babies in a sod house, where my father grew up, where I came to play the happy games of childhood, is gone. The house, the barns, the tall trees planted along the driveway to the house—all have been bulldozed down, and it is now part of a larger, productive, mechanized farm, a wide field of red Oklahoma dirt. I felt a twinge of sadness as I thought of Grandma's lilacs, the swing hanging from that tall shade tree, the big old house where we sat around the table at harvest, laughing and telling jokes. But then, I thought, when Grandma first saw this spot, it was an empty field of flat, waving grass, more like this present scene than the family home of my memory. Full circle. In a way, it reminded me of my own journey, breaking ground and building a life in new territory, only to return, full circle, to the faith of my forebears. That faith was beginning to blossom, here in the rich Oklahoma earth, and I felt rewarded by being able to share it, through that Enid speech.

∾

The summer was beautiful. The American Cancer Society decided to invest two million dollars to run trials on a new European drug. Maybe it will prove to be the answer. "God help us find it!" I prayed. Dr. Rauscher talked with me about the progress in research one July evening, at a dinner here in Washington: The Cancer Society had been criticized for investing so much in treatment, and no more in prevention. As Dr. Rauscher pointed out, if you have lived in our society for ten years, you already have been exposed to cancer-causing agents. And if we found the one *cause* of cancer at 10:30 tonight, we would still need to search for effective treatment—because 55 million Americans will be coming down with cancer for years and years to come, simply because they have been living for ten years. For any cancer victim, treatment is of paramount concern. I just enjoyed the beauty of each summer day, sustained by faith, while we "bought time" for more effective treatment.

The summer was good for Evan, too, he said. He stayed home, working, and was excited about being admitted to the University of Virginia Law School in the fall. Before classes began, however, he joined me for a cruise of the Scandinavian countries. It had always been a dream of mine to take Evan to the land of my mother's ancestors, the Monsons. Now, I had a feeling of urgency about following a dream: "If there is something you want to do, don't put it off. Do it now, at your first opportunity." I took a chunk of my own earned money, which I had been storing up for my old age, and plunked down reservations for Evan and me to go to Europe. The Senate was in session, so when Birch couldn't join us, I didn't let that stand in our way. It was a special journey, between two compatible friends.

Just before we left, Marie and Walter Ridder, Steve Martindale, and Jane Coyne gave an anniversary party for Birch and me at the Ridders' home overlooking the Potomac River. It was an evening of loving friends, about seventy people, some of whom came a long way to be with us: Mary Lasker from New York, the Enders from Canada, Dear Abby and Mort from California—a glorious evening of music, dancing, celebrating life. Birch and I danced and danced . . . as I hope we'll be able to continue doing.

Evan offered a toast to us that evening: "As a member of the younger generation, I would like to thank my father for being a courageous, idealistic, and compassionate man who has truly made his country a better place for his having lived. I would like to thank my mother for being a courageous and compassionate woman, who has made this nation a finer place due to her efforts. As a son, I would like to pay tribute to my parents, who, in spite of conditions which have often been anything but ideal—have succeeded in fashioning a family which is warm and loving." (Just imagine our exploding pride after hearing that.)

This eloquent person was my shipboard traveling companion through Bergen, Copenhagen, Stockholm, Helsinki, Leningrad, Visby, the Kiel Canal, northern Germany, and Amsterdam, on the Greek cruise ship *Danae*. Evan's company and his enjoyment of the trip were worth all my retirement years put together. On the ship's deck, watching the magnificent mountains reflected in the blue waters, I read Oral Roberts' book, *How to Get Through Your Struggles*—and I thanked God at every turn for the health and well-being to spend this precious time with my son. It was like seeing one Monet painting after another, being so aware and appreciative of the life within each one. A big orange moon decorated our last evening on ship; the orchestra played, of all things, selections from *Oklahoma*. God blessed that trip, I felt. The bond between my son and me grew tighter. Evan and I planned our trip for next year: We'd hogtie Birch so he couldn't beg off, and plan another cruise. No more deferred dreams.

⤜⤏

In the fall, the pain came. Two weeks after we returned—in my legs, in my back, a sciatic nerve, the most awful, screaming pain I had ever known. I prayed that it was only a pinched nerve, somehow not related to the cancer, but the doctors were not encouraging. Even though Dr. Cifala, the osteopath who had helped with so much neck pain in the past, was able to alleviate some of the sciatic pain, he was convinced that it was from spread of the cancer. My cancer doctor showed us the x-rays and compared them to those in June. "It is quite obvious, I'm afraid, that it has spread," he said. Seeing it with my own eyes was rough. There would be another confusing decision about therapy. The pills were no longer working—if they ever had.

I called Janie Bayh in Indiana. I would be there in a few days, making a speech for the ACS. "Tell me about God's love," I said. "I'm really *down*." The visit she arranged to Martinsville Ministry Center was a therapy for my soul. And for two nights, I slept without pain.

⤜⤏

There would be an article in a national magazine, prepared months earlier, attesting to my new-found comfort in prayer, as well as the testimony on Rev. Schuller's television program, taped months earlier. Would this terrible pain, coming from tumors growing within my bones, make a mockery of my witness to God's healing power?

We continued to question the experts about chemotherapy, and also were flooded with advice from all corners to take the unorthodox cures that some people absolutely swear by. Kind, well-meaning people have taken time out of their lives to write me about these things, to document different approaches, to offer a helping hand. There were also new, more medically acceptable methods being tested. There was a doctor in the Bahamas . . . one in New York . . . one in Indiana . . . one in Scotland, another in Greece. We were fortunate, because of my experience with ACS, and because of Birch's position, in being able to consult with this country's most eminent specialists, at the National Cancer Institute, as well as with doctors in private practice. And then we were faced with making life-or-death decisions in the face of conflicting medical advice.

I read each helpful letter offering a story on how someone had been cured of cancer from such-and-such treatment, listened to each doctor's educated guess on which method of treatment I should employ, and I had a great urge to try each and every one. But there wasn't time. This enemy was on the march. I had to make the right choice.

I remember lying in bed at the time of President Carter's talks with Prime Minister Begin of Israel and President Sadat of Egypt at Camp David, praying for God to touch my throbbing knee, praying for peace in the Middle East, praying for forgiveness, praying for a sign to guide me toward the right medical direction. In the night, there came to me, clearly, the outline for a speech that Arvella Schuller had asked me to make, in California. I guessed that was a sign to say, "Don't worry."

By this time I was getting accustomed to speaking with my God. I speak to Him as a friend. There is nothing I can't discuss with Him. Sometimes I feel like saying, "Have You been too busy? Have You forgotten me?" And then, when I am in great pain, and feeling that I am losing ground, the prayers are hard prayers: "Where *are* You? Are You listening to me? I am right here and I need You, *now*."

But in the last analysis, I learned to leave it all to Him—put my problems and my pain at His feet. And He took them and brought me a great love, and a peace and quiet.

Reading the Bible helps. I find that a modern translation in the rhythms and cadences of our own language is easier for me to read than the familiar and beautiful King James version of another century. The words are more immediate, more alive to me. From the Psalms of David (50:15), I read, ". . . I want your promises fulfilled. I want you to trust me in your times of trouble, so I can rescue you and you can give me glory." I have to believe that is the Lord's promise. And, again in Psalms (118:17–18), "The strong arm of the Lord has done glorious things! I shall not die, but live to tell all His deeds. The Lord has punished me, but has not handed me over to death."

There have been other books that have helped me, such as

those of Oral Roberts and Father MacNutt and Reverend Schuller that I have already mentioned, *How Can I Find You, God?* * by Marjorie Holmes, *Lord, How Will You Get Me Out of This Mess?* † by Kay Golbeck with Irene Harrell, *God's Will for You* ‡ by Gloria Copeland, books by Norman Vincent Peale and Kenneth Hagin, and many, many more, as well as Kenneth Copeland's tapes.

Alone in the country, reading and seeking God's presence, I learned from a telephone call late one September afternoon that the C.E.A. test (a controversial test in itself) which had so alarmed me in May by shooting up to 10, was now up to 120. At that point, I wrestled with the ultimate test of faith: that my greatest desire be to come closer to the Lord and Father, and not to be so concerned about healing.

At one of my lowest points, I wrote Evelyn Roberts a letter. After I mailed it, however, I listened to some of Kenneth Copeland's taped sermons Shirley Boone had sent me. He is a former student of Oral Roberts University who has formed his own evangelistic association in Fort Worth, Texas. His homey Texas voice brought me strength and courage. When I came home, I wrote Evelyn Roberts that I was feeling much better, and apologized for my earlier low mood. She wrote back:

"Never apologize for being deep in the valley. That's where the soil is richest, and the most growth takes place. It's all right to be on the mountain top, but the soil for growth is pretty thin up there."

How true, in my life. My personal growth, after the valley of my mastectomy, had been significant, learning to stand on my own feet, take charge of my life, and accept responsibility for my own actions. Now, from this new valley of pain, valley of the shadow of death, came the next burst of growth—that which is taking place spiritually. From this valley, I learned that my relationship with God is more important than my healing, although I continue to pray for healing. I want it so much.

I don't want to be cheated of this time of my life. But there really isn't much I can do about it, is there? I *have* to let go—to try not to hold life so tightly, to rest and relax in the Lord. It is not

* Doubleday, New York, 1975.
† Chosen Books, Lincoln, Va., 1978.
‡ Harrison House, Kenneth Copeland Publications, Forth Worth, Tex., 1972.

always easy. "It is a battle for faith," I wrote on a little notepad. "If you can win this, it makes the other battles easier."

I have been blessed with the strength to carry on my important professional life for the American Cancer Society this year, between the intermittent periods of pain, and to enjoy some of the rewards of my earlier work (with my husband) in behalf of women. Life as they say, goes on.

October 4, 1978

Today I hurried to my Cancer Society office in the rain. I had moved our meeting up an hour earlier so that I could dash to the Capitol in time for the vote on granting the states more time for their ratification of the Equal Rights Amendment. It was the first time I had been to the Senate gallery in over a year. Sharon Rockefeller and Liz Carpenter, now co-Chair of ERA America, sat beside me. Sharon, the West Virginia governor's wife and Senator Percy's daughter, has been up here buttonholing every senator. I was so disappointed in some of our best friends. I was thrilled with the votes of others like Senator Magnuson and Senator Sparkman, bless his heart, and Pell, who had been undecided. Muriel Humphrey, the heroine of the Senate floor, guided them to the right decision. Senator Hodges, from Arkansas, appointed to fill McClellan's seat, was absolutely fabulous. When he started speaking, Sharon said we didn't have him with us, but she was wrong. He is a minister who turned out to give a strong speech for us. He said that some people use the argument that the Bible says that women are the weaker sex and should be subservient. But he said that the Bible also says that the sun goes around the earth. Then he quoted from Paul in the Bible: "There is neither rich nor poor . . . nor male nor female. Everyone is one with Christ." He was fantastic. Last night it was nip and tuck, and didn't know if we'd make it. We ended up with 54 votes. We got Packwood at the last minute, which was a big surprise. Birch set me a note in the gallery which said, "Hi there Shotsie. I don't know why we are voting to give you equality. There is no question that you are much more equal than I. You are everything to me."

Birch was the hero of the hour. When we went to the reception room off the Senate floor, it was filled with ERA supporters. When Birch came through on his way to the press gallery they began to applaud and cheer him.

Jill Ruckelshaus was there, and very nice to me, inviting me to stay with them whenever I come to Seattle. Liz Carpenter asked Sharon Rockefeller if she would make a good first woman senator from West Virginia. "Oh, no," Sharon replied. "I have seen how their lives are—I would rather have another baby."

We went to dinner at Pat and Mary Munroe's, to honor Attorney General Griffin Bell. Barbara Eagleton was there, without Tom. He has gone, along with Miss Lillian, to represent the U.S. at the funeral of Pope John Paul.

At the dinner, I was seated next to Hugh Carter, whom they call Cousin Cheap, because he keeps a tight rein on White House expenses. I said to him, "Aren't you the one who is known as 'Cousin Tight'?" On the other side was Pat Munroe's sister. I asked her if she and Pat had any other brothers and sisters, and she said, "Oh, yes, there were eighteen of us." I met Charles Kirbo, about whom I have heard so much, as the man who has the biggest influence with Jimmy Carter. He is mild-spoken and certainly doesn't seem like someone with much power.

I wore my old black velvet tuxedo pants suit and everybody raved about it and thought it was new. Olga had taken the big full legs and made them straight. It was a big day; Birch was the man of the hour.

October 6, 1978

Seven years ago today is when I checked into the hospital. Seven years ago tomorrow is when I had the biopsy. Seven years ago the next day was the major surgery. We have always celebrated on this date before—so many down—but not this time.

Birch loves to surprise me but this day he outdid himself. His favorite ploy was to leave notes in outlandish places, leading me on a treasure hunt. This time the notes led from the refrigerator, to the glove compartment of the car, to the jar of instant coffee, to the umbrella, to a framed photograph, to the washing machine, to the furnace filter, and finally to the piano. They instructed me about a package which I took from the refrigerator and had to put in a warm oven. The last note (signed with five hearts) told me to open the package.

By the time I did, I was convulsed with laughter. Inside the package was a beautiful porcelain music box, which played a cheery tune, "Buttercup," from *H.M.S. Pinafore*.

It was a fine October day, in which I cherished my love, and my work, and all ordinary days, and life itself. That was what I had to celebrate this year.

But I came down with a cold.

Or at least, with temperature and cough, it seemed like a cold. And for the next two months, my active life as I had known it ended.

I sniffled in California, where I spoke to two thousand women at the Garden Grove Community Church at Arvella Schuller's request, at a conference called "Light Up Your Life." Pat and Shirley Boone were there, speaking too. When I returned home, however, I felt worse. There was fever, but after prayer over the phone with the Martinsville Ministry Center, the fever went down. I decided to keep a speaking engagement in Omaha, Nebraska. Birch had left for Indiana, to help Democratic candidates campaign for the '78 elections. On October 15, I arrived in Omaha, checked into a motel—and began to suffer pains in the left shoulder and chest. By morning I was worse, uncomfortably hot, and could not lie on my left side.

On the way to the speech, I stopped at the emergency room of Nebraska Methodist Hospital. They wanted to keep me there. The x-rays showed fluid built up in my left lung. But against the kindly doctor's advice, I went to the theater, pulled myself together, and gave a Town Hall speech for one hour. At the close of my speech, in which I talked about life in Washington, and about cancer education, I talked about God—and I prayed as I spoke. And I went home to Washington and to the hospital. There, ten days after that speech in Omaha, they tapped my lung, drawing five pounds of fluid. The cancer had spread to the lining of my left lung. It had to be drained, dried out, and then treated in the hospital, an excruciatingly painful experience.

There seemed to be another sign from God, in the middle of that painful October. The response to my public witness happened suddenly, all within a few days. My taped testimony on the Schuller program was shown on television. The November issue of *Good Housekeeping*, with the article about my faith, appeared on the newsstands October 15, heralded by an announcement which had gone out to the news media. A news story reported that "Marvella Bayh says she is dying of cancer." Walter Cronkite, a respected friend, mentioned it on the CBS evening news—and the phones at Birch's office lit up. Though I had not said it, the publicity allowed me to say, on the news program that evening, that I am living, cherishing every moment of life, with the knowledge that I have cancer—and I am walking with my God every step of the way. David Hartman, of ABC's "Good Morning America," later came to my house for a candid ten-minute interview, in which I repeated the message: "I, along with many others, am living with the knowledge that I have cancer, but I am growing in the knowledge of God's love—and I have never been happier in my life." And there was a syndicated article by Myra MacPherson in the *Washington Post* which went out to newspapers over the country, in which I reiterated the message: "My walk with God is growing each day. You know that you are not alone, that you will *never* be left alone. That God is the same. Yesterday, today—and tomorrow."

The reverberations from those television appearances bounced back, a hundredfold, in letters from people praying for me or asking for help, reaching out for a connection to the kind of peace I described. There was also an immediate and overwhelming outpouring of letters from strangers in response to that magazine article, some just offering love, but most from suffering people, reaching out for a helping hand from someone who has walked that road before. I answered those more than 800 letters, sharing the books, tapes, what words of comfort I could impart. Those letters fed me with a purpose.

Many of the letters brought up the problem of encounters with insensitive doctors and hospitals. It was one I could sympathize with; though some of the people working at hospitals have been wonderful to me, others have been thoughtless. Once an employee neglected to offer a wheelchair when I needed it; another time one forgot I might require a pain-relieving medication that had been prescribed. Perhaps after seeing so much illness, some doctors and nurses become discouraged, or inured to it. They ignore the hypersensitivity of cancer patients who cling to and magnify shreds of hope, and can be wounded by every word. A patient ought to be able to tell a doctor or nurse, "I feel awful," and know that he or she will understand, and not turn away. There should be more nurses like those I have met who have a soothing, healing touch; more doctors like Susan Mellet of Richmond, Stafford Hawken, and LaSalle Leffall of Washington, who are saints.

Dr. William Regelson, from Virginia, once told me, "I never tell my patients that something has failed. I never take away one thing that they are holding on to, unless at the same time, I give them something else." Dr. Leffall told me about being in the room with a woman when the doctor told her she had only a few weeks to live. But during those few weeks, a new drug came out, the cure for her illness. "That was fifteen or sixteen years ago," he said, "and every time I see her, she looks at me with a cat-who-ate-the-canary expression on her face, and we smile together."

I found myself using up vast amounts of energy that I could be using to fight the disease, just fighting depression after each new set of facts had been delivered to me by my second cancer doctor in Washington.

Talk about stress? It is much better to have a doctor who will say, "Okay, we've got a problem. We are going to walk this road together; we are going to search out every clue, every alternative; we are going to leave no leaf unturned; we are going to keep exploring the new things that come out of the laboratories. It is an exciting time to be involved in the fight against cancer because there is so much on the horizon that is going to break through before too long. We have come so far, we know so much more now than we knew three years ago. We are going to know so much more in three years than we know now, and I just want you to know that I am going to be there. And I am with you."

And I now have found a doctor who will walk that road of hope with me. I left that second cancer doctor, as I had left the first, because his words tore me down.

A cancer patient's worst enemy is passivity. A recent study at Johns Hopkins Hospital reports on the effect of a woman's emotional state on her prognosis after she has been told she has breast cancer. It was found that women who expressed a higher degree of anger toward not only their disease but also toward their doctors lived longer than those who were pliant and cooperative. It appeared the fighters had a better chance, which makes the role of the physician even more difficult.

I have placed my life in the hands of this new doctor. When I told him God was working through him, he said he was glad to be in such good company. Now whenever I experienced pain in the legs, I knew it was from my body and his medication destroying the tumors. And the pain did come. I was grounded. I must add my present cancer doctor to the list of "saints." He is patiently walking every step of this rough road with us. He is always available when I need him; he understands when I vent my anger at this disease. He offers me hope.

Although I have continued my public speaking both for the Cancer Society and for God, I have also been deeply gratified by the one-on-one contact with those other hurting human beings, who have reached out for my help. They know that I have suffered, that I have been hit in the head with tragic, almost unbearable news. When people have cancer, and ask me what they can do to bear it, they know I have walked that road.

If you're facing a situation like this you need somebody to listen. The family, caring and protecting, sometimes pats you on the shoulder and says, "Everything is going to be all right." But you are not dumb. You know that everything may not be all right. A sympathetic listener who has been down the same road opens the door for real pouring-out of your pent-up emotions, resentment of the situation, and anger. Hurting people need somebody just to listen, to be there, not to judge.

The second thing you need to know is that all of these emotions you are feeling are normal. Tom Harper, the Annapolis student who won the ACS Courage Award in 1978, told me about a retired admiral out at the cancer wing of the Naval Hospital, who came to him, crying: "What's the matter with me? I could face the Nazis. I could face the Japanese under fire. But I can't face this cancer without sobbing. . . ." Everybody needs to know that this is normal. You feel cheated. You feel hate and fear at the situation. That's normal. Cry it out! That's normal, too.

I saw Katharine Hepburn on television, vibrant, active, productive at seventy-one. I want that. I see people who are well at eighty, with great-grandchildren, enjoying holidays with their families. I want that. Birch and I sat at the Kennedy Center for the national tribute for Bob Hope's seventy-fifth birthday, and wept with memories as Lucille Ball sang, "Hey, Look Me Over." I want a seventy-fifth birthday party. But I was forty-five, and when that phone call came from the doctor and I reeled from the bad news, from the matter-of-fact predictions of future surgery, from the gloomy prediction of "we always expect the worst," there were a few times when I went into my bedroom alone and screamed and screamed as if somebody were attacking me with a knife and my life depended on raising the neighbors. I have screamed with anger, with feeling trapped—and I believe that is normal, too. It helps to cry out the frustration, the bitterness, the resentment. And then it's easier to pull one's self back together again.

Everything has its advantages, I suppose. When your strength is sapped by pain or shortness of breath, you learn to simplify your life, to eliminate some things that once took up your time and to save your energy for those events that are really important to you. But in their place there are great books to read, more time for reflection, and time for prayer, for reading the Bible.

I think about all the wonderful friends I've had in my life—from those I knew in my earliest childhood and those in Indiana, to the new ones who have helped me walk with my God. I am overwhelmed by acts of kindness—from our neighbors, for example, who for months on end have brought in food, when I've been low on energy—and from Birch's office. His present staff—all of them—have been caring, thoughtful, understanding, supportive, reaching out to me as a friend.

I have gulped life. Now, I have time to savor it. Although I still have a will, a strong fighting will, I have relaxed. I have changed. I can turn off the telephone. I have willingly released Birch from his promise, made back during his presidential campaign of 1976, that he would not run for office again.

Birch has matured from this experience with me, too. He has grown spiritually, as well. You can't walk through the Valley with a loved one without feeling a great impact. Birch knows my thousands of shortcomings, he knews how awful I am. I am eternally grateful to him for standing with me the way he does. He has traveled all over the country searching for medical help for me, he has held me and cared for me when the pain has been heavy, he has listened to my fears. The other day, when I was talking to my doctor on the phone, Birch walked in and scribbled on a piece of paper in front of me, "Tell him your husband loves you very much."

Today, I am celebrating my forty-sixth birthday, wrapped in love. How fortunate can one be? It has been over a year now, and all in all, not a very good year. But there has been growth in those valleys. I have been born again. And I am resting in the assurance that God loves me, that His love is the guiding force in my life, as it is in all things. I truly feel His power. That, in itself, is the miracle.

I think that I would have gone stark raving mad this year, faced with the medical report I was handed, if God had not come to me. He has been my rock, my anchor, and my salvation. If I have been able to survive emotionally this past year, if I am able to help

other people, God has all the credit. He has reached out to me—
often through other people doing His work here on earth.

And I will continue to praise Him, and to try to be of use to
others of His children, for as long as He gives me the life and
strength to continue to try.

Washington, D.C.
February 14, 1979

Epilogue

On March 2, 1979, Marvella spoke on behalf of all cancer patients to a cancer crusade audience, including our law student son, Evan, in Charlottesville, Virginia. Hers was a message of life and living—of the importance of hope. She was radiant—an inspiration. There was a standing ovation. Only those who knew her well could detect her difficulty in breathing.

She was so thankful to have shared those moments with Evan. Their beautiful relationship of mutual love, pride, and respect grew even more precious.

On March 28, Marvella received the Hubert H. Humphrey Inspirational Award for Courage. Though she was not well enough to accept the award in person, the thoughts she expressed say much about her values and her life: "Courage? If I have shown courage, it has been saying, I alone am not strong enough, and I need help from God and others. I am blessed for they have been, and always are, there."

In the days that followed we talked and held hands. We reminisced about the past, thought of the future. We prayed for a miracle.

Marvella so wanted to know the lucky girl who would win her Evan. She hoped to become a grandmother. She was not afraid of dying, but she very much wanted to live.

On April 24, Marvella slipped away. She was at peace and secure in her faith in God. Those of us who loved her, cried. But somehow I have the feeling that those tears expressed only our grief, our own deep personal loss. Marvella must have been smiling down on us.

Epilogue

She was always her own most severe critic, always restless to learn more, to do better, to comfort and help others. Yet deep in her heart she knew that she had been able to comfort those who were distressed or in pain. She had made many conscious of the importance of good health and how to prevent illness. She had tirelessly championed the belief that in America, each boy and each girl, each man and each woman should have the opportunity to pursue his or her dreams unfettered by prejudice. Marvella believed that each human life could and should make a difference. Yes, she must be smiling, because her life did make a difference.

—BIRCH BAYH

"I have *never, ever* said I was dying of cancer. I am *living* with the knowledge that I have cancer. And my life is rather normal." That was Marvella Bayh's characteristic protest last October, with half a year of life left to her. Her life was certainly not normal, except in the way she perceived it. To the rest of the country hers was the most exceptional life, for both its bravery and practicality, for the way she took the most cruel news about her fate, fell to her knees, then stood up and turned that news into a gift of strength for anyone who ever saw or heard her.

She was a thoroughly beautiful woman. Whatever toll the cancer took never showed, at least while we could see her, certainly never showed while she was going from speech to speech on behalf of the American Cancer Society, or granting television interviews, in which she appeared as a hostess, not a subject. That flourishing beauty of hers was like a feat. We did in fact see a woman living. And if there really was that other, terrible fact, that the cancer in her body was spreading to the bones, then only the force of her generous faith could drive that thought away—which it did.

How or why she behaved so remarkably in her final year is almost beyond understanding. Surely, the option was hers to treat death as a personal business, and spend her last year of life alone with her family and out of public reach. Instead, it was she who did the reaching, which seems always to have been her way. Yet she never gave the sense of eager martyrdom. She said all along she was "praying for a miracle," and, according to a friend, she came to feel her prayer had been answered by the serenity granted her.

She also said the disease had taught her "how little control we all have over our own lives." What Mrs. Bayh did with the amount she had was enough for a lifetime.

The Washington Post, April 26, 1979

Index

Index